THE CONDOR'S FEATHER

MICHAEL WEBSTER

THE CONDOR'S FEATHER

TRAVELLING WILD IN SOUTH AMERICA

1 3 5 7 9 10 8 6 4 2

First published in 2022 by September Publishing

Maps by Liam Roberts
Typeset by RefineCatch Limited, www.refinecatch.com
Printed in Poland on paper from responsibly managed, sustainable sources
by Hussar Books

TPB ISBN 9781914613005
EPUB ISBN 9781914613012

September Publishing
www.septemberpublishing.org

To Paula, the girl with the golden hair

CONTENTS

PROLOGUE

There is one week of my life that I remember extremely vividly, but it's one that I strive daily to forget. Every important thing that followed was triggered in those few days – endings as well as beginnings.

On the Monday I was on business in Johannesburg, the richest and poorest city in Africa with the highest concentration of guard dogs per head of population in the world. The threatening sun beat down, a day hotter than molten gold in which a long sultry afternoon sagged into an eye-popping thunderstorm. Returning to my hotel bungalow the outside door was ajar. I entered, facing a wrecked room and two armed robbers. With a gun pointing at me, I was waved over to sit on the bed and keep quiet. They left quickly, each with a bag, inside which were my camera, computer, some clothes, cash and, far more dear to me than anything else, my passport.

A shock, yes, but consular officials respond automatically and efficiently to such 'mundane' situations, while the personnel director of the multinational food company I worked for was sympathetic.

On the Thursday night of that week I flew to Cape Town. I'd been there many times, I knew the score, the places to avoid, so I hugged my new passport close – no way was I going to lose that again. The taxi dropped me off unexpectedly on a quiet, dark street and pulled away too quickly for my liking. A man grabbed me; I struggled to get free. The savage mugging was over in what seemed like moments, but I had felt a final, vicious stab.

When my eyes opened it was quite dark. 'Electricity cut again,' I heard someone say. People shuffled around, attending to one part of my body or another. The hospital resembled a scrap yard. Someone held up a bloodied syringe for me to see. 'They stuck this in you. There's little we can do for you here.' This was the time that HIV rates were at crisis point, out of control in a country where the disease was thought by most to be a curse from God.

The first incident had been traumatic enough; the second had much longer consequences.

My company flew my wife, Paula, over and she took me back to the UK, where immediate hospital treatment fought the virus. Weekly visits to a specialist HIV ward became an unremitting nightmare. How many blood samples did they want? I would sit in a queue of mostly young people, all with vacant, ill-looking faces – yellow, pinched and furrowed. Some were walking skeletons, others handcuffed between police. Treatment with a battery of antiretroviral drugs crushed my energy. A nurse told me, 'This place is a zoo. The only way to prevent you coming here forever is with these,' and handed me a week's supply of drugs. 'Most people can't put up with the regime. Come back next week.'

Every week I returned without fail.

Severe panic attacks meant cities, towns and shops became places of intense distress. Cars would aim to run me down. I conjured the faces of everyone who walked by into feared people from the past. Strangers became spectres. Crowds sent me cold then hot as I floated in detached fear. I became a ship without a rudder, lost, storm-tossed and careering on an unknown ocean. Night-times were worse, the solace of sleep rent by hideous dreams of all the sadness I was inflicting on those around me. I was locked in a box of past memories. No one could do anything to help; I needed a new brain, a new head. I lost four stones in four months.

In the mornings Paula would reluctantly leave for work –

running a busy maths department in an inner-city school. I would sit at home and tear up bits of paper, hour after hour, or I would wander the valley meadows around my home. Fearful of others, I would climb trees or seek out hedgerows suitable to hide in if anyone came along. I lay hidden in the long grass looking up at buzzards overhead. I watched the antics of a pair of blue tits busily feeding their young. But, twice a day, I had to return home and force drugs down my throat, knowing that they would make me retch for hours, sending me dizzy and scared.

This regime lasted six months, but it was worth it. The same nurse seemed happy: 'No need to come back here, your blood counts are back to normal.'

But I didn't feel normal: the toll had been high. A trust in science and drugs had repaired the systems of my body, but I still felt an irrational mess. The incident had dug deeper into my soul than I realised. Slowly I realised that my career was finished, and a life that I had loved had disappeared.

A further year of cognitive behavioural therapy and a library of self-help books did help, but quick fixes are easily undone. Far more sustaining was the uplifting song of blackbirds and the joyful sight of skylarks parachuting through the air. The arrival of swallows swooping low over the garden reminded me that a new beginning was possible.

The birds had started to pull aside the hazy curtains from my mind.

All my life nature had been at my side, now I realised it was being my saviour. There was going to be a debt to repay.

Cats have nine lives; people normally have one. I was lucky – I had been given two, and a chance to learn from the previous one and try not to make the same mistakes. I decided I would now take it slower, make life more meaningful, make the most of every day. I would follow my heart, do something I'd never before thought possible. Now could be the time to become deeply immersed in the wild, to fully embrace the natural world, no longer be a mere bystander.

Could I communicate my love of nature to others? The skills Paula and I possessed as lifelong and near-professional photographers and film-makers could be put to good use. It was a dream, but still, would I grab the opportunity, take the risk?

It was over a year since I had walked out of the hospital doors for the last time. Now I felt able to step out of the contained and protected world I had built around myself. As for Paula, would she step into the unknown with me?

Paula gave the answer a few months later: early retirement from her demanding job.

Spending more time together was key to our new life plan. We went to Spain, wanting to find the heaviest flying bird in Europe – the great bustard – and make a film about the declining cork oak forests. I had been a photographer since a teenager and had made a number of films for the international company I had worked for. With the natural world flowing through our veins, we knew the warm Andalucian breeze on our cheeks and the smell of bougainvillea would be enough, even if we never found the birds we sought.

But we did find them. At a metre tall and with red neck feathers reminiscent of a Viking's beard, they were magnificent.

Hiring a car, we stayed in rustic hostels, but therein lay a difficulty. We needed to be out early in the morning, sometimes very early, when birds were singing and shadowy light illuminated every crevice on the bark of the trees – the perfect light for filming.

Early starts meant we liked to be asleep well before midnight, the time many tavernas were still taking diners in.

'Can we eat early this evening?' we would ask.

'*Si, si*. What time?'

'Eight?'

'Oh. Maybe a little later,' the owner would suggest.

'How about nine, then?'

'Umm, you come, we will try,' and they would disappear into the kitchen.

We would go out for the day and, returning to the dining room at nine in the evening, would find the lights out and no one yet in the kitchen. Around nine-thirty we would hear shuffling. Dinner was served at ten, often later. This is the norm in Spain but to us, who had never dreamt of taking a siesta, it seemed extraordinarily late. But there was nothing we could do.

In fact, this experience was helping shape our future, for we had plans germinating inside us, plans that would shape the direction of our new life. We wanted to fly, to live free as birds, close to nature, supporting bird conservation, but to do that we would need to be our own masters.

To be truly independent, we would need our own home on wheels.

For bird lovers, there is nowhere like South America. Nearly a third of all the bird species on the planet are to be found in this moderately sized continent. It has the largest remaining stands of primary forest, it has one of the smallest populations of people, and most of the countries speak the same language – Spanish. That's where our new life would take us. Friends told us it was crazy, but that's what dreams are.

We would travel the length of the Andes, a smouldering series of active volcanoes scattered between peaks and plains for 7,000 kilometres. We would seek out its exciting birdlife. The Andes split the continent in two. 'Divide and conquer' is the mantra of a destroyer, but for the Andes it's 'divide and create' – these mountains are givers of life and represent one of the significant reasons why South America is home to so many bird species. One of the main aims of our journey, too, was to support bird conservation organisations by making films for them, an undertaking far too expensive for small conservation NGOs on their own. We would travel wild, and savour every moment. We would make the most of every day.

Life was starting to look up. We had a purpose, as well as the time.

A year later we were ready to go back to Spain again, this time for a practice run. Now we were driving our own Toyota Hilux truck on top of which we had fitted a tiny camper, shipped over especially from California. We removed the back seat from the truck, giving us space to store essentials like five tripods, half a dozen cameras, lights, binoculars and laptops, and luxuries like clothes and food.

Having penetrated the icy Pyrenees, it took us a few weeks to explore them fully. Like a cork in a bottle, we successfully pulled ourselves through the narrowest alleys of medieval hilltop villages. Following ancient equine paths across Europe's only true desert, we eventually returned through France over rippling lavender hillsides. Travelling wild, we ate and slept when and where we wanted, watching the sun rise and set. Following animal trails and living at the behest of nature grounded us in reality, and brought freedom and joy to our souls.

The other reality was that we returned to England with two broken leaf springs, leaking shock absorbers and a list of engineering tasks urgently needed to make us 'Andes ready'.

Our son Richard, who lived in Canada, now realised we were deadly serious about leaving for South America and, in a parent–child role reversal, told us: 'I want to know where you are, who you're with, and if you're all right. I insist you get a Yellowbrick.'

'A what?'

'It's a global satellite tracking system. If you can see the sky it'll send my computer a message with your exact location. It's even got an emergency button which sends out a distress signal.'

We were ready.

We tried to see as many friends and family before we left, knowing it would be a couple of years before we saw them again. Paula's brother was to collect our post and look after the house. A myriad of jobs bombarded us in the final few weeks. We had never realised how difficult it would be to separate ourselves from the hi-tech world in which we lived. Freeing ourselves to travel wild sometimes seemed unattainable; the reality of achieving it was almost impossible.

It was another reminder to us of our disconnect from the natural world.

One spring morning in 2014, as the cuckoos were arriving in England, we were departing. At Tilbury docks we slowly edged our Toyota camper into a shipping container, chains and straps securing and locking it down. Like a heron scooping a frog from a marsh, our container was hoisted high over the dockside. Inside was everything we needed, our new life bound for Montevideo, Uruguay.

As for us, we put out of the safe harbour at last, and set sail to follow a dream.

PART ONE

A NEW LIFE

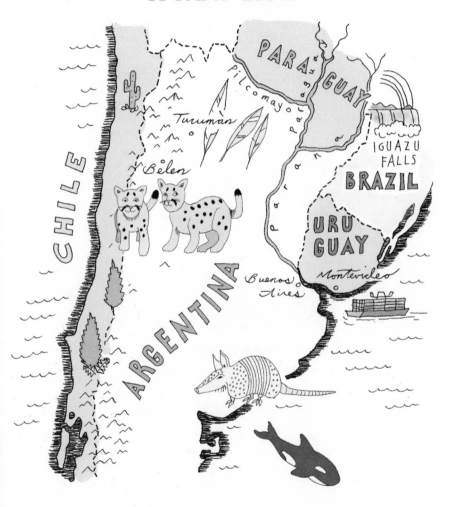

CHAPTER 1

NOMADS IN A NEW LAND

It was June, winter in Argentina, when the great adventure started. Our new life was a blank sheet ready for writing on. We had little knowledge of what we would find or when it might end. If we found somewhere we liked we'd stay for days, even weeks; in forests, on beaches and mountaintops, on the outskirts of villages among cultures new to us; perhaps with people but, we thought, more likely with birds.

Time and governance had not been kind to what was once called the Paris of South America, Buenos Aires. Peeling stucco, rusting balconies and graffiti scarred the graceful neo-Classical buildings. Concrete pillars thrust urban motorways high in the air between apartment blocks – residents' washing waving on balconies alongside speeding trucks.

All of my life I have lived in the shade of an oak wood. I don't really enjoy city life, so we gave ourselves two weeks to clear the truck through Customs, change our money and make the necessary contacts. After all, we had the greatest mountain chain in the world to traverse.

We rented a small apartment above the Café Manolo in San Telmo. Its stone balustrade was brushed by jacaranda trees. Each day the *menú del día* was written on a chalkboard which stood on the cobbled street. The local policeman visited throughout the day, eating, sipping coffee and shuffling his papers. I never saw him pay for anything. The restaurant closed at half past two every afternoon, and the streets became quiet. It was siesta time.

At five in the afternoon the shops, cafés and restaurants reopened. At ten in the evening, a side door below our balcony opened and a hallway led people down stone steps into a dim cellar under the restaurant. There was a bar and a stage for musicians: a double bass, a piano, three violinists and three others sitting down, each with a small concertina called a *bandoneón*. The resident band of young musicians was the well-known Orquesta Típica Andariega. This was a *milonga*, intense, musical and magnetic, where locals came for one thing: to dance the tango, as traditional in Buenos Aires as a folk session in a wave-lashed pub on the coast of Donegal.

We timed our early morning walks to be after the city streets had been washed but before the demonstrations in the main square started. Scattered between the spreading buttress roots of rubber trees was a group of disgruntled veterans from the Falklands War of the 1980s, their banners and placards leaning against trees. We didn't want them to catch sight of a lone English couple chatting away. Decades after the end of the war, it remained a very sore point in some sections of Argentinian society.

On quieter streets I made my first friends. A brown, thrush-sized bird, the rufous hornero, Argentina's national bird. The bird goose-stepped along the edges of the flowing gutters like a fascist general and made its ostentatious nest, looking like an oven of mud, on the elaborate buildings, cocking a snoot at passers-by. In complete contrast was the monk parakeet, a small, bright green rascal of a parrot, groups of which squawked loudly at the ragged families who collected the mountains of city rubbish for recycling, stuffing it into great white plastic bags piled onto rickety handcarts. Later in the day, the monk parakeets would hang out with gangs of street pigeons, raiding picnickers on park benches.

BirdLife International is the global agency that partners with passionate yet often underfunded national bird conservation organisations. In Argentina, the partner organisation is Aves

Argentinas, and on our third day we had a meeting with its director, Hernan Casañas.

'How can we help you?' asked Hernan, a tall, laconic figure with an engaging smile, who fortunately spoke English well, as my Spanish was limited.

'Thank you, but really it's how can we help you.' We explained that we had always worked as volunteers for wildlife conservation back home and wanted to do the same in South America. We were birdwatchers, photographers and film-makers and could help them if they needed these skills.

Hernan seemed a little lost for words, understandably perhaps. Strangers don't often turn up on your doorstep from the other end of the world with ambitious offers of assistance. He cleared his throat, thought for a moment and finally smiled. We could come back to the office the next week, he said, and give a talk to members of their local Buenos Aires group.

In fact, the talk was videoed and the event transmitted live to all the other eighty clubs that the organisation had throughout Argentina. In doing so, we were introduced to the thousands of nature conservationists and birdwatchers spread throughout the eighth biggest country in the world. By the time we were back at our hotel, our Facebook page was filling with messages of welcome, offers of help and people to meet. Now it wasn't just the two of us against the mighty Andes. We had a nationwide support team.

As we had left the talk, Hernan had come to say goodbye. 'Where will you start?' he asked.

'We have a family friend who lives in Tucumán. That's where we're heading tomorrow.'

'Then travel safe, and I will remember your kind offer.'

We ought to have noticed the flashing lights earlier. Instead, we drove along the earth road until the thought of turning around occurred to us too late. With a barricade in front of us and a dark figure waving at us to slow down, there was no going back.

As we were used to living in a country where people never encounter road blocks, this was more than a little unsettling and my thoughts immediately filled with the endless, dire warnings that had been pressed on us when we told people we were planning to travel the length of the Andes, northwards to the Caribbean.

'Are you crazy?'

'Of all places, why South America?'

'Beware of the people, they're all crooks.'

'After all you've been through?'

'Colombia is full of drug smugglers.'

'Don't trust the police.'

'Never stop for people waving you down at the side of the road.'

'South America? The spiders are as big as footballs.'

'Dream on, you'll never go.'

After a while we had begun to wonder if anyone had travelled to South America and returned alive. Was Gandalf correct when he warned Frodo that going outside his front door and stepping into the road was a dangerous idea; one that could lead to all sorts of unwanted adventures?

We were fast approaching the man.

Paula whispered, 'It might be the police.'

I slowed down.

'He's got a machine gun.' We'd never seen a traffic cop with a gun, ever.

'Quickly,' I said, my heart racing. 'Hide the binoculars on the floor. Where's that emergency distress gadget that we bought?'

With the truck slowing to a halt a camouflage-wearing, machine-gun-toting man walked towards us. I gulped, my throat dry.

The man moved the gun off his shoulder. A shiver ran down my neck, sweat on my forehead feeling cold. Deeply hidden and unwanted memories flooded back, and my fingers trembled. Years of planning, and we were at gunpoint before we'd even started.

Of course, we had discussed and planned for situations such as this, as much as you can ever plan for an armed robbery. Cut into the floor of the truck, under the carpet behind the driving seat, we had fitted a small safe the size of a robin's nest. This metal box held our most important papers: passports, vehicle ownership documents, vaccination certificates, a list of our camera equipment with serial numbers, insurance documents, credit cards and thick wads of cash. Lastly, in a waterproof envelope was a list of next of kin and emergency phone numbers. And we had a plan B. Underneath the front passenger seat, readily available, was a cash box containing $500, old passports, a watch, two phones, a selection of Paula's less desirable but very glittery jewellery, and photos of our nearest and dearest. We were ever ready to hand this over at a robbery without quibbling, hoping it would satisfy the average bandit.

Was this the time to do it, just six hours into our journey?

Our British vehicle was right-hand drive, a rare and bizarre sight in South America, so as the man approached us, he did so from our left, where Paula sat as the passenger. I realised this would leave me, as the driver, free to drive off in an emergency.

The last element of our plan was to speak in English, though Paula's Spanish was good.

The man, camo-peaked cap low over his eyes and gun levelled from the waist, stepped nearer, his knee-length black boots scraping the gravel. He walked slowly up to our white truck camper, not quite sure what to make of it. Across the side doors were decals of mountains and flying Andean condors.

'*Abran, abran!* Open, open,' the man commanded, tapping on the window.

I nudged Paula. 'He needs a shave.'

She hissed at me to be quiet and lowered the window. He looked surprised at there being no steering wheel.

My foot hovered over the accelerator.

'*Documentación!*'

Taking our papers, he disappeared to a large unmarked truck parked under a tree. We waited.

Some minutes later a tall, confident-looking man in a dark green uniform with medals and pips all over the place approached us. He held our papers in one hand, a baton tucked under the other arm. 'Good morning, my name is Major Xavier Hernandez,' he said in BBC English. He looked at us keenly, his eyes flicking from us to our equipment stacked high in the back.

Only then did I turn off the ignition and relax a little. This was no robbery: it was our first brush with the military.

'I see you are British. Why are you here?' he asked.

A little affronted by the directness of the question, I leaned over to Paula's window. 'We're visitors.'

'What are you doing here?'

'We're going to Tucumán, we have a friend there. We took this back road to watch for birds.'

The officer paused for a moment, glancing at the papers again. 'My father fought in the Falklands war.'

My heart sank. There was nothing we could say in reply to that. We had seen plaques at every village we had passed through: '*The Malvinas are, were and always will be Argentinian.*' It seemed the 1982 war against the British had not been forgotten.

'He was captured by the British and held prisoner,' the officer continued slowly.

I feared the worst and wished I hadn't switched off the ignition.

'He was held by the Scots Guards. They treated him really well. He and his men hadn't had decent food in months.'

We sighed with relief.

'You're the first British visitors I've met. On behalf of my father, thank you very much. Please enjoy our country.'

'Thank you,' we both said, quickly.

The major continued, 'We have a situation ahead, so you will have to turn back. In a few kilometres there is a right-hand track, take that, it will be safer.' He saluted us, passed the papers back to Paula and turned away.

I started the truck and started to drive off, slowly.

'Well!' Paula said. 'Perhaps we might return home alive after all.'

We both laughed, nervously.

CHAPTER 2

FEATHERS

We had left the Argentinian capital at last, following route 9 through foggy marshlands by the River Paraná. After 500 kilometres and with the road block well behind us we looked for our first camp for the night. There had been fewer villages or towns along our route than we were used to at home, and we had seen hardly any shops. Though we had plenty of food, we had no fresh bread.

On a narrow minor road between fields of maize we stopped by a bridge over a stream where an area of dried mud allowed us to park safely. Eventually, a small blue van came slowly along and we waved it down.

Paula hesitantly tried out her Spanish: 'Hi, is there anywhere nearby to camp?'

The driver looked thoughtful. 'Go back towards the main road. In a few kilometres, look for a track, a sign that says "Museo". Go down there.'

'Thanks. And is there a shop nearby, somewhere to get bread?'

'No need!' He reached behind him and handed Paula two baguettes, flour sprinkled along their crusty brown length. Surprised and not knowing what to say, we stood and watched the van disappear.

Taking the golden gift in her arms, Paula smiled. 'Welcome to Argentina!'

From the 'Museo' sign we found ourselves on a dead straight track, short grass down the middle. After a while a building appeared in the distance, and as it neared we realised it was a disused railway station – the grassy track we were driving on was where the railway lines would have been. We stopped in front of the station, a sandy-coloured, craftsman-built, rectangular stone building with big windows. We clambered up onto the platform. It felt strangely familiar. Ornate ironwork supported by meaningful pillars held up a wooden veranda roof decorated with crenulated edges. The clean but otherwise aged and riven slabs of the platform were in contrast to the unkempt grass stretching either side, and several large trees were drooping their boughs low over the abandoned building. A large round double-faced clock hung from a rafter. A couple of benches faced the empty track, and a small wooden hand-cart held a collection of old boxes. If it hadn't been for our truck neatly parked where the carriages would once have stood, we might have been waiting for a train at a Cotswolds village station.

'*Hola!*'

We jumped. Standing behind us was a couple. A tall, burly man with an open shirt revealing a hairy chest was accompanied by a smaller woman in a purple T-shirt, her black hair tied back in a ponytail.

'Can we help you?'

I said that we had been told we might camp there and that we were British. On hearing that, the man relaxed, with a beaming smile. 'Ah, the British built this station; not been used for years, though. Italians put the tracks in.' He waved his arm around. 'We look after the place – live opposite in that house through the trees.'

We glanced across to a small, single-storey building.

'This is a museum. Want to look inside?'

His wife unlocked the door. Inside looked like a second-hand shop of train memorabilia, lamps, fire buckets, badges and ticket machines. The walls had photographs pinned to boards as well as oval brass plates off trains, each with the name 'Ferrocarril Nacional' and a number. A rack of clothing contained uniforms, caps and coats. One corner was a library of books, documents and maps; the other end of the room, looking like a café, had three small tables set with damask table cloths, bentwood chairs forlornly tucked underneath.

The couple told us that everything had been donated by people who lived in the area. 'It keeps the place looking alive, though few people visit these days.'

I walked over to the books and was surprised to see two whose spines were decorated with a gilt title and inlaid bird motifs: *Idle Days in Patagonia* and, next to it, *The Naturalist in La Plata*. Both were by W.H. Hudson, one of the earliest writers to publish tales about the natural history of Argentina. The books were first editions from the 1890s.

'They were donated by a local man. If we're given stuff we feel we have to accept their generosity,' the man said.

'I've read them,' I said. 'We're interested in birds and wildlife, that's why we're in Argentina.'

'Oh?' the woman said. 'The man used to work in Buenos Aires. He sent us all sorts of stuff, even some feathers. Want to see them?'

She disappeared off to a back room, returning with a roll of newspaper that she laid out on a table. Sticking out of the end we could see three long, dark brown spikes; unwrapping the yellowing pages, more feathers appeared.

Drawing out the largest was like unsheathing an Arabian scimitar. Longer than my arm and almost black, its curving bow shape gave it elegance; its weightlessness gave it power, a supernatural feel. I knew instantly that it could only belong to one bird – the Andean condor. I stroked its vanes reverently.

The vanes lie either side of feathers' stiff hollow midrib. Each vane is made up of hundreds, and in the case of the condor feather thousands, of hair-like strands, the culmination of 150 million years of trial and error. Each of these strands has aligned along its length a multitude of tiny hooklets that zip it tight to the strand next to it. When a bird like the condor is cutting through air currents four miles high, it's this gloriously simple design that enables the bird to control the astral vibrations of the air. When the bird is not flying or feeding, the rest of the time it's tending its feather vanes, zipping them back and lubricating those that have come undone. The one I held was a primary feather that had no doubt carried the bird to the edge of our troposphere and back. Would we see this legend of a bird? We hardly believed it possible.

Two other feathers were in perfect condition: one as long as my hand, its colour a deep red gently fading to pale salmon, like an evening sky; the other being a diminutive finger length, the colour of a beech leaf tipped by autumn's first blush.

'You can have them if you want, they're just gathering dust here,' the man said.

As we left the building it was locked up again, its memories from the past secure and quiet once more. The couple showed us where we could get water then returned to their house.

Finding a bench on the deserted platform, we sat and quietly looked around us. It seemed eerily auspicious that we found ourselves at a place built to help move people across the country, as we were doing ourselves. Years before there would have been a great train here, belching smoke, steam swirling, the smell of burning coal and hot metal. Crowds of people would have been hurrying, shouting goodbyes, carrying baggage, slamming doors. Argentina is a country built on immigration; the passengers who had sat on this seat would have been adventurous souls seeking a new life, just like us.

We had left behind us a comfortable home. Family and friends had teased us we wouldn't leave, but we did. I had certainly never expected to ever leave our beloved oak wood, but we had. Since time immemorial, people have always journeyed on personal searches for truth and meaning. They've gone to mountain tops, caves, islands, the extremities of land and sea. This was my own pilgrimage into the wild, to live close to nature.

Beyond the platform, where our truck stood, the shadows of a long-departed train taking the last passengers had gone. I looked at the gently swinging clock, its delicate hands frozen. Not us, though – this was our time to move on, and we were raring to go.

One thing was for sure: there was no going back. Nothing in life is constant; perhaps that's its meaning. If we didn't change now we'd risk being left behind, chained like prisoners to diminishing certainties. That was not going to happen to us.

Still in my lap lay the bulky rolled-up newspaper. I gently placed my hands on top as if to warm the feathers from their long sleep.

'What are we going to do with those? We've hardly got room,' Paula said, ever practical.

'They'll be OK. The feathers will fit somewhere.'

The small ones I popped into a pocket at the back of my red notebook. The condor's feathers I slid behind the windscreen visor, trapped for the time being, but close to us both.

I've always loved feathers. As a young child walking home from school one day with my mother, I saw a flash of colour when kicking a heap of leaves high into the air. A glint caught my eye. Diving my hands into the crispy golden pile I pulled out a tiny feather, the length of my little finger. Turning the feather over, one vane was blue, finely barred with black. Blue, black, blue, black, blue, black – a bird's ladder into the sky. It had belonged to that wary woodland bird, the jay. I taped it into a book, a captive memory.

Since then I always turn over feathers that I find, in the hope of seeing another flash of magic.

In Tucumán we stayed with Leigh Cotton, an old family friend, who taught English in the city. The only other contact we had in

Tucumán was Ada Echevarria. We had emailed her out of the blue some months before leaving the UK, having located her name on the Aves Argentinas website – one of those enquiries you think will come to nothing, a shot in the dark.

A rapid, helpful reply to such an email tells you a lot about a person. It was efficient and professional, interested and kind. Ada was just the sort of contact we needed.

Tucumán has a renowned university with a long-established natural sciences institute named after Argentina's most famous naturalist and scientist, Miguel Lillo. The institute has one of the finest bird collections in the whole of South America and that's where Ada worked as an ornithologist.

We met Ada in the calm precincts of the institute, a lush rectangular botanic garden in the heart of the city. For us it could have been a tropical forest. She came down the steps leading from wide, glass entrance doors and, smiling, held out both hands to us. She was a slim, dark-haired woman, dressed as you might expect for a field biologist, in a green gilet, jeans and trainers. 'Great to meet you. Welcome to Argentina. Come up to my office.'

We followed her, up several flights of stairs and past an imposing bronze bust of Miguel Lillo in a recessed alcove. At the end of the hallway, Ada thrust open heavy wooden double doors, ushering us into a large, high ceilinged room with windows looking out over the green precinct. A woman in a vividly coloured dress, giving her the appearance more of an artist rather than a scientist, was in the room, and Ada introduced her as her friend and colleague Valeria Martinez, the curator of the institute's bird collection.

Polished, chest-high antique cabinets were positioned along one wall and also back to back in three rows down the middle of the room. Each cabinet had ten drawers and each drawer a shining brass handle. On top of the cabinets, looking down at us, were stuffed birds in large, dusty glass cases: herons with dagger-like bills, an eagle clutching its bloodied prey, and a brilliant red and green macaw. The room was solemn, churchlike, the fragrance of incense replaced by the faint whiff of chemicals from nearby laboratories.

At the end of one row, a particular bird awaited us. 'Come, look at this one,' said Ada, following the line of my gaze.

The specimen was not in a case but perched on a log, its huge black wings outstretched. It was a condor, dull-eyed, its spirit gone, a wizened creature from which I had to look away.

We walked back down the middle aisle and Ada pulled out a glass-topped drawer. Nestled inside was a row of black-throated trogons, exquisite yellow and green forest birds, now just fading rainbows. With cotton wool for eyes, the sun had disappeared from their lives long ago. 'We have over ten thousand bird skins here. They get sent to scientists all over the world.'

'Migrating across the skies in a box,' I said, and Valeria smiled.

We opened another drawer, this time of meadowlarks, starling-sized birds, black and scarlet. Gently I passed a hand across the glass, as if to wake and bring the birds beneath back to life. They just lay still, line after line, neatly arranged like paired socks in a drawer.

Ada turned to us. 'They're used for research. But these days we get more information from taking a sample of blood from birds we catch and then release.'

'DNA analysis, isotopes and that sort of stuff?' I replied.

'Yes.'

'I've got this feather,' I said, and taking my red notebook from my pocket, I slid from it the finger-length green feather with the red tip we had been given in the train station. 'Any ideas what sort of bird this is from?'

Valeria moved closer. 'Why, yes, I think so.' She passed it to Ada, who put it on a bench, the better to view it. 'See this scarlet tip, it's from a parrot,' Valeria added. 'Yes, a special one, the alder parrot. No other parrot has such red-tipped feathers.'

We told them the story of the feathers from the railway museum.

'You're lucky. Condor feathers are considered sacred by some. Seeing the birds, though, is difficult, as most often they are just specks in the sky.'

'We haven't got much room in the truck. Would you like them?' I said.

'No!' Ada and Valeria said together. 'The feathers have found you,' Ada said. 'They will be talismans for your journey.'

The next day Leigh introduced us to one of her friends, Guillermo Aceñolaza, a professor of geology at the university. Lithe and looking younger than his years, he welcomed us and over dinner eagerly wanted to know our plans.

'To travel the Andes and support bird conservation.'

'And how do you expect to do that? Argentina's in an economic crisis. People are more interested in putting food on the table.' He said this in a pleasant but challenging tone.

'Then that's even more reason why we can help. We will find the people who care. We can make films for them. We will talk to schools.'

'And where will you start?'

'In the wildest place we can think of – Patagonia. Then travel the length of the Andes, north all the way to Colombia. Who knows?'

'How will you travel? The Andes are tough. I know, it's where I work. Have you got oxygen?'

I explained about our pick-up truck with a small sleeping cabin mounted on the back. But then asked nervously: 'Why do we need oxygen?' I pulled out my red notebook in which we had made our plans for the next few months, reeling them off one at a time. None of them included oxygen, however.

Guillermo looked amused. 'Throw your notebook away, free yourself! Listen to people and trust them,' he said, with a flurry of his arms. 'Take each day as it comes, you're in South America now. But you must have oxygen. You'll be going high. I never travel without oxygen, neither do my students. Don't worry, I'll organise it.'

Paula and I looked at each other. Despite our meticulous planning, there were clearly things we hadn't thought of.

A few days later, still doubting we would ever need it, we collected a huge cylinder of oxygen, together with a bag of face masks and tubes, from Guillermo, and took the road south, to Patagonia.

The distance from Tucumán to Tierra del Fuego is nearly 4,000 kilometres, a journey longer than driving from London across Europe to Istanbul. A daunting prospect, but for once in our lives we had time.

One of our first stops was at Belen, a small town in the Argentine province of Catamarca. Tired and with a pounding headache, I wanted to find a chemist. The streets were lined with small shops whose collections of multi-coloured ponchos and blankets spilled onto pavement tables. As lunchtime beckoned, the displays were taken in, doors and shutters starting to close. Argentinians take their midday meal seriously, their afternoons commencing with the main meal of the day, followed by a siesta. Soon the streets were deserted and, with no chemist in sight, we returned to the truck.

There, we found a tall man leaning against the bonnet. He was muscular, in his forties with a tanned, healthy complexion, and dark hair with the first tinges of grey. 'This truck yours?' he asked, pointing to the condor logo on the vehicle.

I nodded warily and with a little apprehension. My head still throbbed and, facing this big man now, I started to tremble with feelings and thoughts I had not had for a long time.

'Are you interested in condors?' he added.

'Of course! We've not seen one yet but we have got some feathers.'

At this the man looked surprised but smiled, highlighting a number of missing teeth. 'Condors only show themselves to you when they're ready. If you have feathers, it's a good omen. How did you get them?'

'It's a long story, but from a railway museum.'

The man gave us a strange look. 'I'm Claudio. Come into the café, let's have lunch and tell me about it.'

The meal was a hesitant, disorderly affair as Paula wrestled with Claudio's thick accent – rapid village Spanish was difficult to grasp.

I was wrestling too, but with the food in front of me. 'What are we eating?' I asked.

'*Locro*,' Claudio said, surprised we had never heard of it.

Looking down at the thick, yellow and glutinous soup in front of me, which contained a range of strange, indistinguishable objects floating in it, I decided this wasn't going to be in my collection of favourite recipes.

Claudio, it turned out, had a passion for protecting the local population of Andean condors. He was a warden in the nearby provincial park and, together with some young people from the town, ran a small ecological group looking after injured animals. The result of this hastily convened meeting was that he would find us a chemist, and we would then all return to his house where he would show us an injured condor.

Paula turned to me. 'At least, I think that's what he said.'

Leaving the café, Claudio jumped into a vehicle resembling a child's homemade motorised go-kart and sped off down a series of quiet streets with us following. Everything had happened so quickly. We had no idea what Claudio's surname was, where he lived or, for that matter, whether he was the local axe murderer.

Claudio apparently knew the chemist but, to open up the shop, had to rattle hard on the door and shout up to the man's top-floor window to wake him from his siesta. We sheepishly entered, and bought our few small items.

The shop owner and Claudio parted shouting excited and happy goodbyes to each other, and the worry we had of being enticed off to the woods by a serial killer receded. Claudio was a man obviously well known and liked.

Sitting astride a garden chair, holding a steering column jutting from his large wooden box of a car, the wheels spinning, Claudio continued off down the road to where he lived. He pulled into a side street littered with rubbish, typical of most Argentinian villages. We followed him through a gap in a fence and parked in tall grass. His home was a small, grey-block building amid a tangle of trees and large ramshackle pens and cages. Claudio pushed open the door to the house and a chorus of voices shouted a greeting, 'Hola, hola!'

Claudio beckoned to us. 'Come in, sit down,' and he introduced us to his friends.

Most of the room was taken up with a huge heavy table around which sat four others: two young men and two women. In front of them lay an assortment of large knives on a rough block of wood, and stacks of papers, posters and wildlife books.

'Maté?' asked one of the women. We nodded and she opened a flask and poured hot water into an apple-sized calabash gourd, passing it to one of the young men sitting next to me.

For the English, the etiquette of drinking tea has been finely honed over generations but fundamental to the occasion has been the desire to sit down and talk. In Argentina, the ritual of drinking yerba maté (pronounced 'jerba mattay') is similar. Historically, it was the indigenous Guaraní people, found in Paraguay, Brazil, Uruguay and Argentina, who picked the leaves of the native yerba bush from the forest undergrowth to brew a strong, bitter but sustaining drink; it was the Argentinian gaucho who turned the brew into the mainstay of their diet. A gaucho's life is hard and maté is the drink that enables them to endure the privations of months in the saddle, following their cattle across the windblown pampas and sunburnt, thorny prairie. Now, three centuries since the gaucho made his appearance, the culture of maté is an integral part of everyday life in Argentina. The calabash is passed around from person to person, each of whom sucks up the drink through a shared, finely crafted silver straw, a *bombilla*. The calabash is refilled between each person and resumes its circuit. This close act of communal drinking helps develop a sense of deep intimacy and friendship among the circle of drinkers – crucial to *gauchos* working together in a harsh environment, or to immigrants freshly arrived in a foreign country.

Sitting immediately to my right was a tall, stocky young man who introduced himself as Miguel. A more distinctive person I've rarely seen. He was big, had a large, tanned, oval face strikingly framed by jet-black silky hair, a neatly trimmed moustache and a wispy beard. His demeanour was quiet. It was like sitting next to a gentle bear. Tapping my arm, he smiled and passed me the *maté*. I sipped and passed it on to Paula. The gourd continued its procession to Claudio. Sure enough, the passage of the *maté* around the group extended the hand of friendship and widened the conversation.

At one end of the room a curtain discreetly hid a very basic bathroom. Next to it, a rickety wooden ladder disappeared into a hole in the ceiling. From his humble home, it appeared Claudio masterminded the surveillance and protection of the province's condor population as well as other wildlife that came his way. The other people in the room were part of his village team of helpers.

After some time, Claudio disappeared into a corner, opened a fridge and hoicked out two large pieces of meat, slapping them down on the table.

'Why do you watch birds?' Miguel asked me quietly, sipping through the *bombilla*.

At that moment Claudio brought down a machete with a resounding thump on the table. As he chopped the meat I tried to explain that birds bring colour and music to the world. No matter where you go – any country, any city – there will always be birds close by, often ones you've never seen before. I told Miguel I was never lonely, never bored, when watching birds. Looking more directly at him I emphasised: 'Birds have changed my life in many ways. They are my touchstone to nature.'

At that point Claudio stopped chopping and glanced at me.

'I'd love to go out birdwatching with you one day,' Miguel replied, thoughtfully.

Claudio, having dealt with the meat and put it into a large bowl, now asked Paula and me to follow him. *At last*, I thought. *Our first encounter with an Andean condor.*

Round the back of the house was a shed. Claudio opened a rusty metal door and ushered us in quietly. Inside was a chaos of stacked wood, buckets and wire. We could hear what sounded like a series of low growls. Cameras at the ready, we were pushed through another, much smaller door.

We found ourselves in a large wire enclosure with small bushes. We heard the door shut behind us.

Once inside, to our horror it dawned on us that Paula's comprehension of Claudio's Spanish had let us down, and that in fact he was not looking after a condor at all – but two young pumas.

The two cats crouched low, snarling. Their dark ears, each with a white patch on the back, were pressed flat down on their necks. Submissive or fierce, we couldn't decide.

We opted for the latter, backing off instinctively and whispering to each other how ridiculous this was, finding ourselves inside a cage with a pair of some of the most savage animals on the planet. We could hear Claudio whispering assurances to us from behind the door, but we were more intent on watching the wild cats – it was time for their meal, and they looked hungry. Seconds later, a hatch in the door behind us opened and Claudio slid the bowl of meat between our legs and then slammed the hatch closed.

As the two pumas, the colour of wheat, moved cautiously forwards, their eyes only on us, we moved slowly away from the food bowl, edging around the cage's sides to the wall furthest from them. But now we had no means of escape.

The pumas started to eat. Crouching low so as not to

intimidate them, we gradually moved closer and closer to watch. Completely awed by what we were seeing, we didn't speak, not even a whisper, instead listening to the crunching and gnawing as they ate. The larger male puma was more dominant and aggressive, constantly snarling at us. The smaller female was hesitant and cautious, eventually taking some meat, turning away from us and eating it out of our sight – she didn't even want to look at us. Seeing that the male's claws were retracted, we crept even closer, but his hypnotic topaz eyes watched our every move.

Having eaten the meat, the two siblings bounded across the enclosure, played a little, then retreated under a bush and watched us, their upright ears twitching. Now more relaxed, each lifted its huge sandy-coloured paws one at a time, gently licking clean the five leathery pads, just like a domestic cat.

Back in the house, Claudio told us the sad story of how he had come by the pumas. An out-of-town hunter had tracked the mother and shot her, taking the two cubs. When he had tried to sell the cubs he was arrested by the police and the animals were sent to Claudio for safekeeping. 'We're hoping the cats are going to be released back into the wild,' he said.

I had my doubts – I knew the animals would need to be taught how to fend for themselves by their parents.

Later that evening, Claudio asked to see our condor feathers. The big man cradled the longest feather as he would a young child, then slowly held it up, closely peering along its length. 'This feather has a story to tell.'

'What do you mean?'

'These pale parts are where the strong sunlight has taken its colour.' He pointed out small patches on the vanes to us. 'This bird has flown high, close to the sun.' Then he drew his hand carefully along an edge. 'See how perfect this is, very little wear. It's new.'

'So?' said Paula.

'Birds don't drop feathers like this, without reason.'

'Such as?'

'Don't know, but you must keep it. It was meant for you, no one else.'

We camped overnight in Claudio's garden and prepared to continue our journey south towards Patagonia the next day. Before we left, he mentioned that if we really wanted to understand more about condors we ought to attend a condor liberation, when a bird, either recovered from injury or bred at Buenos Aires zoo, was released into the wild. 'They're special, but don't happen often.'

Before leaving we swapped email addresses and phone numbers. Travelling wild and alone in a whole new continent, we needed as many contacts as we could find.

Energetically waving goodbye, we pulled into the village road. From behind us, Claudio shouted, 'See you soon. Look after the feathers!'

Some time later, we understood that the pumas had been transferred to Buenos Aires zoo and, on a visit to the city a year on, we went to see them. I wished we hadn't. It nearly broke my heart to see them as adults padding up and down in a cage smaller and dirtier than the one where we had spent a marvellous hour with them as energetic youngsters. As we stood watching the cats, the now huge muscular male, whose eyes seemed to have lost their sparkle, paced closer and stared at us for a few magical moments.

Perhaps early memories are the most meaningful for us all.

PART TWO

PATAGONIA

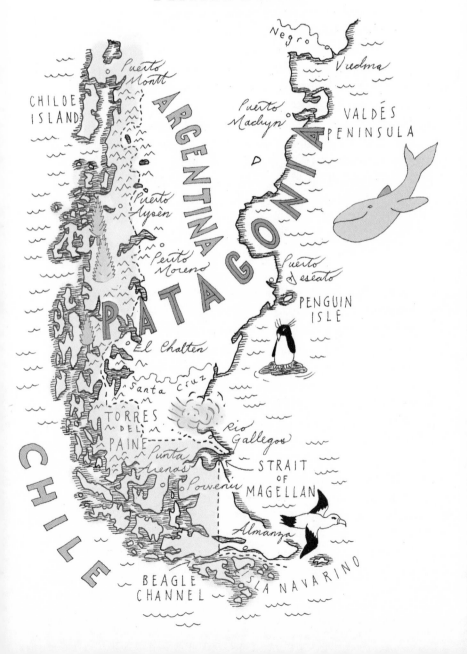

CHILOE ISLAND

Negro

Vuedma

Puerto Montt

Puerto Madryn

VALDÉS PENINSULA

ARGENTINA

Puerto Aysén

Peuto Moreno

PATAGONIA

Puerto Deseato

PENGUIN ISLE

El Chalten

Santa Cruz

TORRES DEL PAINE

Rio Gallegos

Punta Arenas

Porvenir

STRAIT OF MAGELLAN

Almanza

CHILE

BEAGLE CHANNEL

ISLA NAVARINO

CHAPTER 3

THE PENGUIN SHOW

From the town of Belen we headed south in the shadow of the parched Andean foothills, deeply cut by ravines. Once into the province of La Rioja, rows of lush green vineyards stretched across the lower slopes, the home of Malbec and Syrah wine. We continued until it was nearly dark and, unable to find a suitable and safe place to camp, drove into a large pull-off full of parked trucks, sandwiching ourselves between the two largest and longest.

The drivers were huddled together cooking their meal on a small stove. We asked if it was OK to stay and they nodded, asking where we were going.

'San Luis and then Santa Rosa,' we replied.

'Oh, you can't trust the people there,' they said. 'We know, because that's where we come from!'

We slept soundly till five in the morning, to be awoken by the sound of air brakes hissing loudly as the trucks started to leave. After a breakfast of porridge, we also left. A long drive took us to Santa Rosa then we turned due south, taking route 9 as far as the River Colorado. There we stopped, and not just to look at the arching ironwork of the bridge over the fast-flowing water and listen to other vehicles as they rumbled over its thick wooden sleepers. This was not just any ordinary bridge; we knew that by crossing that stretch of water we were entering Patagonia, and stepping into the unknown.

Once over the river, we noticed a subtle change in our mood.

Perhaps it was the air, because from that moment we knew this was where our longed-for quest for birds would truly start. In front of us lay a whole new continent, and no return ticket home. Buoyed by this feeling of utter freedom we followed the road to the coast.

Like so many late afternoons that were to follow, looking for a place to camp and sleep safely was all-consuming. Finally, we edged the Toyota camper along a level area of grass on top of the high sandstone cliffs beyond the town of Viedma.

Under a roseate sky and with the deep blue Atlantic pushing chevrons of white surf onto the rocks beneath us, we stepped from the truck. Parallel to the road, telegraph wires sagged under the weight of thousands and thousands of burrowing parrots, crotchets and quavers of birds on their wire staves as far as the eye could see. Their deafening staccato noise was music to our ears. And then, suddenly, as if at a conductor's command, the birds stopped calling, and a crescendo of swirling rainbow colours – bright yellow and red underparts, sky-blue wings, green heads with prominent white eyes – erupted over our heads. Circling the grassy cliff top, they dropped low, to be absorbed back into their nesting holes in the cliffs beneath us. All that remained was the gentle, repetitive sound of waves rolling onto the shore.

This was our introduction to the birds of a mysterious new land, and they were already weaving their spell.

The Valdés peninsula juts into the Atlantic like a mushroom. It is a arid place, whose red earth is wind-scorched. While the land appeared sterile, this was where we saw our first maras – otherwise know as Patagonian hares – and a stranger animal you couldn't expect to see. Looking like long-legged terriers with pixie ears, they live underground and are closely related to guinea pigs.

The long winding coast held our attention the most, as it abounded with wildlife. We peered over the cliffs at hundreds of wallowing elephant seals that sat like fat potentates. As heavy as a car and rippling with blubber, the males proudly guarded their harem of females lying on the beaches. Further along, we saw colonies of sleek sea lions, whose pointed noses and long whiskers made them look like haughty colonels barking out orders. However, the sheltered bays of the San José and Nuevo gulfs held the greatest surprise. Behemoths rose from the waves in all directions. Southern right whales, rolling, twisting over, taking giant gulps of air. In these calm waters the females give birth and then mate again. Juveniles of the previous year frolic and socialise with each other. This was the whales' winter holiday before the Antarctic summer beckoned them to more southerly and ice-free feeding grounds. And then there were the dolphins. Whenever our binoculars scanned, trying to count the endless whales, our eyes settled on weaving, skittish wraiths. There were so many: dusky, Peale's, Commerson's and bottle-nosed dolphins, all apparently vying with each other to jump the highest or land without a splash.

The best place to spot these animals was Caleta Valdés, and luckily we had an invitation to stay with its two wardens, Luis and Laura, for a few days.

Theirs was a lonely outpost on the Valdés peninsula, except that most days in the whale-watching season, regular coachloads of visitors descended on them for a brief spell. The town of Puerto Madryn, a hundred kilometres away, was a favourite stopping-off point for cruise liners heading down the coast to Antarctica, and passengers would be taken on day trips to the few surrounding attractions. Caleta Valdés was several hours' drive away so the visitors would stream off the bus for fresh air and a look around, but unfortunately were only allowed 30 minutes before having to board the coach again. During that short spell up to a hundred people could file down the cliffside walkways to the vantage points. They had been primed to look for something special.

Above all else, Valdés is famous for one thing: killer whales, known as orcas. During our time there, we visited the marine research laboratory in Puerto Madryn to speak to the people that knew most about them. They told us that they had studied them for over twenty years and during that time had developed an intimate relationship with several of the pods. In the early days they used to swim out and talk to them. They discovered their unique behaviour of catching young sea lions by running themselves aground on the beaches and grabbing the youngsters, then rolling back into the sea, a difficult and hazardous hunting technique.

'There are only three killer whale pods that use Valdés as territory,' Laura told us. 'Only three individual females know how to successfully hunt by beaching themselves.' We later found out that these females teach only their own youngsters, keeping their secret hunting technique very much within their own family.

During our three days of watching from the cliff tops at Caleta, orcas came by on two occasions; together, the sightings amounting to nearly five minutes. Laura and Luis considered that fortune was smiling on us.

Considering the astonishing variety of wildlife to be seen at the Caleta, many of the visitors went away disappointed. We would hear a few say so and see it on their faces, too. They had been sold an orca experience which was likely never to happen – expectations were raised and then dashed. Finding the real thing takes patience and an open mind, a slow mindfulness of the world around us. It's not like switching on the TV or logging on to social media with their instant images of spectacular wildlife.

Caleta Valdés also overlooks a lagoon thirty kilometres long and a third of a kilometre wide which is separated from the Atlantic by a low sand and gravel bar. The sea rushes in at high tide refreshing the water, otherwise for half of the time the entrance is almost closed. Killer whales find it difficult to gain access to the lagoon and so it remains a peaceful haven for sea lions and elephant seals to loaf about in when not feeding.

We would sit on the low cliffs for hours at a time. Arrayed on either side of us were some of the 40,000 Magellanic penguins that breed along the cliffs of Valdés. Inquisitive to the point of being confiding, the black and white birds would approach within arm's reach and peer at us, cocking their heads to one side as if about to disclose to us a family secret. Penguins, like all birds, have incredible senses: they can swim for thousands of miles to known feeding grounds and they can detect the call of their spouse among a multitude of other calling adults in a breeding colony – but what do they think when encountering a human being? The penguin a metre away, looking at me – what was it thinking and what memories would it hold of us? I could not imagine.

Setting up our camera with its giant lens enabled visitors to look at sea lions and elephant seals with their pups on the beach beneath. The shrubby cliff fell away 50 metres to the beach where Atlantic waves sent plumes of spray high enough to be caught by the wind and somersaulted back. Large chocolate-plumaged birds used the updraft from the cliff to glide steadily and silently, low over our heads. They were southern giant petrels, almost the size of albatrosses, with long narrow wings and prominent, hooked tube-nosed bills. As they floated by, their heads moved from side to side, looking for food on the beach. Afterbirths from the seals and sea lions made a tasty snack. They also went for the newly born pups that fighting male elephant seals, the size of small cars and double the weight, accidentally crush. Like ravens on a battlefield, they clear and clean up the carnage of massed animals living together. In the absence of orcas, this was what we showed to the visitors.

Luis wouldn't lend out his own ancient binoculars. He was embarrassed and tried to hide the fact that the two halves were held together with Sellotape, the lenses badly cracked. 'Surely the authorities give you decent binoculars?' I said to Luis. 'This is a World Heritage Site, you're being visited by hundreds of people from around the world every week.'

'No way, they give us hardly anything.'

It is the little, almost inconsequential things that throughout the decades of my life I seem never to forget, memories that surface at odd and unexpected times. I vividly remember a time when I was ten, waiting to catch a bus home after school with my mother. Behind us was a shop that sold army surplus equipment, as well as tents and outdoor clothes. In the window was a pair of binoculars and I asked if I could have them for an upcoming birthday. They were 6x30 Taylor Hobson and the gift lit up my life with patterns and colour: a teal duck suddenly had a bright green eye stripe, kestrels had a yellow ring round their eyes. I used those old binoculars so much that the steel eye cups gave me black eyes.

In the UK, before we left for South America, we had asked members of local wildlife groups to donate their old working binoculars to us. Birders always have unused pairs stashed in the back of a cupboard and we knew they could be put to better use. The company Opticron even gave us two pairs to donate to a worthy cause. Argentina has a ridiculously high import duty on luxury goods and we knew we would be meeting people who couldn't afford binoculars.

On our last night at Valdés, Laura invited us in for a meal. We were joined by a girl from the local gift shop as well as the driver who graded the sand roads on the peninsula. In the corner of Laura's room was a large open fireplace in which a heavy-duty iron grate straddled a sackful of glowing hot charcoal. On the grate, half a lamb sizzled invitingly. In the other corner rested a crate of Malbec. The three of them could speak no English and I virtually no Spanish, so Paula tried to navigate between us all.

Unlike me, Paula, who had been learning Spanish for quite a few years, was taking every opportunity to use it, revelling in mastering the subjunctive. But as the bottles of Malbec emptied, more was lost in translation. At one point Paula said, gesticulating to the driver: 'That gentleman over there says he knows the roads round here so well he could drive them blindfold,' whereupon the other three fell about in hysterics. It seemed Paula had inadvertently used the word *caballo* (horse) instead of *caballero* (gentleman) . . . The evening didn't recover after that and we all went to bed in the early hours, still aching from having laughed so much.

On the morning we left Valdés, we visited Laura to present her with the shiny new binoculars from Opticron. She was stunned.

'They're for you to show visitors your wildlife,' Paula said. 'Give a pair to Luis, as well.'

'I'll do better than that. He's off for a few days, gone to see his mother,' Laura said, as she picked up her phone to ring him.

After the conversation we chipped in: 'What did he say?'

Laura composed herself before replying: 'I've worked with Luis for three years. We've had many rough times out here, such a long way from our homes, but never have I heard him cry until now.'

Heading south on the coast of Patagonia's Chubut province, we looked out from the cliff tops over the Atlantic. In the distance, small black birds skimmed low over the sea, banking their wings one way then another, black and white, a semaphore message that conjured up memories.

In my teenage years I had spent many weeks living on the remote Welsh island of Skokholm catching and ringing these birds. The physical act of holding a bird can tell you a lot about its personality: blue tits will be angry and chisel crossly at your cuticles; bullfinches are so docile they will lie in your hand like a cat on a sofa. The seabirds I had held and ringed had been rightly suspicious of being caught, the wildness of the ocean echoing in the feral gleam in their eyes, so how could I ever forget them? How could I forget the dark, rainy, misty nights stumbling around, torch in hand, searching for the birds on the ground? They had come to the island to feed their young as they huddled in burrows. How could I forget the scary *churr . . . churr . . . churr* sounds through the rain, the sudden *thwak* as one of the disoriented birds flew into me in the blackness? How could I forget the disgusting smell from their fishy vomit on my clothes as I picked them up and tucked them inside my coat, ready to take them to the ringing station?

Despite all that, I hold these birds dear: they are as much a part of me as a robin might be to a lonely pensioner. They were Manx shearwaters, a bird whose life is spent circling the North and South Atlantic Oceans, pulled and pushed by the trade winds.

I was gratified to have stumbled across the birds again at the other end of the world. Like them, we had circled the ocean, not so much in search of food as they were doing – their diet of plankton, molluscs, crustaceans and squid was brought to them by the ice waters pulsing northwards from Antarctica – but more to find mental sustenance. Seeing the birds, understanding a little of their lives as well as marvelling at our unexpected reunion was what I needed – a renewal of a very human desire to connect with the wild.

Paula and I were curious to spend a month up and down this coast to see for ourselves how Patagonia's seabirds were faring. In the time since I had been a teenager ringing Manx shearwaters in Wales, the oceans worldwide had been depleted of 90 per cent of their fish stocks. We knew that South America's penguins were under threat. Two-thirds of Earth's oceans fall outside any national laws. They are a free bar to all comers, and overfishing in the southern Atlantic is a real concern. In recent years Chinese fishing fleets have become more numerous. According to Global Fishing Watch, a non-profit organisation that tracks fish stocks and fishing activities, China is logging 17 million hours of global offshore fishing a year, which is more than the next ten biggest fishing nations combined. Tensions on the high seas are increasing.

Global warming is also affecting penguins. Sea temperatures

are rising. These fractional increases in warmth are forcing fish stocks to move away from long-established penguin breeding sites, towards the colder waters the fish need in which to spawn. Fish can cope with this temperature change, but penguins cannot.

Puerto Deseado is situated where the Santa Cruz coastline of Argentina bulges out into the ocean, like a dolphin's fin. Reaching it means coming off the main north–south road linking Comodoro Rivadavia to Río Gallegos and driving another 120 kilometres towards the sea. The road follows an old disused railway line, another British construction project from a hundred years ago. Puerto Deseado used to be the main sea port from which to ship wool out of Patagonia but those days have long gone. Fishing for squid is the prime industry now, but eco-tourists eager to see penguins are bringing in new money.

The town lies on the north shore of the graceful estuary of the River Deseado, whose waters originate from the high Andes 650 kilometres to the west. Gathering power from numerous tributaries, the Deseado crosses the ochre steppe, the dry leathery land of the *gaucho*. In places the river disappears altogether, draining through fissures into a watery underground of fairy caverns. Kilometres further on, the river re-emerges and, pushed by the relentless wind, flows through wide gravel beds feeding itself with a multitude of minerals, eventually pouring into the wide estuary and the sea. It's these minerals, from ancient glaciers and the passage of the water through a thousand rock formations, that bring nutrients to the estuary and provide food for the birds. Rising sea levels have engulfed the river and led to a striking geography of steep cliffs, rocky shores, peninsulas and islands, some of which connect to the mainland at low tide.

In Puerto Deseado we arranged to go on a trip with a local boat company, boarding their rigid-hulled inflatable with others, including a party of school children. We left the land, eager to find out what birds were making this place their home. The estuary is ringed by low sedimentary cliffs whose many ledges make ideal nesting places for a variety of seabirds, in particular cormorants. Four species of cormorant breed within the estuary and a fifth, the imperial, on islands just beyond. One might imagine that each species would be in competition with the others but clearly they are not.

Understanding the reasons why something like this is so is what biologists do best. Most people look at wildlife for the sheer wonder and beauty of what they are seeing; the satisfaction and happiness that this brings is enough to make the pastime both worthwhile and beneficial. It's different for field biologists. Instead of saying, 'Wow!' they say, 'Why?'

The natural world is changing and diminishing at an alarming rate. It was no different on that remote and little-visited coast of Argentina. One of the species of cormorant, the red-legged, had such a low population it was classified as 'near threatened'. What a bird it was, too. Its face was scarlet, its bill sunshine yellow and, adding to the bird's allure, is its eye, a swirling wheel of luminous green, like a child's lollipop. These flashing traffic lights of colours followed us over the surf.

Back on shore we met up with Annick Morgenthaler, a precise young Swiss woman and accomplished biologist who has been studying the seabird colonies of the estuary for many years. Annick spends day after day watching the minutiae of cormorant behaviour.

I wanted to know how there were five species of cormorant living there.

'They all feed differently,' came her reply. 'The red-legged cormorant feeds inshore, close to the cliffs, in shallow water, where they find their favourite food, sardines. The rock cormorant feeds a little further out, taking fish from deeper water.'

'What about the imperial?'

'That flies out for food in the company of others and dives deep down for squid.'

Annick had discovered that the birds' serious competition was from the fishing fleets that scoured the nearby waters for fish and squid.

There was a scattering of low islands, both in the estuary and around the coast, perfect for penguins, gulls, terns and ducks. Back out on the water, as we skimmed over the waves towards Penguin Island, a fleet of small dolphins emerged, jumping excitedly in the surf that trailed behind us. Turning over and over like dominoes, they were Commerson's dolphins, twisting, jumping and finally darting under our boat, piebald spinning tops one minute, gone the next.

Out into the open ocean, it was a fairground ride, bouncing and careering from one wave to another. There was no proper landing point on the island to disembark, so the boat's skipper manoeuvred the boat into position and judged the best time to close in to the slippery green rocks. On a sudden command, we jumped off, one at a time, scrambling and slithering, eventually tottering onto the beach.

As the noise of the boat's engine died away there was a momentary peace – then the cacophony of sounds and the overpowering smell from the guano of a seabird colony assailed us. In my opinion, the smell of a colony is as good as Chanel No. 5 but for some of the people on the island that day, it was nothing short of disgusting.

The schoolchildren were amazed; for them it was a real-life adventure, they were explorers where everything was new. Imagine their reaction on seeing a bird half as big as themselves! Birds that waddled not flew, birds with cute chicks that they could see close to. With suppressed gasps and giggles, eyes bulging, they watched the Magellanic penguins. The children's reactions added to our own excitement. Watching them reminded us of the time we had shown our own son, Richard, his first puffins.

The penguins' nests were close to each other, some in a small depression on the ground, others under a bush or tight against a stone. Fights were common and there was a lot of flapping and flying feathers between neighbours. Penguins pair for life and when one returns with food, they will caress each other, bill to bill, or point their thick black bills to the sky and emit a raucous donkey-like braying. Some birds walked about the colony like smart soldiers in black and white uniforms, while many settled themselves close together on the ground, a regimented keyboard. Others tottered as if drunk, slipping on rocks or falling backwards. To the children, they were true clowns. In one direction a bird emerged from the waves and returned to its nest with water still running down its silky back; in another, a dark grey furry chick emerged from under its parent, who popped a juicy morsel into its mouth. Others looked asleep but always had one eye open.

We went over the hill, past a ruined lighthouse and down to a more exposed part of the island. Waves were crashing against great boulders along the shoreline. Swimming is what penguins do best, but getting back onto land is a different matter. The birds were tossed about in the surf, using the frothy bubbles on the final wave to trampoline over the rocks, somersaulting in all directions. Once on shore they progressed to a tussocky arena where the fancy dress party unfolded: the rockhopper show!

Rockhoppers are smaller than Magellanic penguins. They have red bills and a headdress that would make any punk rocker jealous: a tuft of bright yellow feathers either side of the head ending in a perky black and yellow spray, a hairstyle forged by a bolt of lightning. They jump, not walk, half-bird, half-kangaroo. The children were laughing out loud, the show a great success.

All the penguins were on their guard – not from the children, but from predatory Antarctic skuas. The skuas breed on the island because a penguin colony means food. They steal unguarded eggs from unwitting penguin parents; even the young chicks themselves are vulnerable. They are airborne attackers, swooping across the island like fighter jets, harassing terns, gulls and penguins. Their strategy is to cause havoc because out of havoc comes confusion, and confusion creates opportunities to rob or kill. The island is as much a battleground as a breeding ground.

As we returned to the Deseado estuary, the boat cut its speed, travelling more slowly and more steadily than when we came. We were all tired, slumped against each other; the children had their eyes closed and I'm sure that penguins were jumping around in their dreams. I just hoped that one day they would be able to bring their own children to see the show we had all seen that day.

When I was those children's age, twelve or thirteen, I was sent away to boarding school, a mill-like grey stone building on the forbidding Yorkshire moors, often not seeing my parents for months at a time. I did not have one happy day there, ever. I did not know what friends were. Every evening I spent working for other boys – eighteen-year-old prefects. Daily I would clean their rooms, polish their shoes, iron their shirts. In winter I would scrub and wash their filthy rugby kit by hand; in summer, the same for green-stained cricket whites. Night-times were spent in terror, beaten and abused.

My only relief was at weekends. Then, I would escape beyond the school gates, past silent mills, their clattering machines now stilled, to wander high up into the bleak, sparse hills. No matter what the season the wind bit my cheeks and legs, always cold. Sunless valleys. With squelchy bogs and ankle-turning tussocks, those moors should have been the saddest of places, ones I could never return to – but this was where the magic started for me.

As I sheltered in the lee of hilltop cairns – pyramids of sharp millstone grit that guide shepherds in the snow – I would lean back against the stones and search the sky, wishing myself a bird. Thinking, crying sometimes, but watching and listening. The wind's plaintive wails could have been my own, but it also carried more comforting sounds, ones that at first I couldn't track down. But then, one Sunday, at the end of a particularly tough week, slumped against a high stone wall, the sharp rocks pressing into my back, from behind those stones it started again: first, like the chattering of children, a series of playful calls slowly rising to a bubbling climax, eventually trailing away in hauntingly soft notes. I listened, scarcely daring to breathe. And then, a large grey-brown tweedy sort of bird, the same colour as my school jacket, swept over the wall and landed close by among some ragged-looking sheep. The bird's long legs matched an absurdly long curved bill that probed searchingly between the waving grasses.

My first curlew, a friend, a moment of joy.

On another occasion I sat riveted as I watched a bird so indescribably gorgeous that a king's tailor couldn't have created a more stunning attire. One whose spangled gold upperparts and black underparts were separated by a band of purest white feathers – a golden plover. The colour and the sounds these birds brought to those dank, miserable hills were a revelation.

Every weekend more birds became my friends. It was the lapwings I loved the most. 'Green peewits' I called them, for that's what their colour is and that's the sound they make. With black and white wings waving like flags, they were tumbling clowns, dancing with the wind. Their cries – which no one heard but me – were my sounds.

It was as a young boy I learnt that nature soothes. Lonely no more, an unknown debt to repay.

After weeks of exploring the Valdés peninsula and Penguin Island we left the coast behind to continue south into what the locals call the 'empty lands' of the Patagonian plains.

Heading south, the gravel road was as straight and unending as a Chicago boulevard, the difference being that instead of a vertically congested city, here we moved through a horizontally wide, open and deserted world, the epitome of emptiness. We saw few people and were thankful for the additional long-range fuel tank – it would usually take us 700 kms before needing a refill –

we had had fitted on to the truck. Running short of fuel was never a worry for us. The few truck drivers that passed us always waved and we waved back.

The sky remained a perfect blue, the land ever-changing: one moment we swept through a vast, grey, forbidding desert of waxy-leaved jarilla bushes and spiky festuca grass; next a shimmering golden haze, as if someone had thrown down a flowery Persian carpet of intricate silken colours. Patagonia is as spellbinding as it is wearisome.

Much of the flat lands had been grazed to death by sheep, and the wind used the earth to take its revenge: for an hour, we watched twisting dust devils hop-scotching across the landscape. The wind was strengthening all the time, and our truck, which weighed nearly three tonnes, was pushed from one side of the road to the other several times.

We were still a couple of hours from Río Gallegos when a dark yellow curtain was drawn down from the sky.

'Michael, look over there; what is it?' exclaimed Paula.

'Where the heck has that come from? It's a dust storm.' I gripped the steering wheel, grimly. 'I'll speed up, hold on.' We accelerated away, gravel and stones ripping away behind us.

Paula craned her head to the side. 'It's closing fast.'

Looking back, I was shocked, unsure what to do – grains of sand were already specking against the windows. I pulled over, right off the road, and grabbed the binoculars. I wished I hadn't – some things are best not seen close up; the horizon was a rapidly advancing wall of rolling, swirling, dark yellow and purple dust.

'It's coming towards us!' screamed Paula. 'What do we do?'

'Stay put, don't get out!'

Within seconds the truck was rattling. As we were shaken about, rocking front to back, side to side, a pit in my stomach brought nausea rising in my throat. Balls of vegetation hit the doors, some rolling over the bonnet. Like being on a station platform as a high-speed train whizzes past without stopping, my ears hurt. I felt a corner of the truck lift a little into the air then bounce back down. The windscreen was bombarded by sand and grit, bigger stones made me instinctively pull the sun visor down for protection, the condor's feather dropping into my arms. Through the windows, I could see nothing, it was a swirling yellow fog. Were we going to be tipped over? I gripped the steering wheel again, eyes tight shut, clenching my teeth, expecting the worst.

After what seemed an age, everything went quiet. We stayed still, and only then did I open my eyes. Paula was clutching her seat belt with both hands. It was over. We looked out onto a different place: the road had disappeared under sand, there was brush all over the place. Gingerly we got out, leaning against the camper, legs wobbly. We walked around the truck to assess the damage.

The stormiest part of the sky was receding into the distance. A car pulled up behind us and a man got out. 'You OK? I watched it from way back. We get them at this time of the year. That was a bad one, though.' The man went on to tell us that a friend of his had been out walking with his dog when one of those storms had caught up with him. 'Never did find the dog,' he said, casually.

We walked around the truck again. Our windscreen was coarsely etched and chipped; every bit of chrome – the back of the wing mirrors, the front grill – was pitted, dull. In the days that followed, we experienced all sorts of intermittent electrical problems in the camper and later, when we to took it into a garage, they found the engine and components full of sandy grit.

For the first time since arriving in South America, we had encountered danger that no amount of planning could have prepared us for. On the outside we both remained calm, but my stomach churned as if I'd had too much to drink. Rustling balls of twigs careered along, the wind at last clearing an outline of a road. I've always loved to feel the wind in my face, soft and refreshing. Not this wind, though, hot and gritty.

We got back into the truck. Our crazed windscreen splintered the sunshine into a frosty fog. This had been our first real challenge; we knew there would be more. But we had escaped the duststorm unhurt. We were alive and happy, and nothing else mattered.

How couples first meet indicates a lot about whether a relationship might last. I was twenty years old and looking over a lake through my binoculars, following the buoyant flight of black terns delicately flitting over the surface, when I saw a golden-haired girl. She was lying on the opposite bank also watching the terns. Later she admitted she had also been watching me.

Paula has always liked the great outdoors. When she was a teenager, the only way to explore wild places and nature reserves had been to join a club and go on their coach trips to places like Norfolk and Yorkshire. It was on one of these trips that we met.

Several years later, when both of us were at university, I asked her if she fancied backpacking across Turkey to Iran. I wanted to go to the Caspian Sea, a known hotspot for bird migration, yet rarely visited. I knew I had picked the right girl when she responded with a positive, 'Yeah! Sounds like fun!'

Travelling together through dangerous country didn't bother us, but we were young and that we were together was all that mattered.

In our thirties, while Paula was pregnant, we camped completely alone for weeks on end in Tanzania's Mikumi National Park. I remember the padding of elephants' feet metres from our heads as we lay in our small tent. The elephants must have known we were there, and we could hear their low, contented grumblings. As the great beasts tore up the fresh grass close to us, our hearts pounded. We were thrilled, not afraid.

Fear is a peculiar emotion. The older I get, the more fearful I find I have become. Maybe it's due to having more family responsibilities: the fear of losing a job, status, material things?

Maybe fear was the reason I had got myself in such a state years before.

Living as we were now, close to nature and in the moment, the warnings that people had impressed upon us before we left seemed trivial.

CHAPTER 4

THE END OF THE WORLD

At last, one December day, we found ourselves on a stony, bumpy track that simply gave itself up to squelchy moorland beyond. The air spat rain at us, an icy wind perforated our gloves, and we stared in disbelief over one of the most desolate scenes imaginable. Around us, shattered and twisted trees pointed towards a shore battered by surf, nature's battleground, and the wind blew. Oh, how the wind blew!

No road on any continent other than Antarctica goes further south: this was Tierra del Fuego, the true starting point of our journey. In the distance were the Andes, but not the soaring snow-capped peaks that we had expected to see. Here, they were low grey hills – the Andes cowered, tamed by the elements, some fragmented into a scattering of islands and jagged rocks, swallowed periodically by the swirling Southern Ocean. But we knew where the grey hills led: northwards. There they grew in stature and ferocity into the longest mountain chain on Earth, an unbelievable 7,000 kilometres, all the way to the sultry Caribbean.

Lying to the south, like a brooding silver slick, was the Beagle Channel. Beyond it was Navarino Island, Chile's last outpost, and further still, Antarctica. The channel, named after Darwin's boat, is a deadly stretch of water. Gale-force winds rip down from the mountains to the channel beneath. Seamen call them 'williwaws'. Even the sea fights with itself as water surges from opposite ends, the Atlantic and the Pacific Oceans pushing against each other while maelstroms and vortices lurk beneath the surface.

Standing in this bleak spot we needed inspiration, a sign, something to snap us into action. Suddenly, a shape appeared out of the mist. Startled, we first imagined it to be a white flag waved from a boat in distress: quite the opposite, this was from something that both commanded and ruled the elements, a white bird wheeling over the waves and scything through each squall-driven gust. We cheered and punched the air in celebration urging the bird on – our first albatross, a wandering albatross, a bird that vies only with the Andean condor to be the biggest flying bird in the world. Watching the albatross cut through the gale was hypnotic – undulating spirals in controlled slow motion.

Driven upwards by accelerating air off the waves, the bird then gently tilted its wings, driving it downwards, one wing tip touching the surf and then upwards again. This dynamic, low-energy rhythm sustains an albatross in flight for weeks and months at a time. It only stops to land on the water in order to feed – and that has been its downfall.

The main threat to all albatrosses is considered to be long-line tuna fishing. The vessels in these fleets lay out up to fifty miles of hooks, baited with bits of squid just below the surface, a favourite food of the albatross. The birds dive down to grab the morsels and are themselves caught by the hooks. Hundreds of thousands of albatross are killed each year. In recent times there have been international efforts to prevent this waste of life. Conservationists from Aves Argentinas have been working closely with fishermen operating out of Mar del Plata, and now buoyant coloured tags are fitted to the lines of hooks hidden underwater. These scare the birds away from the trawler cables – some good news for the albatross.

Birdwatching on the Beagle Channel reminded us of being on the Norfolk coast of Great Britain. Before Paula and I were married we would be there every October, sheltering from the easterly gales in the lee of dislodged and tilting Second World War anti-tank blocks, a good opportunity to snuggle close. On days when the fog rolled in off the sea we would count passing Arctic and great skuas. They would hug the shore a few metres off the sand and pass right over our heads.

The weather here was much worse; the invisible force of the wind physically grabbing and shaking us. With teeth rattling, I closed my eyes. It really did seem like the end of the world. I shook my head and opened my eyes. The tempest was bringing us birds. We crouched by a huge boulder and counted them: southern giant petrels like huge bombers, bluish and stiff-winged southern fulmars, black-browed albatrosses and delicately dancing Antarctic prions. All were spilling and spiralling over the waves from west to east at a rate of ten birds a minute. We were more than excited, we were ecstatic – to be alive in such a place and witnessing nature in the raw. Our fingers numb, noses like mini icebergs, we stayed at our post like sailors on the bridge, tossing laughter into the face of the gale. This was living wild, close to birds; this was why we had come, to have the freedom of life-giving blood pulse in our veins, to refresh our spirits. If this was the first hour of the first day of our new life – a journey to explore the length of the Andes, to travel wild with birds – bring it on!

Exhausted but content, we put our backs to the end of the world and headed for the small hamlet of Almanza. Almanza is a fishing village of fifty wooden shacks that hugs the shoreline of the Beagle Channel. We parked half on the grassy verge just above the high-tide mark and half on the narrow gravel track that ran along the shore, spray from the waves assaulting the side of our truck.

Looking through the window by our bed, the wind rocking the vehicle, we might have been a boat bobbing on the channel. On the far side lay the Chilean island of Navarino, lights from its only town, Puerto Williams, clearly visible. Beyond and above the town, as far as we could see in either direction, reared monochrome mountains with a distinct treeline, as if someone had drawn a pencil line across the landscape above which snowy slopes popped out between low dark clouds. This was the ancestral home of the Selk'nam and Yahgan people, the last of whom died in the 1930s, following a hundred years of genocidal harassment.

Opposite to where we were parked, blown tight against the hillside of trees, lay a shack with red corrugated sheets for walls and rough wooden windows. A grey rusting tin roof was held in place by lengths of wood. Fishing nets draped the fence and by the entrance door an inflatable boat was weighted down with heavy timbers. Two other lengths of flotsam had written on them in garish paint: '*Cerveza*' and '*Parador*'. Nailed to the door, a sign read *La Sirena y El Capitan*, 'The Mermaid and the Sea Captain'.

'Fancy a beer?' Paula asked.

'Yes, but it won't be the sort of *parador* we're used to.'

Once inside, however, it was better than the best of Spanish *paradors*. For us it really was a palace. Warmth from a wood-burning stove wrapped around us, we could get half-decent internet and eat freshly caught king crabs for the price of a pizza at home. No one else was in; in fact, we hadn't seen anyone all day. We sat at a small wooden table in the window. From a room at the back, our hosts' voices rose and fell like Italian chefs in a hectic kitchen. Alicia came out first. She was small, with dark curly hair. 'Hello,' she whispered, in a surprised and smiling tone, and glided back into the kitchen with our order. The wind rattled the outside door. Alicia peered out from the kitchen but no one else had arrived. She went to the door and looked outside. No customers were in sight.

Sergio, her husband, came out and welcomed us warmly. He was tall, receding hair giving his high forehead a priestly appearance, a grey hoodie only adding to it. Clearly he didn't mind our muddy boots and dishevelled, windswept appearance. He waved to the corner of the room. 'If you want music, choose your own. I'll get the drinks.'

In the corner on the wall was pinned a yellowing poster of Carlos Gardel, a famous Argentinian tango master. On an adjacent shelf sat a black 1960s Columbia record player. Another shelf beneath was stacked with LP records in tatty brown sleeves, a few in their original glossy but equally worn covers: Abba, the Supremes, Glen Miller, the Chieftains and Smokey Robinson. It was all vintage music that some would call classical, the only rap coming from the wind-rapped door. The deck turned and the black disc twirled with the familiar, scratchy *chick – chick – chick*, the Moody Blues' 'Nights in White Satin' played, while outside the clouds turned as dark as the musical vinyl, the sea as choppy as the needle.

Alicia returned with our drinks and retired to a high stool at the bar, humming to the music.

'You from round here?' I asked.

'No, Buenos Aires.'

'Why are you here?'

'Waves and wind. You?'

'Birds.'

Alicia turned to us, cocking her head to one side, still smiling. 'That's good. That's very good.' Then she walked to look out of the door again. Still no one was to be seen.

The windows shook as the rain beat upon them, and more southern giant petrels and a few piebald Cape petrels swept by.

Paula's Merlot was smooth, my Cape Horn beer strong. We couldn't have been happier; we were warm, and wished for nothing more.

The next morning we walked the shoreline where a curving shingle bar gave shelter to a few small boats with outboards, all painted the same mustard colour. It was not so much a harbour as a place of retreat. Further on, a high shell-and-pebble hummock hid a small brackish lake from our view. As soon as we topped the ridge a pair of yellow-billed teal and a couple of kelp geese flew off.

The male of the kelp goose is completely white, the female by contrast is black with a throat, belly and breast of white shimmering ribbons, her legs and feet the colour of a lemon. We backed off and settled at the end of the spit, huddled amid a heap of washed-up bladderwrack, waiting and watching. That's what we did best, and as birdwatchers, photographers and film-makers this worked well. Much though we loved the company of friends, often you have to tune out from people in order to tune in to nature. There was no better place to do that than there on the tideline of the Beagle Channel at the end of the world, hidden behind a heap of seaweed, surf-blown salt invading our nostrils, immersed in the wild.

In the channel an occasional ship made slow progress, waves crashing over the bow. First was an elegant French liner, with deck upon deck of round windows, then a much smaller, businesslike ship, sporting a yellow National Geographic logo. The channel is the route from the port of Ushuaia to the Antarctic and South Georgia, taking scientists away from loved ones for months at a time, or tourists from armchairs at home to armchairs travelling over the ocean.

A noise close by alerted us to a rufous-chested dotterel which had alighted on the shore and started to pick at tiny insects. If ever there was a bird that looked like a ship's captain this was the one: an upright wader with longish legs and an orange breast with a black stripe beneath, and on its head a brown cap with a black and white peak.

A pair of large black and white Magellanic oystercatchers paraded about, piping and displaying to each other, or was it to the dotterel? The kelp geese that we had disturbed earlier returned to the tideline, searching for food. Still we waited. Small movements often betray secrets. Further away we suspected something was watching us as we watched the shoreline. We detected movement close to a sea-bleached log and a tuft of flowers. Our thoughts of a nest were proved correct when a kelp goose swam by a little too close: a plump greyish duck with a large orange bill hurtled out of the tufty vegetation, across the stones, straight into the sea, wings flapping wildly, and attacked the much larger goose by torpedoing it with a body slam. After much splashing and with feathers flying, the goose quickly departed. Now we knew what had caused the movement: this was a flightless steamer duck, an uncommon and quite aggressive bird found only in the far south of Argentina. The duck swam off and joined its mate some distance away and we used the opportunity to quickly go towards the log. Like pirates, we discovered a hoard of treasure: seven large beige eggs cosseted in exquisite white and grey down feathers.

Flightless steamer ducks are the southern hemisphere equivalent of eider ducks. Both use heavy bills to crush shellfish and mussels, their favourite food. Our pair, out in the channel, stopped feeding and started to paddle in our direction. We made our escape quickly; we didn't want to mess with these birds.

Back at the truck, we decided it was time for our twice-weekly showers. I boiled a few kettles of water and decanted them into a bucket of cold water. Hiding behind the truck, spray drifting in off the Straits of Magellan, Paula stripped off as I ladled tepid water over her. In temperatures close to zero, she didn't linger.

By now Christmas was only a week away, and Richard had decided to visit us. He lives in Ottawa, Canada, where winter temperatures regularly plummet to minus twenty and snow lies on the ground for months. Thinking that a Christmas visit to us for midsummer BBQs might be a perfect holiday, he decided to fly due south 11,000 miles, taking advantage of Earth's tilt to relive summertime.

We collected him from Punta Arenas airport. At the foot of the steps leading from the small aircraft we watched as he dived into his rucksack for a coat. 'Think it's warmer in Ottawa.'

We had no fixed plans so asked what our son would like to do.

'I just need a break – I've had a crazy few months at work. It's all emails and online calls. Non-stop. I would love to get into the Andes. Before I left, I looked up the campgrounds and trekking routes in Torres del Paine national park but everything's been booked up for months.' Richard sounded disappointed.

'No worries. This place is vast, the mountains wild; we'll find our own adventures.'

We crossed the Straits of Magellan and drove into Tierra del Fuego. I wanted to show Richard something special.

En route we passed through the small town of Porvenir, the biggest one on the Chilean part of the island and home to a few hundred military as well as sheep-farming families. From a misty Fuegian distance the settlement could have been a hillside of flowers. The small wooden houses, all with corrugated roofs, were painted a hotchpotch of colours, white and blue or yellow and orange or just weathered wood and rust. Hand-cut picket fences leaned into the wind, some held upright by abandoned cars or dog kennels. By the shoreline a children's playground contained a broken wagon and an artillery gun, both of which could have been centuries old. There was an austere, high-walled prison, though around the walls was a scattering of tall purple and white lupins.

What I wanted to show Richard appeared a few kilometres down the deserted shoreline at the oddly named Useless Bay. We parked the truck on the narrow gravel road and walked through golden marshy sedges. There, on the desolate shore with a backdrop of a tumultuous storming Magellanic sea, stood what looked like a large group of pompous High Court barristers arguing over a heinous crime. They paced up and down, hands behind their backs, head thrown back. They looked askance at their learned colleagues. Pairs had heads craned towards each other as if whispering about which witness to bring on next. They were king penguins, the only colony found on the mainland of South America. Standing one metre tall, they had black and silver coats over bulging white ermine shirts, smooth custard-yellow bibs and matching ear muffs. They are a ridiculously gorgeous, bucket-list bird.

Crossing back over the strait and into Argentina we took route

5 north-west towards the Andes, a 500-kilometre gravel road through the Patagonian steppe. Leaving a funnel of dust behind us we barely managed a speed of 50 kmph.

'Why are you driving so slowly, Dad?'

'Don't want to hit any wildlife.'

Hefty, long-necked llama-like guanaco, able to jump the old fences at the sides of the road, were common and had the unnerving habit of watching us approach from a distance and then crossing the road just as we were almost upon them. We had passed too many wrecked cars not to treat those animals with respect. Then there were two species of fox: the culpeo fox, reddish with a blackish tail; and the more common grey fox. They would always appear from nowhere and dash across the road as our truck approached.

'These animals have a death wish,' commented Richard.

Much of the land on either side of the road was fenced off with old wire fencing. Historically, sheep grazing had been important to the economy in Patagonia though the decline in wool prices had forced most of the smaller *estancia*s out of business – we passed many deserted wooden farm houses, open doors banging in the wind, forlorn *Wizard of Oz* windmills tottering towards collapse.

Patagonia seemed too big to be held even by the sky, the land so unending that our eyes only sat comfortably on the horizon. Below that distant line separating blue from buff, a scene-shifting drama unfolded the further west we drove.

Sedimentary gorges scoured by the wind often had a black-chested buzzard eagle suspended like a mobile over them. Low bluffs reared up in bands of ochre and yellow, ancient seacliffs holding hoards of fossils. Multiple ridges of igneous grey, black and white rock arose with convoluted patterns traced into them like twisted concertinas. Great rocks as big as minibuses, volcanic bombs, lay embedded in the ground, missiles from the heavens. Grey plates of flat rock, ancient lava flows, tipped obliquely one way then another. Every hour of our journey we turned a different page in the picture book of Patagonia's violent creation. From the north rose dramatic, sheer-faced, flat-topped *mesetas*, seemingly impossible to reach, their high plateaus waiting to be conquered another day.

Endless bleached fencing – perches for red-tailed hawks – seemed to keep nothing in or out. After hours of driving, blinking, our sleepy eyes ached for something new to focus on.

As we neared our destination, the sky diminished as the mountains grew. Brilliant white sunbeams pierced through the darkening clouds like arrows. Without warning, our truck was suddenly slewing about like a tiny boat on the Beagle Channel as williwaws hit us.

At last, we found shelter in mountainous shadows and followed turquoise glacial lakes deep into the Andes. We halted by a road sign: 'Los Glaciares National Park'.

'That's where Mount Fitz Roy is,' said Richard, proudly pointing to the logo on his Patagonia fleece. 'Let's head there!'

A cloudless sky on 20th December tempted us to spend midsummer somewhere special. Towering above the village of El Chaltén was the frighteningly sheer peak of Mount Fitz Roy, its top partly obscured by cloud.

It was in 1968 that the first ascent of the notorious south-western ridge was achieved by Yvon Chouinard, who later founded the global brand of Patagonia, and Douglas Tompkins, who already owned the brand North Face.

We hurriedly packed rucksacks – always a dilemma as to what to take: needs versus wants. Paula wasn't going to join us as her back was playing up and serious trekking up steep slopes was not going to help. Having taught upper-school maths for many years, bending over children to coach them in calculus had left its mark on a spine evolved to be upright. Instead, Richard and I would share what we took: a small mountain tent at three kilos, a Canon camera with a 300mm lens weighing five kilos, a tripod, binoculars, down sleeping bags and mats, emergency kit, food and cooking equipment, a few spare clothes and, of course, chocolate. We weighed in at twenty-five kilos each, far too much for a rapid ascent. My suggestion was, 'It's midsummer, let's ditch the sleeping bags.'

'No way! We need the right kit,' Richard replied. So we pared everything back a little, and the tripod was dumped. I exchanged the heavy telephoto lens for a 180mm macro – my favourite lens, and much lighter.

Then I took out the chocolate.

'Aha! No, you don't!' Richard stuffed the outrageously big bar into his rucksack.

Numerous trails radiate from the quaint village of El Chaltén. We took the one that led us towards the hidden Laguna Torre. It rose steeply along the edge of a rocky spur surrounded by thin forest. As usual I was at the rear, always watching the wild, Richard further ahead. Other trekkers passed us; heads down, walking with great purpose, as if on an important mission. We continued all morning, gradually climbing. Periodically, steep forested slopes fell away to our right and opened out into dramatic broad, glaciated valleys, their lower scree slopes ending in a boulder field cut by meandering silver scribbles which pushed the valley into even more distant mountains.

Two specks in the sky drifted overhead, wings like barn doors, primary feathers splayed out like fingers.

'Condors! Condors!' I shouted.

'Condors . . .? Condors!' shouted Richard, even louder, in reply. A couple of day walkers looked back and laughed. At last, the greatest birds soaring above the highest of mountains.

Eventually the eroded, stony path, strewn with thick, exposed tree roots, gave way to a gentler, less trodden trail. The day's blue sky was being replaced by low, dark clouds which draped listlessly over the tops of the snowy mountains in the direction we were heading. Ahead of us a ridge appeared, beyond which the ground fell away abruptly. Off came our packs and onto the low, springy bushes we slumped. Behind us were sharply tilting gale-pressed trees. There was no wind, the air ominously silent. We must have been close to the treeline as, looking around, the dark line separating the forest from the snowy mountain sides came around to the very spot we were at.

Before us lay a panorama of the sub-Antarctic southern beech forests that run for 800 kilometres through Patagonian Argentina. This forest is clutched by vertiginous Andean claws, over the top of which sits the biggest ice cap outside Antarctica. From this pour forty-six glaciers, feeding great rivers that flow west into the Pacific and east into the Atlantic. Opposite to where we sat, maybe 2 kilometres away, a black hanging valley vomited a cascade of dirty ice, etched with heavenly blue crevasses. Along the flat, boulder-strewn valley floor, way beneath us, meandered a river frothing with icy blue water. A lost world.

'It makes me feel insignificant,' said Richard.

'Not surprising, in a place like this,' I replied.

'My office in Ottawa seems a world away. I've almost forgotten about the emails that will be piling into my inbox.'

'Then don't think about them.'

'You're looking better than the last time I saw you.'

'Feel it too, thanks.'

'Not surprising, in a place like this,' he replied.

Both of us started laughing.

Grabbing a handful of berried vegetation I screwed it up in my fist and then held it out to him. 'Smell this.'

Richard inhaled, and we exchanged smiles.

Sliding down rock scree we entered the beech forest. There are many different species of southern beech, but the ones we walked under were the Antarctic beech, with small, dark green serrated leaves. The great mature trees were well spaced out and, except for the many fallen branches and storm-dashed limbs, it was easy to penetrate the brush, our way illuminated by a carpet of star-like white dog orchids and the bright, upright spikes of yellow orchids, which led us along a path of sweet fragrance.

Ancient trees are almost always the oldest living things in a landscape, so it didn't surprise me when we eventually came across a group of huge southern beech trees, sentinels at the very end of their life. The tops of the trees had been sheared off by storms, and gaping holes had been rent in their sides, but some still stretched their last few thin branches towards the sunlight. One had a massive decaying limb hanging from where, perhaps hundreds of years before, a volcano had cast a boulder at it. Another had a deformed curve in its vast girth, perhaps witness to a terrible gale that had sunk a dozen ships. Another had the tracery of letters cut deep in it where a love-sick soul had carved a single heart. All had thick velvet moss cushioning their massive weather-beaten frames. Nature was kind to them in their dotage.

In one of the trees I noticed a gash at the base. In I squeezed, pushing until I found myself comfortably inside. Entombed inside the blackened timber shell, I closed my eyes, leaning my body against its solidity, imagining the long life of the venerable giant. For hundreds of years it had helped sustain the animals and plants of the forest. This one tree had probably done more good for the Earth than any single human. Opening my eyes, sunlight poured through gaps above me, open sockets where the tree's limbs had been, its canopy open to the sky, sunbeams pouring through. I felt a gratifying peace. My mind rode the piercing sunbeams through the tiny cracks, where I could see a younger generation of trees, fresh with their tiny green serrated leaves. New life is always to be found no matter how badly damaged and dying nature is; it constantly emerges with or without us. I leaned a warm cheek against the cold black skin, happy to be close to that greybeard.

And then I saw it: through a small jagged rent in the trunk, a bird on a nearby tree.

Never before had I watched a bird from within a tree; I shouldn't have been there – it was a topsy-turvy experience. The bird didn't see me – it wouldn't have expected me to be inside its own woody world. The bird was completely black, a thin streak of white on her back – a nun with red cheeks, a wisp of black feathers on the top of her head. At last I'd glimpsed my first female Magellanic woodpecker, whose black bill slowly turned aside strands of lichen as if she were reading a prayer book. And then, as suddenly as I'd noticed her, through the narrow telescope of wood, the bird was lost.

Twisting one way and another I crawled out from within the tree, but she had flown.

Richard was a short distance away and had seen her fly off.

'Did you see that bird?'

'Yes, I saw it. A woodpecker!'

'Right. A Magellanic woodpecker.'

This was the peak of the Magellanic woodpeckers' breeding season and we hadn't gone very far before we heard a loud rapping *toc-t-toc, toc-t-toc*.

Magellanic woodpeckers need a lot of food. They feed on insect larvae and these are best found in older trees. Some southern beech trees reach a noble age of 350 years. The older the tree the more insects are likely to be found, so maintaining and defending a territory is vital. Researchers have found that the daily routes the woodpeckers fly in order to feed are the shortest route through their territory while simultaneously visiting each of the oldest trees. A regular tour of its boundary and loud thumping on resonant trees act like an 'audible fence', a warning to other woodpeckers in the vicinity to keep out.

These woodpeckers have also evolved some novel adaptations, enabling them to improve their success rate in food-gathering in such a harsh environment. The male and female each have a different shaped bill: the male's bill is more substantial, enabling it to penetrate deeper into wood to access juicy moth and beetle larvae, while the female's is more suited to prising away thin bark and needling into crevices, hiding places for spiders and other tasty morsels. The birds also have a remarkable social life with each family working together as a team. Pairs will have a low clutch size, usually one or two eggs, and once fledged, the young stay with the parents in their territory, helping to find food and keeping in close contact all the time. The family will roost together through the winter. When the pair nests again, the whole family will participate in finding food for the new chicks, but once these fledge, the older juveniles from the previous year are then ousted from the territory to fend for themselves. By that time, though, the juveniles have learnt from their parents how to find food and therefore how to survive winter in this cold, hostile forest.

Richard and I followed the *toc-t-toc* thumps through the forest, leading us into a dell of old battered and rotting trunks where we saw not only the male, but his family of two other females. Once located, the birds allowed us a close approach. In contrast to the smaller all-black females, the male was huge, as big as a bowling pin. Like his family his body was black and white but his neck and head were blood-red, like a warrior wearing a scarlet headdress. He saw us and moved around, several times popping his red head around the trunk and peering at us with his orange eyes. We watched the birds for half an hour, sorry that Paula wasn't with us. This would have been an ideal filming opportunity for her. Still, I had my camera and had exactly the right lens, for once. The birds moved off.

By now it was late afternoon and we were surprised by a cold wind that sprang up. Richard turned to me. 'We should get a move on, find the campsite? Hopefully it's close.'

We returned to the path and, after another hour's walk, the sight of two other small tents showed us the place.

Thankful to be relieved of our rucksacks and having eaten and warmed ourselves around a small fire, we curled up and slept. Flapping guy ropes made for a poor night's sleep and I drifted between dreams, waking regularly to the rattling of branches overhead.

I looked at my watch; it was six o'clock, yet very bright. *Strange*, I thought. *Can't hear any birds*. I unzipped the tent, peeped out and saw nothing: everything was white, and so quiet.

Perhaps I'd died. Then I put my cold glasses on. Snow! Thick snow covered the tent and it was still falling. We had slept through a blizzard.

The advantage of a quality duck-down sleeping bag is that it keeps you dreamily warm; the disadvantage is that eventually you have to get out of it and the colder it is outside, the worse the shock. The temperature inside the tent was a crazy minus five degrees.

Richard stuck his head out of his tent. 'We'd better get out. We don't want to get snowed in here.' Hurriedly, we got dressed.

One of the most miserable jobs is to break camp in snow and wind, without breakfast, fingers and nose numb, but it's the best time ever for a bar of chocolate. As we hastily dropped the tent and packed up, a grey fox strolled nonchalantly by, sniffed some of our equipment and drifted away.

'So much for midsummer in Patagonia! But I wouldn't change it for anything,' Richard shouted over the wind. I gave him a silent thumbs-up, and we started the descent back to El Chaltén, the snow still blowing around us.

CHAPTER 5

TANGO IN THE WIND

For a field biologist, it's difficult to imagine anything more exciting than to discover a bird that no one has ever seen before, a species new to science.

This happened to the man we were going to meet, Mauricio Rumboll, who in 1974 quite inadvertently discovered a bird that was destined to become an icon in the history of South American ornithology. Nor was it a discovery of a small brown bird that lived in the far-overhead treetops: this was a large, distinctively plumaged bird, found on open water, an event perhaps never to be repeated.

One of our dreams was to find and film his elusive hooded grebe.

Mauricio and his wife, Diana, lived near the town of La Cumbre in Córdoba province, a smart place whose clean streets were lined with stone buildings housing fashionable shops and cafés, quite unlike the majority of small towns in Argentina. He is a legendary character in Argentina's illustrious attempts to conserve its wildlife.

Standing outside his house waiting to greet us when we arrived, Mauricio was a short, elderly man; bald, but sporting a fine grey moustache, a beard and a broad smile.

We sat at his kitchen table and swapped stories of travels in Argentina, our attention regularly distracted by the garden bird table where green-barred woodpeckers vied with brown cacholotes.

I opened out a map on the table.

'Ah, Patagonia!' the old man said. 'Yes, yes, I was working for the Buenos Aires museum. The Ministry of Agriculture was being pressed by the government to reduce the damage geese were doing to wheat crops. So they dispatched me and a colleague, Edward Shaw, to Patagonia, to research their movements and habits.' He paused, sighing. 'At that time the government was paying five pesos for a dead goose, one hundred pesos for a bagful. Every day people wandered into our offices with sacks of dead geese. It was awful. A horrid time.'

Mauricio was visibly upset at the memories. There was a long pause and I glanced at the old man. His cheeks were glistening. I looked down at the map, and Mauricio slowly traced his finger across it.

'Anyway, off we went in an old Citroën Ami. The roads at that time were shocking, all gravel tracks, thousands of kilometres. It took us six days. What a journey! But we were in Patagonia, the strangest place imaginable.' His voice trailed off and then he stabbed at the map. 'There! In the Santa Cruz valley close to the Laguna Los Escarchados. That's where we were catching and ringing geese.'

Suddenly, it was as if his memories were bringing him out of himself, rekindling his old energetic spirit. 'Edward said he wanted to practise preparing museum skins, so took the gun and walked away to find a bird to shoot.' He chuckled. 'Sometime later a figure appeared on the skyline. It was Edward, naked as the day he was born, with a bundle of clothes under one arm and a bird under the other.' Mauricio coughed and let out another soft, sympathetic laugh. 'He had shot a bird out on the lake but the fierce wind had pushed the bird further out, so he had had to swim to retrieve the corpse. Edward was very cold and shivering badly, so I bundled him into the car, covered him in blankets and turned on the heater. I briefly looked at the bird but didn't take much notice of it, thinking it was a common silvery grebe in autumn plumage. For the long journey back to Buenos Aires, we wrapped the bird in an old sack, and stuffed it between the chrome bumper and radiator of the car. The bird dried out in no time.'

Pepper, his lovely black Labrador dog, wandered over to his master for a stroke.

Mauricio then told us how, through comparison and research, it had started to dawn on him and his team that they perhaps had that holy grail of biology – a new species. Mauricio had to provide evidence of the bird: photos and descriptions – 'pages of information!' – and eventually it was confirmed. They named the bird the hooded grebe.

The old man looked out of the window and sighed. 'It's ironic we found it when the bird was probably at the peak of its population. It seems that immediately afterwards, this lovely bird started to tip towards the bottomless cliff of extinction.'

'Why did no one bother with it?'

'Bad times, very bad times. No one went to Patagonia in the 1970s. People were being killed, people were disappearing. The military junta was in control. If you had a job you kept your head down. I lost many friends.'

Mauricio stopped talking about the bird after that. 'Come on, Pepper,' he said. 'Let's go for a walk.'

Mauricio was a special man, a warm, open Anglo-Argentinian, unassuming, happy and content, a lover of nature. We never met again and he passed away soon afterwards.

There is something innately human about wanting to know everything about everything. Maybe our brains have got too big for us. As a species, we're never satisfied in standing still and being content with our lot.

The hooded grebe was a beautiful bird that no one knew anything about. Of course it couldn't stay that way for long – things had to change – but it actually took ten years before anything happened. What followed was a story of extraordinary luck, and tragedy.

In 1982 a biologist named Andres Johnson visited the Buenos Aires museum. In one of the back rooms, the skin of the shot hooded grebe lay in its drawer, every year its feathers fading a little more, one of thousands of bird specimens that rarely attracted attention.

Andres slid out the drawer and gently lifted up the bird. Hanging from one of its short legs dangled a tiny yellowing museum label. '*Shot April 22nd 1974, Laguna Los Escarchados, Santa Cruz. Sex unknown, life history unknown, food unknown. Collected by M Rumboll.*'

The week previously, following a chance discussion between biologists, Andres had been commissioned by the Argentinian Wildlife Foundation to undertake a study of the species. Andres had the job to unravel the mysteries surrounding the bird – no one knew where the birds spent the winter; certainly not on the plateaus, where the lagoons freeze over and blizzards blanket everything in deep snow.

That faded skin and feathers were all the information Andres had. This was a bird rarely seen. And although Andres was a determined and experienced field biologist, even he was shocked by the difficulties he was to face.

Rumours led him to explore the three largest flat-topped plateaus of Strobel, Buenos Aires and Siberia. They rear up from the foothills between the Andes and the Patagonian steppe in the province of Santa Cruz. Camping out in ferocious weather for months at a time, Andres endured hurricane-force winds, snowstorms and bone-chilling cold.

After three painstaking years, his estimate of the population of hooded grebes was between three and five thousand individuals – very low by any standard. More importantly, he discovered two requirements the hooded grebe needed in order to survive: firstly, the grebes depend upon a certain aquatic plant to build their nests – free-floating nests would be blown away on the wind-scoured lakes, so the birds use the long roots of the water milfoil to attach their nests to the lake bottom, much like a hot-air balloon is attached to the ground by strong cables. Secondly, breeding lagoons need a plentiful supply of tiny snails on which the grebes feed.

Even after all this, still only a handful of people even knew of the bird's existence. No legends had been written about it, no poems. No children sitting on their mother's knee were told stories about the bird's beauty or the otherworldly plateaus where they lived.

The hooded grebe remained forgotten, and another ten years slid by, until a local school was looking for a project for its science class.

The only town of note along the Atlantic coastline of southern Patagonia is Río Gallegos and it was here that a young expert birdwatcher lived, Santiago Imberti. Santiago had occasionally seen hooded grebes along the coast during the winter but thought little of it.

In 1994, he was approached by a local schoolteacher who was looking for a science project. It was wintertime, and cold and snowy weather meant young children couldn't go far out into the field. Santiago decided they could carry out bird counts on the estuary of Río Gallegos, which ran through the town, and on other estuaries a little further up the coast.

During that bitterly hard winter the children were escorted to points along the estuaries to locate and count birds and there they found, among other species, hooded grebes. Inadvertently, the science project had discovered the grebes' main wintering grounds.

The children found that the grebes were present throughout the winter, particularly on the estuary of the Santa Cruz, a little way to the north of the town. However, the number of birds they found was disturbingly low – less than 400 birds had been seen. In the following years, hoping the birds had more important wintering sites, Santiago himself widened the search throughout the whole of Tierra del Fuego, even as far as the Chilean fjords, but he found no more hooded grebes.

In 2008 Santiago raised his concerns with his friend Hernan Casañas, now the director of Aves Argentinas. In the summer of 2009, together with Hernan, he made a more thorough survey of the high plateaus and found about the same number of birds – 400. At this point they pushed the red button to alert conservation bodies worldwide as to the potential threat and looming extinction of the bird. A public relations programme swung into action and in 2010 another and more comprehensive survey was organised, involving a small team of people in four vehicles, searching the three biggest plateaus. To their shock and amazement, the team still could not improve on the numbers of birds. The global population was officially placed at 400 birds, a devastating decline. Where had all the birds gone? Why? What was happening? No one knew.

In 2011, Aves Argentinas funded a team led by expert biologist Kini Roesler to find the answers to the hooded grebe's decline. A field station to house researchers and volunteers was established close to the Buenos Aires plateau. Toyota offered the project a vehicle and fuel for the season. The race was now on and volunteers came from Australia, France, Great Britain, Holland and the United States to support the mission to save the hooded grebe, an endeavour to halt the bird's slide towards extinction.

To the dismay of the project team they found ample evidence that populations of American mink had spread north from where they had been released due to the animal rights protests of the 1970s. Hooded grebes had never encountered such a predator.

A second problem for the hooded grebe came from within the water itself: fish, in particular, the non-native rainbow trout. In the 1970s, land-based fisheries reneged on costly fish farms and closed their businesses down. The fish were sold to farmers inland so they could stock lakes and encourage sport fishing. The rainbow trout is an alien fish from North America and without its natural predators grows to gigantic proportions. They devour the native wildlife of the lakes, altering the chemistry of the water, which leads to the death of many of the aquatic plants, including the important water milfoil. The giant fish even feed on waterbird chicks, including those of the hooded grebe.

A third problem was gulls. Prior to the 1980s gulls were essentially seabirds and seldom spent much time inland. But for a bird to fly out to sea and be buffeted by freezing gale-force winds in the search for food is costly in terms of energy; a much easier way of life was appearing on the gulls' doorstep – food waste in the guise of rubbish. Rubbish is never good, but in a country where there is little infrastructure for waste management the problems mount up and don't go away. A build-up of rubbish means a breeding ground for rodents and a feast for scavenging birds. The gull population soared and eventually the gulls moved inland to smaller towns and remote villages, each with its own waste rubbish problems. It was fast food for all, including the gulls. It wasn't long before birds started to hunt over the plateaus and the tiny hooded grebe chicks became a favourite snack.

Shortly after Richard had returned to Canada in the New Year we had the telephone call we most wanted: Hernan Casañas asked us if we wanted to make a film for Aves Argentinas.

'Have you the time? It could take you months,' he said. Then came the exciting request: 'How about a film on the hooded grebe?'

At last we had the project we had been looking for.

'Go to Perito Moreno.' Hernan then followed this up with: 'Find the café Iturrioz, and in two days' time, sometime in the afternoon, someone will meet you there.'

That was all the information we had. To meet someone in

a café, hundreds of kilometres away, who would then take us somewhere else.

What else could we do but set off immediately?

On the long drive to Perito Moreno, Paula and I talked excitedly about the forthcoming film. Would we be able to find the grebes? Would our cameras cope in the ferocious wind? When we weren't talking we wiled away the tedium of endless straight gravel roads listening to BBC Radio 4 podcasts – a lifeline to our previous life. If we were feeling in need of interesting music and wanted to know what other people had done with their lives it was *Desert Island Discs*; if we felt in need of something historical and even more fascinating, it was *A History of the World in 100 Objects*.

Travelling across the endless flat plains of leathery yellow scrub with the distant jagged Andean peaks always in the west, it seemed an impossible mission to locate so small a number of birds. The current population of hooded grebes was now estimated at 800 – we had seen bigger flocks of starlings in our home town.

Eventually we drove into Perito Moreno, a deserted-looking town of single-storey houses. The only place we could find open was the Salon Iturrioz. Its imposing brick façade gave it the appearance of a bank in a spaghetti western, and the inside could have been a saloon. We pushed between swinging wooden doors into a café full of identical dark wooden tables with matching bentwood chairs. Along the length of one side ran a wooden bar behind which shelves held rows of glasses, bottles of spirits and liqueurs, a small black-and-white television and a few lamps. On high stools we sipped the best coffee we'd had in Argentina and were surprised at the good wi-fi. At the end of the bar sat an imposingly large ornate silver cash till, like some fairground Wurlitzer. But what most caught our attention was the postcard dispenser, in which the only postcards showed images of hooded grebes.

Sure enough, two days after our arrival, we were met by a member of the research team and told to follow them. The first stop was at the village supermarket where they stocked up on pasta, rice, fruit and vegetables to feed the project team, and we topped up our supplies of milk and chocolate.

Two hours' drive outside the town we eventually pulled up at the project base camp, at a rundown sheep *estancia*, now grandly titled 'Estacion Biologica Juan Mazar Barnett'. Accommodation for the volunteers was sparse: dormitories of bunk beds made from recycled fencing. A small kitchen with an ancient wood-fired oven was the centre of activities where people gathered, a warm refuge where food was prepared, cooked and eaten. Outside the wind howled around the exposed walls, tossing grit against the windows.

The three flat-topped plateaus of Strobel, Siberia and Buenos Aires are a feature of the western Patagonian plains. They are of volcanic origin, basaltic in nature and held in isolation by steep, almost vertical slopes that fall away nine hundred metres to the surrounding land beneath. The Buenos Aires plateau is an oval top hat of land about ten kilometres wide and forty kilometres long, a place where no one lives, a lost world. Climbers don't visit (there are no mountains as such), neither do walkers (there are no paths). The shepherds have faded away with their sheep, their economy of wool long passed. Access is via a rudimentary, winding horse track used generations ago by shepherds, so the plateau is left alone, hiding its beauty behind a cloak of silence and only revealing its secrets to the inquisitive.

Inquisitiveness about truly wild places is not that common. Nowadays, the internet and guidebooks instruct us where and when to go, what to see, where to eat and sleep, and to rate the experience from one to ten. Many pay professional guides to move them hurriedly from place to place. But without inquisitiveness we were never going to find our birds – we needed to search.

Eventually, a couple of volunteers spotted two hooded grebes on a small lagoon. At last the birds were arriving from the coast, following the rivers across the wind-blasted steppe. Now the race was on to find where they were congregating. Hundreds of square kilometres needed searching, all treacherous terrain with no roads.

Where the birds chose to gather depended on the snowstorms of winter and the sunshine of spring. The Earth and sky dictated which craters became lagoons of crystal water suitable for the rare milfoil plant to flourish in the spring sunshine. It was these seasonal vagaries that moved the hooded grebes about like puppets, popping them down in one isolated lagoon, then moving them up to another kilometres away.

Lagoon after lagoon was checked. To our eyes, many seemed suitable, but had no birds. Time was running out, and we only had this once-in-a-lifetime opportunity to make a film. At last, the signal came – a search party of volunteers had located a group of hooded grebes on one lagoon. We were given the GPS co-ordinates and dispatched with two American volunteers, Bobby and Kaitlin, together with two weeks' supply of food and water. This was the third year Bobby and Kaitlin had volunteered with the project; they knew what they needed to do to protect the grebes and record the birds' behaviour.

Our job was to make a film, but first we had to establish a camp near to the lagoon. Aeons past, volcanic gas had bubbled up, pock-marking the plateau with hundreds of craters. Explosions had showered rocks haphazardly over the plateau; for millennia the ceaseless wind had ripped, torn and abraded the rock. It was a devilish place to drive over, but we had probably the best commercial vehicle in the world for negotiating this sort of ground. Still, the lava fields of razor-sharp rocks the size of footballs covering the ground threw us from one side of the vehicle to the other. Squeaks and groans came from not just the truck but from us as well. We ploughed through sandy, dried-up riverbeds and slalomed around huge boulders, thankful for the upgraded leaf springs and the 'Old Man Emu' Australian shock absorbers we had had fitted on our return from Spain.

Eventually the landscape beat even our Hilux into submission. Our GPS indicated we were near to where the grebes had been seen, but we could go no further. We needed to stop and find shelter. Spotting a small cliff, we managed to drive down a perilous slope to camp on its leeward side. This was going to be our base for the next few weeks in our attempt to film the hooded grebes. We were excited and happy to have got so far.

The next morning we gathered our camera equipment and prepared to hike in to the lagoon where the grebes had last been seen. The four of us squared up to the trek as a fighter would face a foe: we leaned into the wind as it howled around our ears, buffeting us from side to side, gritty sand making eye goggles a necessity. Walking poles were no use as there was no flat ground, just sharp spiky rock with thick shuttlecocks of long tough grass in between. There were unexpected joyous moments when tawny-throated dotterels rose up off their nests in front of us, before being caught by the tumult and swept away like confetti.

Two hours of this tortuous walking brought us to a crest of rock. Feeling as if I had stepped off a frightening fairground ride, I peered over the rim to see a perfectly blue lagoon beneath us. We scanned the water, where a red flush indicated the presence of water milfoil – a good sign. Then, amidst the milfoil, we spotted brilliant white dots.

Hooded grebes.

The birds were spread over the lagoon in small independent groups, feeding and moving among the bright red water milfoil plants. The strengthening wind forced us below the ridge and we sat leaning against lichen-crusted slabs of rock.

'Oh, my, this is awesome,' Kaitlin said, with a broad smile.

That first day we pitched a small tent 20 metres back from the water's edge, piling rocks on top of the guy ropes. Lying inside, we were sheltered just enough from the wind to keep binoculars and cameras steady as we watched the grebes.

The hooded grebe is similar to the European little grebe in size, but that's where the similarities end. From a distance hooded grebes stand out from their near relative, the common silvery grebe, because they are strikingly black and white. Concealed in our green mountain tent, we watched as the grebes moved serenely around. Each bird carried on its head a feathery amber tiara, their red eyes like the heart of a molten volcano.

The following day we returned to the lagoon early. Even before reaching the crater rim, the wind carried to us a lilting cry. Peering over the crest, we saw the isolated groups of birds had concentrated together in one area of the red-stemmed milfoil. Stretching their necks and heads to the sky, they were calling to each other, and exquisite serenades of flutey, quavering trills were echoing around the crater. Was this the formation of a breeding colony? Had we arrived at the perfect moment?

Most animals have their own unique character; like people, you just need to get to know them. And the next day, our view of this special bird rose to a new level. As we approached the lagoon in the early morning, we were aware of an almost visible tension hanging over the water; as a theatre audience becomes quiet prior to the curtain opening, so the atmosphere in the lagoon had altered. The grebes' behaviour was changing. The sexes are very similar in appearance, so it was impossible to know which was the male and which female, but all the birds were moving about more quickly, looking around, purposeful, quiet.

Single birds searched for other individuals and attempted to lure them out of the vegetation into open water. I noticed that when a bird slipped into open water and stretched its sleek white neck upwards, this sign would be picked up by another bird. The two birds would then sidle up close to each other and paddle in unison, necks outstretched, calling. This activity would immediately alert other grebes, who would quickly swim towards the amorous pair intent on interrupting the couple. Hormones drifting all around the birds, their sexual activity soared.

Our dream was coming true: we were about to become members of a tiny group of people who have not only seen these incredible birds but have also witnessed their captivating courtship display. This was Patagonia's own Broadway stage. Our binoculars became opera glasses as we looked over the lagoon, and the birds became actors, their performance vying between those of both the beauty and the beast.

The opening act was when two birds, some distance apart, turned to face each other. One of them would crouch low in the water, its wings fanning wide with wing tips touching the water. Stretching its neck forward, bobbing down close to the water's surface, it would open its beak almost fiercely, showing the fleshy pink inside. With piercing red eyes, the bird would then flex its orange crest over its head, almost resembling a snarling beast, raw, expectant.

This potent behaviour would enflame its partner into the second act. The second bird, with an incredible backward tip of its head that would have its headcrest touching the back of its neck, would, with an acrobatic leap, then somersault forward and dive into the water.

For a brief moment the stage would be serene. The first bird, still low in the water, would search for the other, moving its head this way and that.

A keen-sighted onlooker would then see a faint white dart underwater, a torpedo streaking forwards, and then the third act would erupt when the underwater bird reared out of the water, upwards like a cannon ball, so close to the other bird – heads together, eyes fixed on each other – it was almost an embrace, tango-like.

For the fourth act, both birds would throw their heads backwards and, in an extraordinary and comical see-saw action, bob their heads up and down in unison.

The finale would bring the two performers closer together still. Belly to belly, they would rise out of the water, paddling fast, toes pointed, fighting against the wind to keep upright. Turning their heads synchronously from side to side, orange feathery headcrests waving in the wind, they glided across the rippling azure stage in a passionate pas de deux.

Then, as if nothing had happened, the pair dropped back to

the surface, regained their composure and drifted away together, heads held regally aloft, side by side.

The following days we observed this behaviour from first one pair of birds, then another. The birds were coordinating their actions, the colony working in unison – as many birds will do, maybe to minimise predation when all the young are close together in age. There is still so much about nature that we don't know, that's its fascination.

By the fourth day the spontaneity and frequency of the courtships declined and after that we never saw a full display again. After a few hectic days of wonder, the show was over.

Being so preoccupied with the dancing displays, we hadn't noticed the nest building which was starting: first one, then another and another. By the end of the next day, fifteen nests were under construction. This aquatic building site became a chaotic scene as each pair wanted to complete their milfoil nest before the next. Stealing, deception and bullying were commonplace. The bricklayers were robbing the electricians; the plumbers were grabbing stalks of milfoil left by the painters; and the masons and roofers were sneakily working together to dismantle a neighbour's nest to use for themselves. Squabbles ensued, milfoil pulled this way and that.

Once the building work was finished and the colony of floating nests was complete, egg laying and incubation commenced, and only then did a semblance of calm prevail.

One week was all it took for the drama to reach its climax and subside. We had filmed the entire courtship dance of a critically endangered bird, a display to rival anything the Royal Opera House or the Teatro Colón could stage.

The title of the film for Hernan and Aves Argentinas was obvious to us: *Tango in the Wind*.

Each morning, as we stepped out of the truck, we never felt alone.

Waiting for us were our American friends, Bobby and Kaitlin. Then there were the grebes, always present as a soundscape, talking to themselves and perhaps to us, all day long. Lastly there was the wind, which, if we hadn't made it our friend, would have destroyed us – it was an all-consuming, tumultuous relationship. Every five or six days it became so intolerable we dared not raise the fabric top of our pop-up camper. Paula had to crawl into the truck and sleep on the seats inside, a sardine in a tin, while I retreated to the small mountain tent we had on the shore and slept alongside our cameras and tripods.

Mid-afternoons usually heralded a cessation of the wind, with warmth radiating from the crater cliffs that wrapped around us. The air became crystal clear; distant Andean peaks appeared nearer; and elongated, pure white discs, lenticular clouds, hovered like ghostly spaceships above them. That was the time a puma would emerge on the horizon, sitting, watching, a silent, sandy killer. These large cats clearly knew of our presence and many times we sensed we were being watched – we hoped it was the guanaco they were after, and not us.

As dusk approached, I would sit on the rocks by our truck and also watch. This was the time that a family group of guanaco edged towards us: a male, several females and their young. Over the weeks they moved closer and closer; I'm sure they saw us as added security. They found a few large rocks near the truck and bedded down close to them for the night. One of the adults always remained standing, poised, alert, like a boxer in his corner.

The southern summer evenings floated through shades of pink and purple, ending in ribbons of fire. Gradually, a trillion piercing pinpricks of light holding a milky arch of diamonds would light up a new world.

For the Tehuelche, the indigenous nomads of Patagonia, the sky dominated their universe. Kooch was their sky god, the stars their deceased comrades and family, and the night sky their paradise. Perhaps the Milky Way really was made up of the

Tehuelche, who had long since been eliminated in genocides of the late 1800s.

For us the night-time was often as dramatic as the day. The stars transformed the sky's midnight blue across the land, and our world became the fabled colour of heaven. Underneath this cerulean sky lay the sparkling silver lagoon, upon which the grebes quietly serenaded the stars as we listened.

I would turn over in my sleeping bag and nestle closer to Paula, who often joined me in the tent the better to hear the grebes' dueting love song. I would go to sleep cocooned in the thought that if we had had only these few nights, life would have been worth living.

Once the chicks hatched, activity in the lagoon became hectic again. Generally only one egg from each nest hatched, but on our lagoon there were at least six pairs with two chicks. Finding food became the full-time occupation for the adults. The parents would dive to the bottom of the lagoon through the milfoil in search of tiny crustaceans. Thousands of feeds had to be done every day, time and time again, non-stop through the long summer days and most of the night, too.

The availability of food is one of the main influencers for bird distribution. Some species, such as the tawny owl, keep to the confines of the same woodland all their lives, while albatrosses roam the oceans having to follow trade winds. Swallows fly from one end of the world to the other and back again in a year of endless summer. So what was acting on the hooded grebes' food supply that led them to breed on these remote windswept lagoons in Patagonia?

The answer was simple: the wind.

Sunlight warmed the top surface of the water enabling algae to grow, and algae were the food for tiny crustaceans. The winds that blew every day across the exposed plateau created turbulence in the water. This agitated the water, bringing the cold water at the bottom up to the top – where the sunlight warmed it, promoting more algae and therefore more crustaceans ... The lagoons were crustacean food factories, and the hooded grebes knew it. But there were only two or three suitable plateaus, only so many lagoons; the habitat was scarce and so the birds were rare – and probably always have been.

By early March the nights were almost down to freezing, the windy days not much better. The chicks were almost fully grown and it was getting time for them to migrate across the empty lands to the Atlantic coast for the winter.

From a photographic perspective we had achieved what we had set out to do. For the first time the full courtship of the hooded grebe had been filmed and people around the world could delight in the birds' antics. We needed to get the film out to the public as soon as possible. The potential for a bird tottering so precariously on the cliff edge of extinction to fall is never far away.

We quickly returned to Buenos Aires. We needed permissions for music and footage of tango dancing. The budget for the film was zero – everything came out of our own pockets.

We were introduced to one of the best tango clubs in the city and were invited to sit down with the owner. She listened sympathetically.

'This is just for the birds.'

'I'm sorry, but we never allow filming or photography at our shows.'

'But these birds are as Argentinian as the tango. They need everyone's help,' I implored.

The owner rose from the table. 'I'll let the dancers decide.' She walked away.

Good to her word, minutes later three lithe young women joined us. 'We'd love to help,' they cried. 'Come tonight and sit right here!'

Later that evening, the table was ready for us. With cameras on tripods, wine and food on the table, we were treated like royalty. Now we only needed music – that from the tango evening was full of the extraneous sounds of the restaurant.

On our first week in the country we had frequented a tango club in the cellars beneath where we stayed in San Telmo. We returned and asked the owners who the band was. They gave us their telephone number.

When we rang, a woman answered and agreed to meet us the following day. 'My dad's a birdwatcher. It sounds great what you've done. I've already spoken to the others in the band, they say you can use our music. It's for a great cause.'

We couldn't believe our luck. It seemed like everyone loved the birds, too.

Paula started the laborious work of editing the 40 hours of footage. Two weeks it took, stuck in the confines of the truck camper.

Following conversations with BirdLife International, we offered to give them the film as publicity for their 'Saving Species' programme. They were overjoyed. We also sent the film to Richard for him to make a meme and add it to our Facebook page.

After a few more weeks the film was launched and, almost immediately, our screens filled up with hundreds of messages. Astounded, we watched as the global views of the meme escalated by the hour – 100k, 150k, 250k up and up. The downside was that other websites were capturing our footage, adding their own soundtrack and relaunching it. To stop this happening, Richard contacted a lawyer friend and they worked through the night writing legal contracts and 'taking down' the offending pirated videos.

Photographers from all around the world wanted to know where we had found the birds. We said nothing – after all, this was a critically endangered species and closely protected on private land.

By this time our truck was like a communications centre

for NASA. Total viewing figures eventually topped 50 million worldwide. Footage sold to National Geographic became their second most popular video of the year; Cornell University sent a team of scientists to the plateau to carry out further research; and Toyota Argentina gave the project another Hilux vehicle, enabling them to extend their surveys.

The fantastic work being done by Aves Argentinas and the hooded grebe team is saving a stellar bird, hopefully ensuring that it is one species that won't become another star in the sky to join the deceased Tehuelches.

CHAPTER 6

CHILE'S SILK ROAD

Under our speeding wheels lay dusty plain. In our side mirrors I was sorry to see the flat-topped Buenos Aires plateau disappear. Rosettes of ground-hugging white junellia flowers and delicate yellow calceolarias dotted the ground, stepping stones towards what lay ahead. The gigantic wall of parched mountains was sucking us westwards.

We crossed over the formidable mountains from Argentinian into Chilean Patagonia at the southernmost point possible, the Paso Roballos. We were 'border ready', Paula having cooked all our raw food, meat, vegetables and fruit, the day before. Regulations between the two countries were strict.

The *paso* was a seldom-used track following a cleft between snow-swathed mountains that led us from one world to another. From an open landscape of airy lightness where hawks hover, held by the wind, we drove towards a misty, dripping dankness where birds crept and scuttled below mossy branches. It seemed unbelievable that mountains could make such a difference but these ones did. A geologist would call them young mountains, at just 10 million years old, and, like all young things, they were full of life, volcanoes still growing.

Straddling the apex border between the two countries it was sobering to consider what lay ahead. By now Paula and I had been away for nearly a year, and most of that time we'd spent in parts of Patagonia rarely visited by anyone. I felt our time on that isolated plateau had been among the most meaningful of my life.

I also knew that a little bit of my debt to nature had been repaid, and this made me happy.

In my mind, however, the Andes seemed to be getting bigger every day, and the enormity of travelling their whole length now seemed an impossible challenge. 'Just remember,' Paula would remind me, 'we're going to take every day as it comes.'

The Andes constitute a haphazard series of parallel mountain chains. From this southerly point and stretching north for the next 5,000 kilometres to the Colombian border, the land that lay between these mountain chains was flat plains, over 3,600 metres high. From where we were now and north to Peru, those high plains are called the puna. In Peru and Ecuador they are termed the Altiplano plateau.

The width of these high plains varies. Those in the south and north are narrow; those in the middle are enormous, up to 500 kilometres across. And then beyond Ecuador, in Colombia, the Andes are quite different in nature – a dreamy destination we aimed for in the same way that NASA aims for Mars.

Ominous dark clouds hung over us, and streaks of rain made for a welcoming rainbow; this was as good as it was going to get. Our four wheels splashed an insignificant stream high and away, but for us it was our Rubicon. The steep mountain track levelled off as we turned onto a wider, straighter one. Our sat nav indicated we were over the highest point; from now on, it was downhill through the western slopes of the Andes, a land of rainforests, not arid plains. We had entered Chile.

The brilliant red dot, a speck on the raggedy road ahead of us, stood out long before we realised what it was: we needed to concentrate our eyes on what was directly in front of us, for we were now driving the legendary and unpredictable Carretera Austral. This 1,500-kilometre route weaves between the glaciers, lakes, rivers, mountains, forests and fjords of southern Chile. The road – if you can call it that – meanders from the town of Villa O'Higgins in the far south, to Puerto Montt.

It seemed strange to me to come across an Irish surname celebrated in this way until I discovered that while O'Higgins's father was born in County Sligo, Ireland, his mother was of the Chilean aristocracy. His revolutionary ideas had led him to become an outstanding general and one whose military prowess had secured the independence of Chile from the Spanish.

The stretch we were driving was particularly bad as it lacked the two requirements of an acceptable driving surface: stability and evenness. Loose stones meant that at speeds over 40 km per hour vehicles were likely to slalom and shift off course, an unnerving experience which might have a nervous driver's foot twitching over the brake pedal. Braking on such a surface, however, could be likened to trying to stop while running down a sand dune, the result being that you just keep going only now out of control. Straight sections of road were manageable; corners, however, especially those on a mountainside, were exciting, in the same way that parachuting is exciting – knowing that death is a distinct outcome. The crashed and upside-down cars we passed were always on bends. And on the rare occasion when the driving wheel and your nerves were in equilibrium, and usually as we were absorbed in listening to a BBC podcast, a wheel would drop into a pothole, launching us into a slithery slide. Dust clouds enveloped approaching vehicles such that you never quite knew what to expect until they were close. Local cars were battered and old and sped towards us, unconcerned by the stones and gravel that sprayed up from their wheels. Large transport trucks were oblivious to other drivers, taking the centre of the road and rarely slowing down. Moments before we met them there was always panic, with visions of smashed windscreens and headlights. These concerns were balanced somewhat by the spectacular scenery, but to enjoy that we needed to survive!

East of the Andes, where we had been for the past months, Argentinian Patagonia is cold, arid, windy and monochrome.

Now we were travelling through a Technicolor frontier country of turquoise rivers, lush with velvet-green forests; its meadows, full of flowers, reminded me of looking into my mother's old tin of shining, colourful buttons. Streams babbled down the mountains to roadsides lined with tall blue and pink lupins. Rustic wooden cabins with attendant guard dogs, chickens and impressive chopping blocks flickered between the trees. Ramshackle villages – homes for *gauchos*, shepherds and fishermen whose livelihood is bound by the wild – looked as if they had long given up their struggle against the elements.

Like the fabled Silk Road travellers, no one came here by accident, all had a purpose – exemplified by the red dot in front of us transforming into a scarlet, hi-tech, Lycra-clad cyclist.

We waved him down as he came towards us: 'Hey, want a coffee?'

'Sure, great stuff!' said the cyclist, slowly edging himself off the thin saddle.

We always had flasks of coffee made up and were happy to chat to another traveller. Handing him a mug of coffee and some chocolate, we introduced ourselves.

'Thanks, I'm Marc, from Belgium. I'm heading for Ushuaia but I started off in Alaska.'

'Wow, well done!'

'Cheers! This road is the best, fantastic. The people you meet are incredible. Any more chocolate?'

Reluctantly I handed over two more squares of my favourite chocolate, Cadbury's Fruit and Nut. Generosity only goes so far.

'Had any trouble?' I asked.

'People's ideas of what is risky and what isn't are blown out of proportion. I've never had any problems.' He paused to sample some chocolate, swallowing it down seemingly without tasting it. I looked away. 'Everyone's so kind, some even want me to stay with them in their homes. That wouldn't happen to me in Belgium.'

'So, what are your thoughts now it's nearly over? Would you do it again?' I asked.

'You bet! But you need balls – not only to make the decision, but to cope with the stunned faces of friends at home.'

Paula and I exchanged a glance. That sounded familiar.

'I've told people,' continued Marc, 'if you have a dream, ask yourself, what are you really afraid of? Happiness is complex but it has little to do with money.'

We finished our coffees and said our goodbyes, driving off to follow our own dream.

I thought about what Marc had said. He was correct in saying that happiness had little to do with money. One of the questions we were most often asked was, 'How do you afford what you are doing?' I usually laughed and said, 'Paula funds me and I fund her.' In truth we found that travelling wild in South America was cheaper than being at home. We weren't spending money on entertainment, fancy restaurants and buying stuff. We had simplified our life. We had made decluttering into an art form. Money couldn't have bought what we were seeing and doing in our new life.

The landscapes of this new continent were speaking to me in a way I had never imagined, in dreamlike whispers. Knowing what lay on the other side of the distant mountains – the arid plains, the dust and the birds – was strangely comforting. For now though, we were entering new and unknown territory.

We turned north towards Coyhaique, heading into a forested region second in size in South America only to the Amazon. We were going into the unsung, rarely visited Valdivian temperate rainforest.

Unsurprisingly it's rain that makes a rainforest, and the more the better. Heat, as well as rain, makes for a burgeoning biodiversity, and that is what a tropical rainforest has. Temperate rainforests have the same amount of rain but, being colder, are less biodiverse.

There are only five temperate rainforests in the world. The biggest is in British Columbia, and is known as the Great Bear Forest after the white Spirit Bear that lives among its 2,000-year-old giant redwoods and cedars. Second in size is the Valdivian temperate rainforest of southern Chile, whose overshadowing mountains drape a cold misty mantle over the narrow coastlands, fjords and islands.

The Carretera Austral is the only road through the region for good reason. A geographic colour palette conspires to isolate this region from the outside world: to the west lies the greatest expanse of blue, the Pacific Ocean; to the east lies the mighty white of the Andes rising to snowy peaks of 3,000 metres; while to the north are the yellow sands of the driest desert, the Atacama, second only in size to the Sahara. These three formidable geographic barriers, immutable for the past 25 million years, restricted the incursion of many plants and animals, making it a closed land of biological opportunity, a cauldron for self-generating biodiversity and full of so many plants and animals that occur nowhere else that it is classified as a global biodiversity hotspot and ranked on a par with the Amazon. Norman Myers, an Oxford ecologist, coined the term 'hotspot' in 2000. To be considered for hotspot designation, an area must contain a minimum of 1,500 endemic plants and be severely threatened by human activity.

The most noticeable natural force along this coast is the rainfall. Warm westerly winds from across the Pacific collect moisture off the cold Humboldt Current. These humid winds drive a mass of dark billowing clouds inland until they are met by the vertiginous wall of the Andes. Like hot-air balloons they try to rise over the mountain peaks, whose powerfully icy winds toss them back again, causing a tumult in the sky. As the clouds are pushed back, more roll in, somersaulting over each other. Eventually gaining sufficient height they cool and release deluges of rain. Time and time again this happens, until the empty clouds dissipate and flow over the Andes into the flat, parched lands of Argentina.

Every month of the year rain drenches the hardwood forests of southern Chile's coastlands, a rainforest at the end of the world. The trees love it, particularly the alerce tree, also known as the Patagonian cypress or *Fitzroya cupressoides*, named by Charles Darwin after the illustrious captain of HMS *Beagle*, Robert Fitzroy.

The Valdivian rainforest was unlike any forest I had previously been in: dark, forbidding and magical. We had not seen the sun for several days: misty drizzle made for short breaks in the fresh air, the more usual torrential rain making such breaks bearable.

Our first steps into this realm found us kicking up golden orbs of weightless lichen. Like slow-motion balloons at a children's party, they floated in front of us before gently descending again. Had we interrupted a fairy game? I had no idea how they came to be like that and I was content not to know, this place fostering our imagination. We were surrounded by tree trunks of such height that looking up to their tops made our necks ache. An evergreen temple of Karnac was lifting the sky away from us. Every surface – stone, rock and fallen wood – was covered in soft insulating plants, mosses of every hue. As befitting a natural sanctuary, it was peaceful and yet vibrant with nature, the only sounds those of a distant gurgling stream, constant dripping and our feet sloshing, a haven for frogs.

We saw no one – few people lived in the area.

As we headed north towards Puerto Montt, the character of the Carretera Austral changed: it got tougher. Unlike the real Silk Road across Asia, made up of a dozen trails and tracks weaving through mountains and deserts, much of our road was a single route and constantly under repair. Occasionally a sign instructed us to stop as a passage was dynamited through great hunks of fallen rock. After the explosion we would creep forward through billowing dust as massive diggers cleared a path in front. Sections of road were little more than ledges cut into cliffs whose sides cascaded with water. We drove alternately beneath waterfalls and then tall mossy trees that created tunnels of darkness. At one point, the road was diverted down a track to a rocky shoreline. Here a small ferry awaited us. Paula chatted up the captain and I wasn't surprised to see her steering the boat for a few kilometres down the coast. From the deck we could see the reason for this diversion: a rockfall had swept the entire road completely away into the sea.

We were happy to reach Puerto Aysén. To continue our journey north by boat seemed a sensible decision.

Navimag is one of the regular shipping lines moving people and goods along the waterways from Punta Arenas to Puerto Montt. Puerto Aysén is one of many small harbour pick-up points. The ships service many remote communities and experience sea conditions that one might expect from seas that are not far from the treacherous waters of Cape Horn, so it's not easy to keep to a schedule.

We arrived at the quayside in Puerto Aysén as requested, one hour before sailing, at 7 p.m. As the hours came and went we occupied ourselves by catching up on diary entries, poring over maps, deleting unwanted photographs and listening to more podcasts, before dozing in our truck. Woken by lights and movement, we saw several cars and more trucks arrive. Piercing arc lights sent welcoming beams across the water to an approaching ship. Eventually, at two o'clock in the morning, we drove into the cavernous hold of the ship, parked between two huge beer trucks and, as the first glimmer of dawn indicated a clear sky, we were underway.

The incoming ship's journey had been delayed by storms and rough seas but now the weather had changed and our journey was to prove smooth and sunny. The time aboard was a joy, with blue above us and blue beneath. The ship zigzagged between a maze of glacially scoured islands and cruised through wide fjord-like channels and gulfs, the surrounding mountains an unending green bubbly tapestry of trees.

We stood alone on the deck, engrossed in the fullness of the wild seas and the wildlands beyond. We saw no signs of habitation. The only visible lights in the endless twilight of summer were the reflections off distant glaciers, making the waves a shimmering silver and grey tableau. Small fishing boats drifted between the islands while larger supply vessels disappeared down narrow inlets. Where they were heading we had no idea – our maps showed no settlements or roads, just hundreds of miles of land accessible only by sea.

The incessant dry Patagonian winds had blown us here; grit had been replaced by the scent of salt, the refreshing wetness of the sea rejuvenated our cheeks. Binoculars in gloved hands, wrapped in all our clothes, beguiled by the stillness, the tranquillity, we kept vigil on deck. We cared not a jot that the sun had disappeared, fusing day and night.

The sea was now a silver salver upon which silent crystal goblets passed up and down; so close to the railings they came, we could have grasped them and sipped their spirit – the black-browed albatross. They were floating with us, following us, their incredible wings marginally longer than the condors', and as steady as a soldier's salute. Occasionally these companions would soar down and dip their long, orange, squid-catching bills towards the silver sea, in expectation. The ship's wake was ridden by mere dancing dominoes, petrels and prions.

Most of the travellers remained inside the canteen and lounges; only a few took an occasional walk round the deck. A lone man approached us: 'What are you looking for? You've been out here for hours.'

'Birds, maybe whales,' we replied.

'Ah. Where are you going?'

'Chiloé.'

'Oh, the dark island.'

'What do you mean?' It was a puzzling thing to say.

'Oh, so much forest, a land of little things, though I've never seen any. But it's the rain – boy, that's something else.'

'What little things?' We were intrigued.

'In the forest, you'll see. That island's a strange place. My wife's family comes from there and there's none stranger than them.' He chuckled to himself. 'Now we live in Puerto Montt.' After a pause, the man wandered off towards a doorway.

We popped into the canteen for dinner and were surprised to discover the boat was dry. No alcohol was available. We later learnt that some truck drivers had got drunk one night and decided to have a BBQ in their cabin, setting fire to the ship. Not surprisingly, alcohol was banned after that.

The ship comprised three distinct groups of people, each keeping apart from one another. There were the burly, unshaven and tattooed truck drivers who carried on animated and loud conversations interspersed with bouts of laughter. Then there were the backpackers, arrayed in colourful technical clothing. They sprawled, fast asleep, in corners around the ship, like a scattering of Lego pieces, their bright rucksacks oozing plastic bags of food, coats and sleeping bags, travellers on their own personal Silk Road. The final group were ordinarily dressed locals, families with children. They carried shopping bags of food and boxes of household items: one a microwave, another an electric iron.

The ferry dropped us off at Chiloé Island, the biggest of the inhabited islands in the region and one we knew to be internationally important as feeding grounds for North American shorebirds.

The island's only significant town is Castro. As we approached it, the road passed over a causeway crossing a tidal inlet. We pulled over and stopped. To our right, the shoreline echoed pages from a child's colouring book: a line of matchbox houses, yellow, brown, orange and blue, teetered on poles suspended over the muddy water beneath. Called *palafitos* or 'stick houses', they edged into the water, with ladders and steps to the shore behind – the *palafitos*' tenuous hold to land seeming to diminish every minute as the incoming tide flowed underneath. To our left and into the distance stretched a marsh-edged estuary. We settled ourselves down among causeway boulders, cameras ready on tripods, and waited as the rising sea filled the slippery channels and raced across the mud, chasing the birds.

Sanderling ran up and down like children teasing the advancing wavelets. In the distance a hazy movement of swirls and contorted patterns in the sky indicated many more birds were being harassed by the rising tide. They were Hudsonian godwits, large, centurion-like shorebirds, upright and alert with long, spear-like bills. One cohort at a time, the birds rose upwards as the water overran their feeding grounds and then resettled with another group. Eventually, in a vast, seemingly well-rehearsed formation, they all took to the air, legion after legion, sweeping back and forth across the bay, looking for higher land. At last the flock twisted in our direction, landing not far away from where we sat.

As the birds settled, we saw a sprinkling of other shorebirds from the northernmost parts of North America. For us, each of these species had their own story to tell. There were the long-billed greater and lesser yellowlegs, birds that had bred in the mosquito-rich bogs of the tundra, whose neighbours were moose and caribou. Their migration carries these birds down the centre of the United States, over prairies being harvested, skimming the tops of oil rigs in the Gulf of Mexico, through Central America and over the lines of container ships passing through the Panama Canal. Finally, down the west coast of South America, numbers diminishing as flock after flock finds its favourite spot to rest. Eventually, large numbers end up here in Chiloé Island.

Among the yellowlegs were flashes from chestnut-coloured birds. A little smaller, fatter and with shorter legs, they were red knots whose face, breast and belly were the colour of a sugar maple tree in October. These birds are declining due to a range of manmade threats, the most serious being the urbanisation of the birds' coastal resting and feeding places. The birds have been global travellers, lovers of sunshine and rich food for 10 million years, but for many their time in the sun may be coming to an end.

The island of Chiloé lies at the easternmost rim of the saucer-shaped South Pacific. At the other side of the saucer lies New Zealand's South Island. Westerly winds circling around this expanse deposit more than six metres of rain on Chiloé every year. This aids the creation of a particular type of Valdivian forest – not so much a rainforest, more a massive sphagnum moss swamp with tall sticks of long-dead trees in it. The forest has a dazzling variety of evergreen hardwood trees of the laurel family, among them tepa, tineo and ulmo, most unique to this forest.

We had the chance to visit a private nature reserve, Bosquepiedra, owned by Elena, a botanist trying to preserve a piece of the unique rainforest. And she introduced us to this very different aspect of the forest – its mosses. This place is so wet that there are 900 species of moss in Chile, almost all in this area. We moved gently to avoid crushing the ancient miniature worlds of moss and lichen: smoky grey cladonias; a knobbly needle with scarlet fruits on top; cushions with plumes of feathery umbrellas, aptly named umbrella moss, the height of a matchstick. Then there were the ferns such as the Magellanic fern that tickled our ears and sprinkled water on our faces as we passed by. During a downpour we sheltered under the forest's own beach umbrellas – the biggest leaves in the world, belonging to the native Chilean rhubarb, or gunnera. Gaps between tree trunks were choked with thin, spiky bamboo. Again, massive trees clothed in a multitude of delicate filmy ferns soared into the topmost vaults; weaving and twisting around these shaggy pillars were vines and creepers dotted with red tubular flowers. Glistening waxy green leaves reflected the bright shafts of watery sunlight struggling to pierce the domed canopy. Higher up, orchids draped the boughs like sparkling vestments; it was a vertical water garden.

A lone bird, a chorister, periodically startled us. The short, strident, throaty calls came from a special and uncommon bird, the chucao tapaculo. The notes were softened, even slowed, by the velvet surroundings. Calls that seemed far off in the forest were actually from birds that were very close.

In such a place, we found the act of photography – pulling out tripod legs, unzipping bags, clicking on lenses – almost disrespectful. So we did it carefully, more slowly than usual, unconsciously whispering to each other.

Eventually we settled down, cameras at the ready, and waited. Reverence was a requirement. The hours ticked by as we sat, our thoughts interrupted only by nature: a distant flock of slender-billed parakeets screaming over the forest then descending into a firebush tree and gorging on its flowers; the loud crashing of a bough laden with its own aerial garden of plants hitting the ground; a pair of a astounding birds, Des Murs's wiretails, which sport six preposterously long filaments of tail feathers.

These brief, sometimes explosive moments were interspersed with long silences. I even thought I could hear the soft munching of insect larvae from inside the logs we were sitting on. My falling eyelids wrapped me in darkness for a momentary doze. Then, with a sudden sense of alertness and an uncanny knowledge of another presence, my eyes blinked open. A motionless chucao stood in front of me.

The chucao tapaculo is a cautious but inquisitive bird that silently moves through the undergrowth with lightning speed. It senses the presence of people and other animals in its territory and investigates intruders. The bird was so close, an arm's length away, tail erect, peering, its head cocking to one side then another. An elf of a bird that had cast off the dark dripping colour of the forest, adorning itself instead in a warm brown cloak, a bright orange breastplate and striking black and white vermiculated flanks. With my heavy eyes still flickering in wonder, the chucao withdrew into the mossy darkness.

In contrast, a high-speed boy-racer with a charmed life

ricocheted between the trees. How could the green-backed firecrown, a tiny hummingbird weighing the same as the water in a teaspoon, live in these wet forests? No other hummingbird lives so far south in the Americas, every day a challenge to its survival. Hummingbirds need a regular supply of fuel – sugary nectar – to power their supercharged lifestyle. But how, we wondered, did they find it in this sodden, dark forest?

Forest plants usually rely on a breeze to carry their pollen, but the wind is no friend of this place – the trees are too dense, too tall. So many of them have found another friend, the green-backed firecrown hummingbird. Its eyes have filters which mute the colours of blue and green and heighten those of yellow and red. The Valdivian rainforest has over 200 plant species that produce red and yellow flowers, and these act as flashing beacons to attract birds and insects to their flowers. Added to this, three of these plants have adapted specifically, such that their red tubular flowers are shaped to accommodate the long tongue of the green-backed firecrown. Each flowers at a different time of the year, enabling the hummingbird to survive throughout the seasons in an otherwise inhospitable place. One plant is the delicate copihue, the national flower of Chile, its large red fuschia-like petals so flamboyant that it was named after the beautiful empress Josephine, the wife of Napoleon Bonaparte, herself a keen botanist. Another is the Chilean wineberry or maqui, a plant revered by the indigenous peoples of the forest, the Mapuche, as a medicinal plant. Scientists have recently found this plant to be high in antioxidants as to be invaluable in the fight against colon cancer. The third red flowering plant, the boquila, is parasitic on the southern beech trees. The boquila produces white berries which fall to the forest floor in May. There, they are collected and eaten by a tiny marsupial, the colocolo opossum, known by the locals as the 'little monkey of the mountains'. Only when the seeds have passed through the gut of the small animal and the droppings have been deposited on a branch will a new plant start to develop.

Despite nature's bounty from these three plants – the copihue, maqui and the boquila – the green-backed firecrown still lives on a knife edge of survival. Keeping warm means retaining energy, and enabling its chicks to do the same is a challenge.

Twice we saw a hummingbird dart above a runnel of water in a cleft of the forest, then disappear into the darkness. Pushing under the spreading fronds of massive Magellanic ferns, we noticed a mossy rotting log had fallen across the water. We peeked underneath into the darkness and a green-backed firecrown zipped out. Barely able to see, our torch shone on a green, gherkin-shaped nest no bigger than an eggcup suspended under the log over the water. The microclimate of such a nest position adds a degree or two of extra warmth. This tiny home was made from long delicate strands of moss, plaited and twisted together. From the top, two needle-sized bills peeked out: the next generation for the forest.

This forest has many specialist and unique birds, like the Magellanic and ochre-flanked tapaculos. These species are lovers of the Valdivian rainforest. We had often heard these dumpy, dark charcoal-coloured tapaculos but seeing them was like looking for a black cat in a coalhouse. Like small moorhens, they nervously crept through the dense vegetation, flickering like shadows, playing with our senses.

The chucao tapaculo was different; it had welcomed us to this eerie forest, seeking us out.

The ferry back to Puerto Montt made slow progress through the fierce tidal run between Chiloé Island and the mainland. A drenching mist surrounded everything in sight, the rain lashing down as it had for so many days. As we stepped off the boat, we watched as passengers embarked. Two overlanding bikers from the USA rolled their Harley Davidsons up the ramp. A small tourist mini-bus, faces peering through steamed-up windows, followed. Next came a truck of building materials piled high with wood, insulation and a large plastic water tank. Then a dozen passengers walked on, heads down against the squall, holding their personal goods in bags and cases. All were travellers on the move, some to meet loved ones, some to build a new home and put down new roots, some perhaps to get away from established ones. All, like us, were travellers on Chile's Silk Road.

PART THREE

CONDOR COUNTRY

San Pedro de Atacama

ECO PORTAL RESERVE

Pilcomayo

Asunción

COPO NAT'L PARK

CHACO NAT'L PARK

CAMPO DE LOS ALISOS

Tucumán

Belén

LAGUNA MAR CHIQUITA

Olta

Miramar

URUGUAY

Mendoza

Santiago

Buenos Aires

Montevideo

CHILE

ARGENTINA

Negro

Sierra Pailemán

VALDÉS PENINSULA

CHAPTER 7

CONDORS AND A CHICKEN

Crossing the great mountain chain for the fourth time we moved from the luxuriant forests of southern Chile back into parched lands. Within the first few days of entering the province of Mendoza in Argentina, the thermal layers we had needed in Patagonia were discarded. Life was warming up.

We spent days criss-crossing the foothills of flat ochre plains. Yellow river beds curved through the landscape, waves of pink stratified hills dotted with columns of green-ribbed cardon cacti and smart *estancias*. Converging lines of tall poplars led to manicured vineyards; a David Hockney landscape.

We were becoming accustomed to the slow but purposeful rhythm of our lives, as contented as turtle doves in hawthorn. We spent days without meeting or talking to anyone else, captivated by the peaceful places we passed through. We had given ourselves the rare gift of time, something that had all too often slipped through the fingers of our past life too quickly – parents, children, work, houses, all necessary time takers; necessary, but not sufficient for us. Now it was our time: time for us to support each other, as well as time for us to give back to nature.

Medical science had healed and repaired my flesh and bones, but managing past events remained a daily personal and physical challenge for me. Some days, it was as if I was climbing a mountain, exhausted. Thoughts and memories, those gremlins that whizzed around my head, were so difficult to tame. Paula was my sounding board who listened quietly throughout, and was happy to do so. We trusted each other unconditionally, mutually. Isn't that the unspoken power of love?

It was our love for birds that drove us onwards. We always had our eyes skywards, on the lookout for big birds, especially Andean condors. Those we had seen up till now had been just dots in the sky, just as Ada had said. The attraction of the warm, animal-rich plains in the foothills of the Andes was the hope of viewing these great birds more closely – an avian drug that kept us on the move, scouring the wide open skies for a fix.

The other big bird, so distinctive that its image often graces prehistoric rock art sites, is the greater rhea. Usually the first thing that drew our attention to these birds was when up popped a periscope head with a pair of bulging eyes, looking at us. We would lift our binoculars and off the great bird would run, like an old washer woman being chased down the street. The rhea's long muscular legs carry its round pudding of a body, feathers shake like petticoats in the wind, its long neck and head swaying in unison. It's understandable behaviour – by all accounts rheas are very tasty and have been remorselessly hunted for millennia. Its local name is *ñandu*, a soft sounding word that must have been muttered around many a *gaucho* campfire.

How rheas lived in the extensive open bushlands of the Monte Desert can be compared to elephants in the African savanna, or to great whales in the world's oceans. Rarely heard by humans, male rheas are known to attract females from over very long distances with low-frequency siren sounds. Multiple females then gather together and form a ceremonial circle around a male bird. With leathery feet as large as dinner plates they pound the dirt, fanning plumes of feathers in a mesmeric courtship dance.

Ñandu chicks never know their mum. Every day for a week

or more she lays a single golden nugget, so big that a child would need both hands to hold it. Then she disappears back into the bush and has nothing more to do with her family. Another of the females will then visit the same nest and repeat the process, then another and another, until there are up to fifty eggs in this massive hatchery of a nest. Dad is the hero in this story – he guards the nest and its treasure day and night, keeping pampas foxes and great hairy armadillos at bay. A long neck enables him to watch for predators, of which man is the deadliest. Twice we saw groups of men scouring the bush. Running alongside them was a pack of lean dogs, tongues as long as assassins' knives.

Early one afternoon a road led us into the small town of Olta. We'd heard this was an area to find condors. There was no traffic and the streets were almost deserted, pink blossom from lapacho trees showering us as we parked in the square. Although it was early afternoon we still hoped to find a shop that was open and someone to give us directions. Naturally, the one shop to be open was the butcher's: Argentinians will eat meat any time of the day, every day. We exchanged a few pleasantries and asked if they knew the best place to see condors. Without hesitation the butcher walked us into the street and waved his bloodied knife westwards towards the mountains. 'Not far,' he said. 'Keep going, up, up.'

We laughed to ourselves, as we'd heard that before. But we did as he said. The road narrowed and the ascent steepened; it had been several hours since leaving the town and we glimpsed its houses way down beneath us, out on the green plain. The stony, dusty road wound upwards. Many of the stunted and thorny bushes were familiar to us but the varieties of succulent cacti were the finest we had seen. Some lay prostrate with flat, star-shaped spines and pink flowers; other, taller stemmed ones had multiple arms reaching out like a supplicant; others still were tall and straight with woolly spines and bald white bare patches on top like monks; while smaller ones hid under creosote bushes like round spiky hassocks with yellow trumpets of flowers. To film and photograph them we needed to be on our hands and knees, cameras on tripods. And that's when we noticed the straggly lines of ants.

Ants and cacti have a mutually beneficial relationship: the cacti supply the ants with sweet, nutritious nectar and the ants protect the cacti from animals that would damage the plant. An incongruous team you might think, but when we saw the dark brown ants, we believed it. The worker ants were a centimetre long and processed in columns, each ant carrying a piece of chewed-off leaf above its head. The warrior ants, sparsely spread among the workers, were twice the size and scary to look at, with what looked like plated armour on their thorax. Protruding from their body were eight long spines, five pointing forwards on the thorax and three pointing backwards on their bulbous abdomen – a formidable foe.

Onwards and upwards we continued through steep, arid, cacti-covered hillsides. By late afternoon we were giving up hope of finding anywhere suitable to camp. Then out of nowhere we surprised ourselves by driving straight into a farmyard, scattering goats as we came to a halt.

This was definitely the end of the road. As I opened my door a massive pig sniffed at me before wandering back into a muddy stone-walled enclosure. Back in the cab, assuming we had made a wrong turn somewhere and with our wheels on full lock struggling to turn the truck to leave, we suddenly saw a young man coming out of a rickety gateway. He was about seventeen years old, short and muscular.

Paula opened her window. '*Hola*, we're after a place to camp for the night. We're looking for condors.'

The open-mouthed man looked perplexed, as if aliens had just landed in his midst. '*Un momento*,' he said, and he disappeared.

Looking around us, it became apparent the farmstead had seen much better days. The roof of the main house was covered with a black plastic sheet weighted down with rocks; most of the low stone walls to keep the pigs enclosed were falling down, and a disembowelled car with no wheels lay rusting against a tree. A dog growled.

The young man, smiling as he returned from the house, was followed by his mother, a small plump lady with a round, weather-beaten face. I thought it strange she was wearing a white lab coat with stains and splashes of different coloured dyes down it – mostly reds.

My eyes flicked from her to the car wreck. Suddenly I felt hot, my fingers trembling. The gremlins were whizzing around my head again. 'I don't like this,' I said. 'We're at the wrong place.' And I put the truck into reverse.

Paula touched my arm. 'Remember what Guillermo said. Trust people. Go with the flow.'

'It's OK to camp here and stay the night,' the woman called and, pointing to the young man, added: 'Javier can show you condors tomorrow.'

I looked at the fading sun, it was a lovely evening. Reassured, I knocked the gear stick into neutral. 'Could we go this evening? This light is great.'

'OK,' Javier said. 'But it'll be dark when we get back.'

As we left, I turned to Paula. 'Could you ask her if she can cook dinner for us tonight? We'll pay.'

Question posed, there was a slight hesitation, with glances between son and mother, making me wonder if I'd got it wrong again. Were we being rude? Then she replied, '*Si*, *si*, we have chicken.'

Satisfied that we were going to eat before bed, we followed Javier along a path from the house and up a rocky hillside, almost immediately finding ourselves on an undulating, stony plateau broken by miniature ravines and outcrops of great boulders. This was no longer an imaginary David Hockney land: we were now in the Monte Desert.

At a pleasantly level green area the walking became a lot easier, a tranquil spot, out of the wind yet catching the setting sun.

I paused and ran my fingers over a line of stones and muttered to myself, 'Someone lived here once.'

Javier stopped and looked at me. 'Why did you say that?'

A little embarrassed, I was not sure myself. 'Just thinking it would be the spot I would choose to live. It feels right.'

'Come over here. Follow me.' Javier led us between more large boulders and down to a similar area where, spread about, lay the ruins of a settlement. Tumbledown stone walls and lengths of bleached timber were overgrown with grass. There were larger stones, with finely worked straight sides, lintels from doorways and windows, all scattered about like a picked-over carcass. 'People have always lived here – my grandfather and his grandfather before him,' replied Javier. 'We should hurry, though – the edge is not far and we need to return before it's too dark.'

It was another twenty minutes before we reached a jumble of large, smooth slabs of rock, collapsed on each other like a pack of cards. Sliding on our bums down the last one, our feet thankfully lodged against some vegetation. Beneath the jumble was a huge flat rock, a platform onto which we jumped. Turning around, I saw a dark chasm, half a kilometre across, a deep rift in the mountain. Facing us on the opposite side of the chasm was a sheer, smooth, slate-blue cliff, the vertical cracks and crevices even more striking than its towering scale, colours reminiscent of a Canadian forest with red maples, golden hickories and orange oaks. In front of us was nothing but an airy vista. The darkening plains far below twinkled with the glow-worm lights of villages and towns.

All those people, what were they doing? And what do the birds think about as they circle above?

Flying into Chicago at night, as I used to do occasionally in my previous life, the flight approach was always from the north over the blackness of Lake Michigan. I was always unprepared for what came next, my eyes filling with a dazzling chessboard of brilliant city lights. I would close my eyes and feel the plane bank, climbing and falling as we entered a stack. I could hear the deceleration, wing flaps opening, hear the clunking of the landing gear drop down.

Condors can do the same, all that, simply with a silent flick of their feathers.

On the rock platform I stretched out my arms, capturing a warm breeze.

Javier tugged at my jacket and pointed, 'Look! Birds!'

I couldn't see anything as I strained my eyes in the failing light. Then the distant specks of condors emerged, like black flies floating back and forth. They were so insignificant that without binoculars you would hardly see anything. The largest flying bird in the world was scaled down to the size of a gnat by the mountainous rock face.

'Do they roost over there?'

'Yes, on ledges that catch the morning sun. We'll see them tomorrow, but now we need to get back.'

Like having to leave a party as soon as we had arrived, we reluctantly left. It was getting dark.

Arriving back at the farmhouse we were both starving and weary. I fetched the longest of the condor feathers from the truck. Javier's mother, Sara, beckoned us into a large room. It was cool inside. The ceiling was low, bits of straw sticking out from the rough plaster. From beams, paraffin lamps hung down, which we had to duck between. Pools of yellow, flickering light lay on the stone floor.

There was a large wooden table set for the two of us. Way over on the far side of the room, from where I heard the clanging of pots and pans, was what looked like another table and that's where some others sat, three or four adults – I couldn't see properly, as tall cupboards had been used to divide the room. Already on the table, where Sara pointed us to sit, was a plate of chicken and vegetables, a basket of bread and glasses of wine. An eager-looking dog wandered between the two tables.

I put the feather on the table; Javier inspected it and said approvingly how big it was. He then showed me some others, similar but shorter, lying on a shelf. I put ours with theirs and heard hushed murmuring from the people at the other table, who were watching us.

I have led the life of a poor student with little to eat, learning to cook as a matter of necessity. I've added salt instead of sugar and used too much chilli. I've been marooned on a Scottish island and had to eat road kill and seaweed, but never have I had to pray for a meal to end so quickly as I did that night. The chicken was so tough it was impossible to eat, rolling around in our mouths like an old tennis ball. The bread was like rock and I feared for my teeth after the first bite. Glances between the tables were exchanged, with smiles and nods. Having an English couple in the living room was not a usual occurrence. We were subject to constant scrutiny.

The dog had now crept into its bed putting its head down. I think it, too, had suspicions about the chicken. The meal continued with Paula and I making small talk, smacking our lips occasionally and smiling as if to give the impression that this was indeed a wonderful meal and to distract attention from the bits I was sneaking into my pocket. Eventually we sat back, as if happy and replete. The plates were taken away and Sara insisted on bringing us a bowl of chicken soup.

'I'm famous for my soup,' she said.

I had my doubts, but the first few mouthfuls proved me wrong. The soup was delicious. The scrawny, veteran chicken had been beaten into submission by hours of simmering and the soup was a masterpiece of rural gastronomy that took away the soreness from my worn-out mouth.

Leaving for bed, we asked to pay and after a discussion among the family, the mother suggested seventy pesos. My reaction was measured but surprised; after all, the finest meal in a top-class Buenos Aires restaurant would have cost less. But we paid it – the people were poor, and perhaps our surprise visit had caught them at a time with little food in the house.

The remaining evenings we ate as we normally did, in the living space of our van, roughly the same size as a single bed. A year of being in this confined space had made us adept at cooking and working on our computers at the same time. Paula would prop herself up on the bed platform, balancing her computer on her lap, while I prepared a meal. We ate from two bowls: pan-fried steak or fish with pasta or instant mashed potato and tinned peas. Fresh veg was a luxury; the sort of cheese we liked an impossibility. A small fridge, the size of two shoe boxes, meant we could carry milk and cold beer.

Each dawn and afternoon we hiked with Javier across the plateau to the ravine. Despite his young age Javier had an amazing knowledge of local plants. Wandering along, he would casually snap a twig off a branch or pluck some tiny leaves and explain their medicinal qualities.

'The bark and leaves of quebracho trees aid all manner of stomach ailments. This one's *molle* – some people call it the Peruvian peppertree,' he said. 'It helps to ease anxiety, blood pressure and internal parasites.'

I was intrigued. 'How do you know all this?'

'This is what our family does. We make medicines.'

One day, as we reached the ruined settlement again, Javier lay down on his back and, reaching under a rock, pulled out a tiny piece of lichen. 'We call this "bread of the rock" – it's one of the most valuable medicinal plants. It can help women when they are pregnant and can reduce fat in the blood. It grows nowhere else we know of. No one else knows of its location and that's why my great-grandfather built his homestead here.'

'Do you still collect it?'

'Only in the autumn. My mother uses it in many drugs.'

Paula noticed several very old broken rock pestles lying by a stone wall. 'The last person to live here was my grandfather,' Javier explained. 'This land is so rich in medicinal plants, trees, herbs, edible cacti and fungi. These are only found in the home of the condor.'

'So condors are important to you?'

'Very. This is why our family has always lived here, to be close to the birds and to collect plants.'

'Do you have problems protecting the birds?'

'Yes! Pumas and foxes eat people's goats. So they put out poisoned carcasses to kill them, but condors find the poisoned carcasses and die too. Some farmers are bad, ignorant men but most are good and some locals help us protect the birds.'

'How come?'

'Sometimes if they have a cow that's died they give it to us and we leave it out for the condors.'

We were getting to know Javier and his family better, every morning sharing a gourd of *maté*, then spending the evenings chatting about birds, plants and their life in the mountains. Apparently Javier's family were well known in the area, supplying herbal medicines and cures for people in the villages below.

Mornings were best to watch for condors. As arrows of brightness brushed the curtain of cold air off the cliff face we waited for the condors to move. One early morning we watched one individual particularly. First there was a lift of its head, next a ruffle of wings, energising all 7,000 of the bird's feathers and preparing them for flight. The bird then stretched its calloused neck, looking around as if waiting for a sign. Nothing hurries the King of the Skies. When ready, the bird opened its broad black wings, allowing the mountain air to lift it gently into its arms. With the delicacy of a butterfly, the condor's wing tips flexed, tilted and curved, bending upwards, splaying outwards, sensing the air before harnessing every invisible eddy of wind, every updraft. As varying degrees of heat reflected off different surfaces, they supplied energy and direction to the wind, enabling our bird to move through the air at its command. Condors are the sun's puppets.

Another bird joined the one we had been watching, then two more, until the group was caught in a graceful, spiralling vortex. But then, fast as a bullet, a shape shot through the air. A peregrine falcon fell with closed wings through the group, then up and down again, mobbing one of the condors.

With a flip of its wing, as a king would wave his hand at a trifling courtier, the upstart falcon was sent spinning away.

At times, the condors swooped low over our heads, inquisitively peering down at us land-locked creatures beneath. Javier pressed my shoulder and pointed. 'See that one? The white collar's very small – my father showed me that bird when I was small.'

Condors are one of the longest-living birds. In captivity they are known to reach eighty years of age, so who knows how old they get in the wild, cosseted by the sun and the wind.

'You mean you know some of the birds as individuals?'

'Yes, many of them. We travel these hills together. We talk to each other.'

Staying by the farmstead for a few days, enjoying each other's company, we walked the hills and watched condors. This was not birdwatching, as Javier knew but few of the other birds around him, and neither did he seem overly interested. The bond that bound us together was a love for condors.

One evening, Sara decided to visit us. Climbing into the van was a little awkward. Before we left the UK, we had fitted a smart telescopic aluminium ladder but I had destroyed it one day when I reversed with it still down. Since then we had used a child's wooden chair – it suited us perfectly, as it doubled up as an occasional table and extra seat. We had to be careful when standing on it, though, as it was prone to toppling over.

We took Sara's hand and pulled her inside. She stood up and stared around, mouth open, amazed. 'Oh, my! Oh, my!' she exclaimed. 'You've got everything! But it's so, so small.' She stretched out her hand and turned around. 'I can touch everything.'

Paula pulled out a drawer which had our knives, forks and spoons, then opened the tiny fridge, hardly big enough to hold a six pack of beer. She showed her our packets of vacuum-packed ready meals.

Sara had never seen such food. 'Where do you cook?'

Paula flipped open a top revealing a hidden cooker with two gas burners. No chopping wood and cooking over an open fire for us. Sara was mesmerised. 'How long have you lived in here?' she asked.

'Over two years,' said Paula.

There was no reply, just a baffled shake of the head – this was beyond Sara's comprehension.

Paula gave her a few packs of the vacuum-packed food we had brought from home. Sara hugged them to her chest tightly.

As so often when travelling, our visit had to end. We made preparations to leave. It would take us a couple of hours to pack all our gear away. We would make flasks of coffee and snacks for the journey, then turn off the water and bottled gas. Our small table would be collapsed and stored. Sleeping bags were rolled, even the smallest item tucked away securely. Camera and film equipment was packed away very carefully. Boxes that had been temporarily put on the front seats of the vehicle were put away in the camper. The last thing I would do was to carefully clamber on top of the stacked items inside the camper and unclip the roof, bringing it down on top of me as I scrambled out backwards.

Outside, I would walk around the camper tucking in the fabric sides and clipping the roof tight shut. Lastly, I checked the tyre pressures. Punctures were a constant worry and the way to avoid them was keeping the tyre pressures suited to the variable terrain we encountered. A small compressor enabled us to do that and we rarely had punctures.

Javier popped his head around the truck door and asked us to join him and his mother for *maté* before we left. As we sat outside their farmhouse in the shade of a tree, Sara brought out some homemade buns. I looked around. There were some tall, colourful flowers similar to hollyhocks, chickens outside the gate and a vermilion flycatcher flitting about in the tree above us. Draped across a splintered wooden fence was washing – clothes that were torn, many with holes. As Paula chatted to Sara, I listened, trying to understand what they were saying. A plate of biscuits lay on the table – we could have been in a Cornish tea garden, not high up in desert hills.

Javier joined us and put a box on the table. 'We have few visitors, never foreigners. So, this is a present for you. To remind you of us and the birds we live with.'

Surprised, Paula reached into the box and took out a parcel wrapped in a scarlet cloth. 'Oh, it's heavy.'

Before Paula had finished removing the cloth, Javier said quickly, 'Close your eyes, Michael, and hold out your hands. Hand it over to him, Paula.'

I felt the soft cloth. 'You're right, it's heavy.' Still with my eyes closed, I removed the cloth. The object felt cold and comfortable as each hand fell into a very different grasp. 'It feels like stone, but smooth.' Still with my eyes closed, I turned it over carefully in my hands. Its shape was longish and oval, the size of a small bag of sugar. My thumb and index finger fell naturally into a groove, my right hand moving over one end that filled my grasp like a cricket ball. My left hand moved about, feeling something quite differently shaped. The object tapered on two sides towards an edge, rather like a large canine tooth. I opened my eyes and exclaimed.

It was a heavy stone axe head, painstakingly worked,

smooth as a sea-washed stone and no doubt cherished. 'This is extraordinary, how did you get it, Javier?'

'From under rocks near the homestead. It's very old.'

'Yes, hundreds of years, maybe a thousand. But it can't be for us.'

'It is for you. You have to accept it. Your love of condors is enough for us to know it is going to a good home. You gave us a condor feather, the biggest we've seen. That will bring us luck. This axe head has power – a little of the people that laboured over it remains within the stone.'

We hugged each other goodbye with genuine gratitude.

Travelling was reintroducing me to situations and people I had never imagined. For me, it was an acknowledgement that I was becoming more comfortable to take risks with people. Memories from my recent past had prevented me from moving forward – a fear of young men, violence, even shouting had been enough to trigger bad responses even just a short while before.

'Would you like to leave boarding school and go to another school closer to home?' my father had asked me one day.

The answer – a fervent 'yes' – had been a heartfelt relief for me. Every day that I cycled to my new school, a co-educational comprehensive, was wonderful. The first day there was the first day of my education. I talked to the first girls I had ever met socially, I had my first science lessons, and it was the first time I had ever been issued with homework.

The only thing I missed was my moorland walks to find the peewits.

Life normalised, until the South African incident that is, and then all the horrors of the past returned.

We carefully stowed the ancient stone axe head under the driver's seat, not far from the remaining two condor feathers. We now had a treasure as well as talismans to support us on our long journey northwards.

CHAPTER 8

QUEEN ANSENUZA

Not many friendships start by throwing a bottle of wine over someone, but this happened to us when we attended a gala dinner to mark the end of a South American Bird Fair. It was held in San Isidro, a smart suburb in the north of Buenos Aires, bordering the great estuary of the River Plate.

We were seated at a table; opposite was a man whose name tag identified him as Walter Cejas. I reached out to shake his hand and introduce myself and, before I knew it, I had catapulted a bottle of fine Malbec into his lap.

Jumping up with the agility of a kangaroo, Walter, a big man, bumped into a passing waiter who toppled into the back of a lady on the table behind. Pandemonium ensued. The chaos made the day of several teenagers at the end of the table who were having difficulty suppressing laughter, while everyone else looked around as if a fight had broken out or someone had collapsed in a fit.

For a few embarrassing moments, the restaurant was silent. Walter disappeared to clean himself up and I was left red-faced, trying to explain to those around me how clumsy I was.

When Walter returned, his trousers wet through, he looked as if he had just been hit by a bucket of water. 'Well, that was a strange introduction! My name's Walter – but let's not shake hands again!'

Thankfully, the conversation resumed and we soon started swapping tales about birds. We learnt that he lived in Córdoba and was involved in conserving the birds of South

America's second biggest salt lake, Mar Chiquita, famous for its flamingos.

Waiters brought our second course, steaks so large their sides hung over the edges of the plate. Walter seemed happier now and asked if we had seen many flamingos.

'Very few, only individual Chilean flamingos up to now. I've got a feather, though.' From my red notebook I took out the deep crimson feather given to us at the railway museum and laid it on the table. The activity around us made it flutter a little, as if trying to rediscover its previous life. I gently pressed it down, being careful with the bottles close by.

'Oh, it's so bright! But you'll have trouble finding that bird round here. This is a feather of a Caribbean flamingo. They're the most deeply coloured. You'll have to get up to Colombia or Venezuela to see them.'

Flamingos turned out to be one of Walter's favourite birds. He admitted to wading chest-deep into the water to try to photograph them.

Putting down his knife and fork – which for an Argentinian eating a steak was unheard of – Walter turned to me. 'They're social, colonial birds. Find their food and you're halfway to finding the birds.'

Paula wanted to know how we'd do that.

'That's the tricky bit,' Walter said. 'They're not easy to find. Imagine the finest hair, the sort you find on a baby's head. The width of one of those is the size of the food that flamingos feed on – zooplankton and phytoplankton. You only find it in saline lakes, often high up in mountains. The water can be so alkaline it can take the skin off your hands.'

The look in his eyes as they met mine and the nod of his head was of genuine concern. Perhaps he had forgiven me for covering him in wine, and at least flamingos had brought us together.

In the August of 2017, an ornithological congress had been arranged to follow on from the South American Bird Fair. This was in Iguazu, close to the border with Brazil and the site of the most spectacular waterfall in the world. We were there to present the premiere of our film, *Tango in the Wind*.

On the last evening of the congress we attended another celebration dinner. Sitting with us at a table with eight other people was Annick, the cormorant expert from Puerto Deseado, and our good friend Hernan Casañas, the director of Aves Argentinas. At some point in the meal he asked those on our table to raise a glass to Paula and me, determinedly announcing: 'To Paula and Michael, whose next film will be about the Goddess of Water, Queen Ansenuza!'

Thinking it was a joke, I happily downed my wine. Paula and I hadn't a clue what Hernan was talking about and so, during a lull in the conversation, I asked: 'Who the heck is Queen Ansenuza?'

'It's a fable about Mar Chiquita, in Córdoba, the biggest salt lake in Argentina, a place that teems with birds! That's going to be your next film for us!'

Quietly we remonstrated, 'Hernan, it's impossible! No way. We're heading north, up the Andes, not back south.' We'd been away for three years and were still only halfway up the Andes.

Hernan leaned in towards us. 'Relax, you've got the time. This is important.'

'Why? What's so special?'

'I can't say at the moment but it's a wonderful place.'

'It takes months to make a film, Hernan.' Paula dug her elbow into my side.

Hernan softened his tone. 'Just call in, have a look around. We have people working there who know a lot about the flamingos.'

With the mention of flamingos, I remembered the incident at the Bird Fair dinner. I turned to Paula. 'Who was that guy I spilled the bottle of wine over, the one who loves flamingos?'

'Walter, Walter Cejas. He lives in Córdoba.'

Turning back to Hernan, I shrugged. 'OK, maybe we'll call in and have a look; I doubt we can make a film this year, though. Perhaps when we return from Colombia.'

'We need the film as soon as possible! It's important – it could be massively important for conservation.'

A little frustrated I opened up Google Maps on my phone to see where Mar Chiquita was, only to find that it was a huge lake in the middle of the country. But we still knew hardly anything about the place or the project , although Paula and I had to agree that flamingos were a bonus, as we hadn't seen that many. And perhaps Walter would help us.

Three days of driving south took us from Iguazu to the city of Córdoba, where we had arranged to meet Walter. He met us in the centre of the city, on the steps of the Monserrat College. This school dates back to 1680 and was started by Jesuit priests who followed in the wake of the conquistadors. Walter taught biology at the college as well as looking after its renowned natural history collection.

Walter, smiling, threw his arms wide as he saw us. Hugging Paula, he turned to me and laughingly said, 'I have new trousers on today. Let's go for lunch – no wine though, just water.'

Over lunch we bonded. Walter was turning into a great ally.

We explained as best as we could why we'd come. It was something we were struggling to justify to ourselves.

'Well,' said Walter, 'Mar Chiquita is the best place in South America for flamingos. It's a flamingo factory. They nest there and they visit from all over the country.' He took a mouthful of food, warming to his subject. 'But there are a lot of problems, like pollution and disturbance. The place is becoming very touristy. They are trying to make it a national park, but that's a sensitive issue with the absentee landowners. Better not to talk too much about it.'

'Is that why Aves Argentinas is involved?'

'Yes, them and BirdLife.'

As soon as Walter mentioned BirdLife, we started to wonder

what was really going on. That afternoon we gave our friend Jim Lawrence, their global marketing director, a call. We learnt from him that BirdLife was about to declare Mar Chiquita as the conservation project to receive support from the British Birdwatching Fair. This event raises hundreds of thousands of pounds for international bird conservation projects every year. Now we understood why the film was important and why Hernan had been reluctant to tell us what was happening.

Sometimes it seemed we were going backwards and not forwards on our journey, but following our hearts was something we had promised ourselves to do. And making a film to promote a possible new national park and help its threatened flamingos was exactly the sort of thing we had come to South America for.

Later that week we met up in the small town of Miramar on the shore of Mar Chiquita, and followed Walter along sandy tracks occasionally used by hunters or fishermen, leaving in our wake clouds of dust. We drove as far as possible until the scrub became too dense to penetrate and set up camp. Walter slept in a small tent adjacent to us.

Travelling wild as Paula and I were doing, we rarely had other people with us but it's not impossible to get one more into our camper for a meal, albeit with a squeeze. Paula, being the smallest, crept up onto our bed where she was able to sit up straight, legs outstretched, without hitting her head on the roof. Walter, who was a big guy, sat at the small table, which was only big enough to hold two small dinner plates. I stood by the cooker in a space sufficient to accommodate a crate of beer, and prepared the food.

Walter dubbed it 'The Webster Restaurant', and started to tell us the fable about Mar Chiquita.

'Locals don't call this place Mar Chiquita at all, but Ansenuza.' Apparently, Ansenuza was a cruel queen who lived alone on an island in the lake. She had never found a man handsome enough to match her beauty until, one day, she found a great warrior, who lay dying on the shore. For the first time in her life she fell in love but wept as the man died at her side. She cried so much that her tears turned the lake salty. The gods took pity on the queen and returned the warrior back to life in the form of a beautiful pink flamingo to comfort her, and from that day flamingos had lived at the lake.

The reality is a little different. Mar Chiquita is a huge shallow basin in the western central part of Argentina. It is enormous, about the same size as the island of Mallorca. The shallow lake is fed by a number of mineral-rich rivers, the most important being the Dulce river. These rivers have extensive marshland tributaries, known locally as *bañados*. As there are no outlets to the sea, the high summer temperatures encouraging rapid evaporation make the lake highly saline, perfect for the food that flamingos need.

We were all up early in the morning and before setting off introduced Walter to a breakfast of hot porridge laced with golden syrup, which he loved. Argentinians eat late in the evening and breakfast is often an overlooked meal. Not so for us.

Flocks of noisy monk parakeets were flying to and from their huge communal stick nests high up in a grove of eucalyptus trees, while cream-bellied thrushes sang from the chilca bushes. Once at the muddy shoreline of the lake we walked for several kilometres, becoming more and more conscious of the immensity of the area. The level of the lake changes with the seasons: some years there are massive floods which inundate trees; other years the water shrinks far back, creating extensive saline dust bowls.

I had been walking carefully for a few minutes, placing my feet with some trepidation along the treacherous shoreline, when Walter touched my arm. 'There,' he breathed.

Stretching as far as the eye could see across the water were faint lines of flamingos, wading in between the skeletal remains of dead trees. There must have been hundreds of birds.

To our right lay a marsh waving with tall reeds. We donned wellington boots and walked straight into it, endeavouring to reach the water's edge.

Paula has never liked walking in places where you constantly pull your feet in and out of mud that never wants to let you go, but she gamely kept up with Walter, who was in his element tramping through the swamp. Soon the squelchy mud gave way to a multitude of shallow pools scattered between areas of reeds, so tall they came over our heads. In single file we pushed through them until we came to an open area of marsh interspersed with short clumps of bright green sedge.

A streaky brown bird suddenly zipped up in front of us.

'Painted snipe,' yelled Walter, as another bird followed, right over his head. And then the whole marsh erupted around us.

A dozen South American stilts rose into the air, noisily screaming alarm notes. These birds did not fly away, instead they flew close, black wings held up, bright red legs dangling, almost parachuting in front us, before landing a short distance away. There they embarked on agitated 'broken wing' behaviour designed to attract predators away from their nest. Inadvertently, we had found ourselves in a breeding colony and carefully started to look out for their nests so as not to tread on them. They were in the open, platforms of dead, sun-bleached sticks encrusted with white salty mud. Nearly all had either three or four eggs, the colour of wet sand and blotched with squiggly patterns of black and light grey, their pointed ends facing inwards. Stilts are tall, delicate shorebirds, strikingly plumaged, and have a long black needle-like bill. While we remained they never stopped piping, their shrill notes rising into the air as they skimmed over our heads. For a predator such as a skunk or fox this is intimidating and one of the reasons why stilts nest in colonies: strength in numbers.

As for the painted snipe, an elusive and cryptically camouflaged bird whose appearance had started the commotion, there was no sign, until an excited Walter beckoned to us. He was peering into a dense clump of sedge about half a metre high, inside which lay a different sort of nest containing one chick and one egg. The nest was more like a pile of rotting aquatic vegetation than a collection of sticks. The egg was smaller than that of the stilts', more oval than pointed, much darker and blotchier, with a rough, crusty-looking surface. The chick lay as still as a stone, its plumage a warm brown colour with a buff halo around the top of its head, on either side of which we could see an eye. The upperparts were dark brown streaked with yellow. On top of the end of its bill was a white blob, its egg tooth, which the chick had used to crack its way out of the shell. It was a unique sight, and one I had never seen before as a bird's egg tooth drops off a day or so after hatching.

The behaviour of the painted snipe was quite different to that of the stilts. The adult birds made no sound; instead, they froze, almost dissolving into the marshland. One individual stood close to the base of some reeds, its head and bill pointing into the water, its back end tilted upwards. Clearly the bird was watching us, the yellow stripes on its back mimicking the reed stems. The other adult we saw was standing motionless too. I crouched down only three metres or so from the bird and peered closely, not quite understanding what I saw. The bird seemed to have four legs. But then two legs twitched and out from underneath the snipe came a bundle of feathers – a chick, smaller than a golf ball. It had been standing stock still with its body buried in the underparts of the adult's feathers.

The stilts continued their cacophony of alarm and I supposed that nesting so close to them was a good strategy. The painted snipes had developed ploys that any military commander would have been proud of: camouflage, and the ability to escape under the cover of a military offensive.

In total we found four nests of painted snipe and six of the stilts, an incredible morning's bird walk through a swamp. Walter was ecstatic: 'I've been coming here for years and never found the nest of a painted snipe. To find four is amazing. You've brought me luck.'

In the afternoon we drove around the eastern side of the lake to continue our search for flamingos. Walter led the way. Amazingly he knew his way around the enormous marshes, plains and salt flats surrounding the water. 'I'm OK around the southern half,' he said. 'For the northern half you need a helicopter and a boat.' We were able to park our vehicle at the end of a long muddy track and then walk a few kilometres to the lakeshore.

The wind carried faint gobbling sounds. Large groups of flamingos will make that that sort of throaty noise. In the far distance, close to the shore and a reed bed, we saw a smudge of pink. We circled back on foot, turning inland, and approached through an enormous marshy reed bed. Slowly we pushed our way through, quietly trying to negotiate ditches of water, across logs. All the time the sound of flamingos was growing louder. The birds were close.

We prepared our tripods and cameras and moved forwards, shin-deep in water. Moments later, we pushed aside the reeds and directly in front of us were about 300 Chilean flamingos. We were so close we spooked a few shorebirds, which noisily darted away. Excitingly, mixed in with the Chilean flamingos were twenty or so James's flamingos, the first of this species we had ever seen and the rarest of all the flamingos.

Luckily, the flamingos were too fully occupied in 'marching' to pay us much attention. This behaviour sees the birds parading around as a group in a wide circle, heads held high, uttering their gobbling sound. Flamingos have long, drooping scapular feathers on their wings and those of the Chilean are much deeper coloured than the other wing feathers – imagine hundreds of dancing swans, a metre tall, whose feathers are etched with carmine. Those in the centre of the group bobbed their heads up and down, while the ones nearest to the outside kept moving around more quickly, like a tribe of brightly dressed people engaged in an ancient ritual. New birds arrived, always in pairs, gently pitter-pattering across the water. Before joining the massed flock they bowed their heads, fluffed their plumage and engaged in mutual caressing, intertwining their necks. Pairs are thought to mate for life, so this pre-marching dance must be important.

As the sky's light faded, so the birds on the outer parts of the circle peeled away, departing in groups of twenty or so. Eventually there were only sixty or so birds left and they seemed intent only on themselves, unconcerned by us standing so close. They bobbed their heads up and down, several pairs standing very close to one another. As the dusk sky turned orange the birds quietened down; pair by pair they departed, as did we.

For wildlife photographers, really great days out are rare. This had been one of them. We had got the footage we needed, sufficient for Paula to edit the film into a celebration of pink.

On the drive back to Miramar, Paula's phone pinged with an incoming email.

'It's from Claudio,' she said.

'Who?' I was concentrating on the road and couldn't think for a moment.

'The man who pushed us into a cage full of pumas.' Paula read the email out: 'Condor liberation in Sierra Pailemán, Patagonia, mid-September.'

'Patagonia! He wants us to go back to Patagonia? That's bonkers!'

'Yes, but first pick him up in Belen.'

'Tell him we're in Peru!'

The phone pinged once more. 'He says, "I know you're close, see you soon."'

'Don't reply. We've got to carry on going north. He's crazy.'

Ultimately, we thanked Hernan for directing us to Mar Chiquita: 320,000 of the 'near threatened' Chilean flamingos live at or visit Mar Chiquita, with many of them breeding; 18,000 vulnerable Andean flamingos migrate down from the slopes of the Eastern Andes for the winter; and many 'near threatened' James's flamingos depart the freezing wintry waters of the Altiplano for its shores.

With Walter's help we had captured some great wildlife footage. The film was underway.

We weren't surprised that we hadn't heard about Mar Chiquita before. The landscapes and biodiversity of the continent are some of the finest on Earth, with so many 'celebrity' locations such as the Amazon, the Ecuadorian cloud forests and Patagonia stealing the limelight.

Mar Chiquita is fabulous and its importance is reflected in our film *Mar Chiquita – Why Is This Place So Special?* Hernan was delighted with the film, as was BirdLife International, who used it to open the 2018 British Birdwatching Fair.

Almost no one outside Argentina had heard of Mar Chiquita before. Birdfair and BirdLife International were at last giving it celebrity status, and at the same time ensuring its protection.

CHAPTER 9

THE FOUR GREAT BIRDS OF THE AMERICAS

As the months passed, we travelled through Catamarca and Salta provinces in northern Argentina. July snowstorms halted us in our endeavours to reach Laguna Blanca high up on the Altiplano, and most days we noticed small groups of Andean geese as they flew in skeins above us, heading to their wintering grounds lower down in the lush marshy pastures around Tafi del Valle.

It was then that we received bad news from home. Paula's mum, Doreen, well into her eighties, was very ill. A victim of Alzheimer's, she had lived in her own world for many years.

'What do we do? We're so far away.' Paula's mobile hung loosely in her hand. 'Can we get home in time?'

'We can try.'

We pointed the truck towards Buenos Aires and drove fast.

Four days later, we arrived in England and went directly to the care home. Doreen was a shadow of her self. Paula took her frail, tissue-thin-skinned hand and sat at her bedside. We talked as if everything was quite normal: Paula about her childhood and family holidays, while I interrupted with a few jokes, as I had always done over the years with her. We chatted about our travels and how often we thought of her, as we did all our family. There was little sign that Doreen could hear us, but we were sure she could.

Doreen drifted, and passed away peacefully only a few hours after our arrival.

In a sombre, shocked and tired state we returned to our house, surrounded by oaks, birch and holly. South America seemed so far away, almost a dream.

At breakfast the next day we opened our kitchen cupboard and Paula stood, bemused and bewildered. 'So much stuff! Why have we got all this? I never realised.'

'I know what you mean.' For the past year or so we had existed very nicely on four melamine mugs, plates and dishes. They did all match, though; we did have standards. I could hold all our kitchen utensils in one hand; we needed nothing more, and had cooked fabulous three-course meals with these limited resources. We had been away so long and lived so simply. Now we were back home, face to face with our past life, a life of having too much, too much unnecessary stuff, that had got in the way of actually living and loving life. We were uncomfortable, even in our home in the woods.

We found empty boxes, lots of them, and went from room to room.

'I never liked this vase.' Into a box.

Paula opened bedroom cupboards.

'Not worn this for years.' Into a box.

'Hey, look! My wedding dress. I'd forgotten all about that.' That went into another box and more followed: shoes, shirts, jumpers, books, crockery, a dozen mugs, old camera equipment, lamps that didn't work, toys, old Christmas cards, plastic chairs stacked up in sheds, boxes of plant pots, an old dog's bed, blankets from pre-duvet days, bottles, tins, a table with a broken leg awaiting repair, a hundred paperbacks, a huge radio with its tuning needle permanently fixed on Radio Caroline and jewellery that had escaped being put into the giveaway box in the truck.

By the time several charity shops had given their thanks, we started to feel better, less hemmed in, more relaxed.

A week later we returned to Buenos Aires.

A good strategy for avoiding roadside robbery in South America is to carry on driving – whether you see someone lying in the middle of the road or just trying to flag you down. So, when an excited-looking man ran towards our vehicle waving at us, I pressed on the accelerator and sped past, watching him hold out his hands, a confused-looking figure becoming smaller in my wing mirror.

Slowing down, I thought, *Perhaps that's him, but what's he doing here?* Slowly, with windows firmly up, I reversed and approached, the safety of plate glass between us.

The man's face shone with an unmistakable Claudio smile and I felt like a fool. Anticipating our arrival, Claudio had gone to a stretch of road near his village. He knew we'd have to come this way, and he had waited for us.

My embarrassment at taking him for a roadside robber over, we followed him home and sat around his great table drinking *maté*, talking till late into the night.

Since we had last seen Claudio, we had travelled over 20,000 kilometres in Argentina and Chile, spanning a time of two and a half years. Some of the most memorable days we had had were what we called a 'condor day'. Condors are unmistakable with their great splayed primary feathers, and the adults with white vanes on their upper wings. One day we had watched a group on a hillside. They had feasted for an hour on a carcass then struggled about like old men coming out of a pub at closing time. Having eaten too much, unable to take off, they had staggered slowly to the top of the hill, opened their wings to catch the breeze and were gone.

In our truck, the remaining two scimitar-shaped feathers nestled safely behind the sun visor. Each time we visited a school the feathers accompanied us and we watched the looks of awe and disbelief on the children's faces as they passed them around. There was something about this bird more than any other that left us needing more. Mentioning condors opened doors and brought smiles to faces. So it was no surprise that we had looped back south on Claudio's invitation, instead of pressing north.

Sipping the *maté*, I asked Claudio why he'd come to the road at that time on that day to find us. How had he known this was the day we'd come?

'A dream. After you left, I had many,' he replied. Claudio then disappeared behind the curtain at the end of the room and clambered up the short ladder to his bedroom. He returned carrying an object wrapped up in black cloth, which he laid on the table. 'I knew you would return today. The dream told me. Another dream told me I had to make this.'

The black cloth shimmered like velvet and from within, Claudio lifted out a shining wooden carving, the size of a cricket bat.

'This is a *wara* to take to the liberation. A *wara* is a totem; I had to make this or you wouldn't return. Once the *wara* was finished, I knew you would come for me.'

He handed the wooden carving to me; it felt as smooth as glass and I could see the swirling veins and knots of the surface. It was astounding – I had never seen anything like it, had never *felt* anything like it before. My hands were tense; it felt as if the wara had energy.

Claudio leaned towards me and pointed to one of the carvings on it. 'This is the head of a condor, the king of birds.' I ran my hand over the bird's head. 'The condor sees everything, knows everything. Even now his spirit watches over us. When we die our soul is caught by the condor who takes it to heaven.'

Carved around the top half were three other birds. 'And these?' I asked.

'This one is a bald eagle. That bird represents the indigenous people of North America.' He pointed to the next bird. 'That's a quetzal, to represent those in Central America. And the last one' – his finger moved again – 'is a hummingbird, which are the condors' messengers; they bring the indigenous peoples together.'

Further down the *wara*, a small opaque square was set into the surface with motifs either side. Below that, and tightly wrapped around the wood, was a shining fabric, the multi-coloured Andean flag.

'It's important. A dream has never told me to make anything like this before.'

I traced the swirling veins of wood down to the small, opaque square. 'What's this?'

'A sliver of quartz I found on the ground. The dream told me to go to El Shincal, up there.' Claudio nodded in the direction of the forested mountains behind the town.

By 1530, the province of Catamarca in Northern Argentina was the furthest south that the winding stony roads of the Inca Empire reached. The centre to administer these southernmost regions became the settlement of El Shincal. Stretching across a fertile hillside, it commanded a strategic view over the plains below and was protected by high Andean peaks to its rear. Today its ancient ruins reflect the craftsmanship of stonework seen in Cusco. Few people visit, as it lies well beyond the trail of tourist buses. Thorny bushes of chilca dot the landscape, and black-chested buzzard eagles sit watchful on the hilltop where human sacrifices were once performed; the place exudes a hypnotic stillness.

Claudio continued with his story. 'Behind the quartz cover on the *wara* is a cavity, and inside that is dust.'

'Dust?'

'The dream told me to go to El Shincal and directed me to a spot by a rock. There I had to dig.'

'To dig for what? Why? What were you looking for?'

'I had no idea. But I had to do what the dream said. So I dug and found a skull. I reburied it quickly but first I took a little bit of earth from that very spot and put it inside this cavity in the *wara*. Inside that earth is a tiny bit of that person's soul. This and the condor will guide us to Sierra Pailemán.'

All this talk of the *wara*, of dreams and digging up skulls, made me feel unsettled. However, Claudio was quite relaxed and went on to tell us that in Inca society there were four *wara* rods in every community, held by people at different levels of importance. The first rod was given to the person best able to run between communities to deliver messages, the second to the person best able to teach those how to sow seeds and care for the land, the third was held by a person in charge of the distribution of water and land, while the fourth, of the type Claudio had made, was held only by the wisest men of the community, whose task it was to transmit the relationship between Mother Earth – Pachamama – and Man.

'On each ceremonial *wara* rod there is always a condor,' he said. 'The condor oversees everything in Andean culture.' He paused and looked at us. 'We will go south to a condor liberation, to release condors back into the wild. There we shall hand this *wara* to a wise man, a Mapuche chief. The dream has told me this should be done and you've come to help. I can't do it on my own.'

What had seemed to us a simple journey to see a condor released back into the wild now took on another role, that of delivering a sacred rod from one community to another. How this journey was going to end up, we had no idea.

The next day we departed. The *wara* was carefully wrapped in its black cloth, secure between boxes of food. As we travelled we occasionally heard Claudio talking to it. He seemed thoughtful.

Many of the roads south were rough dirt, fenced on either side. Birds were, as usual, the most obvious wildlife. Red-shouldered hawks were the most numerous bird of prey and used pylons as surrogate trees. On leaving the province of San Leonardo we started to see our first white monjitas on roadside bushes.

Excitedly, we counted them as we drove and by lunchtime had seen over a hundred. They are a member of the tyrant family, one of the largest families of birds in the world and restricted to the Americas, but this information does this angel of a bird no justice. They are pure white except for black primary feathers and black tips to their tail feathers – shining lights on an otherwise monotonous landscape.

For camp sites we were usually able to find somewhere in the wild, up small tracks leading into the thorny bush of the *pampa*. Once we accidentally found ourselves on an oil field surrounded by nodding donkey derricks. Two security cars arrived very quickly and we were escorted off.

Another night we found a secluded spot in the bush, well off the road, though in the distance there were barking dogs. Fast asleep, I was dreaming of dogs and birds, *wara* sticks and flashing lights – and then more flashing lights. Blue ones.

With a start I woke to the sound of a vehicle right by us, and then came a hammering on our door. Zipping out of our sleeping bags and into our down jackets we clambered out to be met by uniformed police officers. It was the early hours of the morning. Claudio poked his head out of his tent. They shot questions at us. Who were we? What were we doing? They needed to check our truck. We emptied our boxes from the rear cab and their torch beams fell across a long parcel, the wrapped *wara*. They pulled aside the black cloth and in the darkness they stared at the totem.

'What's this?'

'A *wara*,' Claudio quickly said.

The two policemen looked at each other and backed off, peering into the front seats.

'Have you any guns? We're looking for guns. Have you been hunting?'

'No, none at all. We have no need to hunt. We have the *wara*,' said Claudio.

With that the atmosphere calmed immediately.

Looking at Claudio, they said, 'Where are you from? What are you doing with this couple?' They seemed uneasy, the whole arrangement just didn't seem right to them.

'We're travelling to a Mapuche ceremony further south.'

'Be careful. It's best not to camp around here. The farmer's dogs heard you arrive and he thought you were hunters. Sleep well and sorry to disturb you.' The police seemed apologetic, even embarrassed. Why that was so I couldn't understand. Perhaps it was something Claudio had said to them – Paula couldn't follow the conversation in detail. Maybe it was the influence of the *wara*.

We journeyed south for five days. Towns were small and we always stopped for lunch because for Claudio it was his main meal of the day. Many of the people do not have well-equipped kitchens in their homes, so have lunch out. Bars and restaurants are always full and convivial, with people chatting to each other while children play. Sometimes customers sit together at large tables; once Paula and I found ourselves sitting next to the mayor of the town. It was often a set menu, and food was there in minutes: bowls of soup, plates of pork chops and small dishes of *chimichurri*, a sort of salsa.

Eventually we crossed the River Negro again. We were back in Patagonia, a windswept expanse of grey-green, where shadows seemed to stretch forever; a place where people could believe the world is flat and trees only exist in their imagination.

Late afternoon on what we thought would be our final day of driving, Claudio suddenly leaned forwards from the back seat. 'Anywhere here will be good to camp.'

'We have daylight left for another few hours' travelling,' I said.

'Yes, but I feel this is the place to stop.'

I was learning to trust Claudio, so pulled off the gravel road to set up camp. He had his small purple dome tent up in five minutes and then disappeared. It took us longer to sort ourselves out, moving gear from the camper into the front seats and preparing supper. After a while Claudio returned and urged us to follow him a short distance. He had found something. He took us to an elevated area of stony ground but we could see nothing out of the ordinary. Turning through 360 degrees he pointed out to us large round boulders, half buried in the ground. Once we had seen them, the evening shadows unmasked their cloak of concealment. A circle became clear, which on our own we would never have noticed.

'This is a sacred place. A Tehuelche campsite. These are anchor stones, used to hold down their guanaco-hide tents to the ground. The Tehuelche people were nomadic, following herds of guanaco. This site is hundreds of years old, perhaps a thousand.'

By now the pink flush of the dying day had almost gone. We sat outside for supper and in silence watched the Southern Cross appear, content to let our thoughts drift between the billion stars that arched across the silent sky.

On what we now hoped would be our last day of our journey, Claudio told us to keep a lookout for a domed reddish hill called Sierra Pailemán. By late afternoon we were starting to tire, my patience with it. The icon on our GPS had long been signalling that we weren't close to any roads.

'This is ridiculous, we have no idea where we are going!' I snapped to Paula.

'We'll be OK,' said Claudio calmly.

But the roads worsened and it started to drizzle, turning them into slippery, slithery tracks, bushes narrowing our way. And then, suddenly, in the far distance we saw a wind vane, the first manmade object we had come across all day, and then a rusty metal drum with an arrow scrawled on it.

We were more than a little fed up but at last we had arrived. Despite the dark, I could see that we were in some sort of permanent camp. To greet us was a small group of people. Four were volunteer biologists – they looked dishevelled and gaunt, as if they had been marooned there for years. Two others had recently arrived: Leonardo and his wife, Valeria, the project directors.

Introductions and a drink of *maté* over, we prepared our truck for the night and then were called over to the main cabin. We were starving.

As we sat around a table I noticed a lack of food or anything that even resembled the start of a meal. Instead, the table was covered with a colourful quilt upon which were a variety of items: small pebbles, shells and a tiny dish of herbs. As other people sat down they added to the collection: a small pouch containing sand, a candle, a book, a tiny statue and a ring. The atmosphere was quiet, conversation muted, the room dark except for a few candles. Eventually the talking stopped and some bowed their heads. I looked up, unsure of what to do. Outside the wind gusted against the door. There were nine of us in the cabin, flickering candles highlighting large cobwebs suspended in the overhead rafters.

Leonardo put his hands flat on the table and spoke. 'We honour the land as animals do. We honour the mountains, valleys, the caves and rivers. Honour is the start of all teaching. We honour mother nature, Pachamama.'

There was a long pause and, one by one, each person around the table spoke of themselves and their experience in the wild and with Pachamama. The volunteers spoke of their heartfelt pleas for better equipment, of their personal struggles against the elements in this desolate land. It was their task to track and care for the juvenile condors released in previous years – the released birds were fitted with GPS tags, so they could be tracked by telemetry. The volunteers recited instances of climbing isolated and steep outcrops in torrential rain, of traversing on foot through kilometres of thornbush in gales. One exhausted young man was in tears.

There were no confessional-box answers, no discussion. We sat riveted by the intimacy of what was being said. The drama was heightened by the heavy rain beating against the walls of the cabin and rattling the windows; sounds that I was thankful for, as they masked my rumbling stomach.

The session continued with everyone in deep concentration, focused on the proceedings. Leonardo reverently unrolled a richly decorated cloth and from this he drew out a long, narrow bone pipe. Valeria filled the pipe with native herbs, lit it, paused and passed it to the person next to her. It left behind a circle of sweet smoke which drifted above her head until caught by a draught and carried away.

There is something primitive and transformational about smoke from a pipe. As each person took the pipe they offered a goodwill message to aid the condors awaiting release, the rising smoke carrying thoughts and prayers. 'May the winds be strong and fill your feathers.' 'May you fly to the coast and find food on the shore.' 'May you build a great nest.' The pipe made three circuits.

If one was to believe that man talks to God through the condor and that intercession with Pachamama was needed to guide the condors, then this was the very place where such mystic messages might be successful.

It had been almost two hours since we had started the ceremony. *Perhaps*, I thought, *everyone has eaten before we arrived or maybe they are ascetics who deny themselves worldly pleasure.* All that seemed to matter to them was the plight of the condor, both past and present. I was all the way with them on that idea, but there was no denying it: I was starving.

At long last Leonardo brought the ceremony to an end. The volunteers left the room and thankfully returned with magnificent dishes of food: rice and meat, vegetables and homemade bread.

I jumped up, eager to help.

Over supper, Leonardo told Paula and me about the condor project and the birds they were close to releasing. 'This project is unique. As the condor has two wings so does this project – one wing is scientific, the other cultural.' He chewed and swallowed before continuing. 'This is Mapuche land. An indigenous reserve of protected land. We need their permission to be here, they need the condors. We need their help and support, otherwise the project won't be a success. We take the eggs from the wild and raise the chicks in Buenos Aires zoo. The chicks never see a human, we hand-feed them with a puppet that looks like a condor's head.'

'How long does that take?'

Leonardo sighed. He had devoted the last twenty years of his life to saving the Andean condor. He looked upwards as if asking Pachamama herself for strength. 'About two years.'

'Two years!' I exclaimed.

Leonardo explained that no other bird species anywhere requires to be fed solely by its parents for so long. Not only that, he said, but the bird then takes a further ten years to become sexually mature, sometimes as long as twelve years before they are able to lay their first egg – and then only one. This was one of the reasons why the birds were so rare, as well as being among the longest-living ones. 'Just before the birds are ready for release they are fitted with a radio transmitter. We track the birds, help them if needed, and leave food for them if required. These volunteers are their surrogate parents and we have a 100 per cent success rate, thanks to the fusion of culture and science.'

'Have the condors started to breed here?'

'Yes, a few pairs are now breeding. It's fantastic. Condors hadn't bred in these sierras for 170 years, and during all that time the ground became poorer. It hardly ever rained. It's different now the condors have returned; the land, the sky and its people are in harmony.'

We sat and talked, more food arrived. Suddenly, the door was thrust open, allowing a sudden gust of cold air to push away the spirits which might have gathered. A crowd of people fell inside, laughing to each other, hugging old friends, the first of many groups who drifted in during the night.

Tired by the extraordinary events, we crept off to bed. Half an hour later, there was a gentle knock on the camper door. Claudio popped his head inside. 'Can I have your condor feathers, please?'

I passed them to him, trusting Claudio to take care of them.

The following day dawned dry and bright. We were woken by slow single drum beats. Climbing out of the truck, we joined a small group waiting for the sun to appear. The rain clouds from the night before had receded. The eastern sky was clear.

Three threads of plaited wool – blue, red and yellow – had been twisted around three black feathers; they hung on a line strung between two poles. The longest of them, shimmering as the brilliant orange rays passed through its vanes, I recognised.

Our connection with the wild is now so tenuous, few of us watch the miracle of sunrise with a sense of awe. Yet this daily act is the one that every human who has ever walked the Earth has seen and once must have marvelled at. This brilliant orb rising over our tiny, obscure speck of dust in the universe means the Earth can be our home. Without the sun we would not exist. That morning, over the dark, flat plains of Patagonia, the sun rose in the same way that it has done for 4 billion years, its perfect rays drying the raindrops, warming the rock, readying the soil for a germinating seed.

The drum continued to beat until the sun was clear of the horizon, then it stopped.

The release of the condors was done on a hilltop. People had started to gather all morning and by midday there were several hundred, including white-coated children from schools up to eighty kilometres away. Cars and buses had to be parked some distance back in a village, as the mud roads were too wet to drive on.

We formed a straggling line to the liberation area, many in warm ponchos, bands round their heads holding back long hair, embroidered bags over shoulders, forming talkative and expectant groups. Having no idea what to expect, we followed.

Once at the top of the hill, a circle was formed around a pile of stones. Many had brought sacred talismans and laid them on the ground. Claudio carefully placed the *wara*, still wrapped in black velvet, on the ground; our last feather with it.

At last two metal crates were brought from within a truck and placed on the ground at the cliff edge. People crowded quietly around, eager to see the release of their birds, messengers to their god; some no doubt thinking to themselves that one might be the very bird that would some day take their soul up into the heavens.

A man stepped out from the crowd. He was draped head to foot in a striped cloak, the colours of the Andean flag: red, orange, yellow, white, green, blue and violet. Along with this he had a multi-coloured Doctor Who-like scarf hanging from his neck to his toes, and a matching hat on his head. Nahuel was his name, a Mapuche chief. He walked to the offerings and pulled the black cloth off the *wara* and stood it up. People shuffled their feet, murmuring, and Andean flags were waved.

In one hand Nahuel held a small ceramic bowl, glowing with embers with a rising wisp of fragrant smoke. Slowly he walked around the ring of people, wafting the smoke from the bowl over the gathering, and then he placed it on the ground. Approaching the crates from behind, Nahuel drew away the blankets that covered them and carefully slipped the catches off their mesh doors.

No one moved or spoke.

First one, and then the other, of the condors stepped out into the mountain air, free for the first time in their lives. The onlookers looked dumbstruck and for a moment my heart lost a beat. The birds seemed monstrously large, taller than some of the children present. Their heads had a skullcap of pale wrinkled skin ending in a long nose tipped with a white hooked bill. Round their necks, a ruff of purest white topped the vestment feathers of black and white.

One bird turned its head towards the people, having the impact of a pope standing in front of his supplicants. All were frozen in hope. The second bird took a step forward. Turning, it looked our way, dispassionate, intense and aloof. I saw a reflection of myself in the bird's eye as the bird slowly unsheathed its long black flight feathers, then folded them back again, unsure what to do.

They stood on the edge of the precipice. Would they fly, or fall to their death down below?

In the silence that only a mountain top can bring, we felt it first. A caress on our cheeks, then a rustling, like passing a hand across the top of growing barley. It was a movement of air so gentle as to not turn the page of a book, but it strengthened a little into a feather-twitching breeze and then into a wind that opened broad dark wings.

Finally, circling the mountain, a fierce gust hit us all. We braced our feet and, accompanied by gasps from the people, the birds were swept upwards, away and upwards, further and higher. Higher still they were taken – until one bird stalled. Stiffly turning and twisting downwards, the wind streaming through splayed feathers, the giant swept low over our heads.

Like the swirl of a magician's black cloak, the birds had gone, transformed into silence.

There were muted cheers, a few clapped, but the atmosphere was far more personal, more intimate; many hugged those close by, some cried, those who didn't held back private tears and many could not utter a word, eyes straining to see specks now high over the peaks. All were lost in their own thoughts.

A subdued anticlimax rippled through the people; no one moved.

Then Nahuel took hold of the *wara*, addressing the people one last time. With both arms reaching into the sky his voice boomed out.

'Bald Eagle from the north, the bird whose kingdom you share with the salmon and the whale. People of Haida, LOVE AND CARE FOR YOUR SEA! Quetzal, the most beautiful, the bird whose kingdom you share with the trees. Mayan people, LOVE AND CARE FOR YOUR FOREST!' Then Nahuel bowed. 'Great

Condor, king of the Andes, whose kingdom you share with us, your people. LOVE AND CARE FOR YOUR MOUNTAINS and send Hummingbird to greet his friends!'

The condor liberation was undoubtedly a success for the scientists, with their calibrated incubators, puppet-show nurturing methods and satellite tracking systems, but standing on that cliff edge it was the cultural significance of that moment that was overwhelming.

The majority of the people had drifted away by the end of the day and there were only twenty or so of us left. Ancient peoples always feast after important ceremonies and Nahuel had come prepared. Out came a new roll of hessian and three long-handled shovels, one each for Claudio and Leonardo, Nahuel taking the third. No instructions were needed – they knew what to do, and set about digging a pit the size of a freezer. Others were instructed to find large stones. Paula and I looked on perplexed, until we were given the task to find wood. Considering we hadn't seen a tree in more than a week this presented a challenge, but by scrabbling under small bushes we managed to find plenty of dry kindling.

I watched the process of construction carefully. Rocks, two deep, were laid in the bottom and up the sides of the pit and a large nest of wood built on the base. When the fire was crackling merrily, more stones were added, and Nahuel then spent his time selecting slivers of wood, passing these into every crevice and niche with the precision of a surgeon, flames licking towards his fingers. More stones were then placed in the pit until they were almost level with the ground. Smoke circled upwards from the gaps between them, and still Nahuel pushed in more twigs and sticks, chanting as he did so.

As the sun lowered so my appetite increased, and I was grateful to see a procession of food bowls appear. Thick triangular wedges of meat stuffed with all manner of herbs arrived; legs and shoulders and hunks and chunks from goodness knows what as well as heaps of half-chickens were piled in on top of the hot stones. Then came buckets of vegetables: red potatoes, orange carrots, bright yellow squashes and green apples, all pushed between the meats, a Technicolored jigsaw of food swirling with smoke.

Standing up to ease his back, Nahuel looked at the sun. When it first touched the far horizon he gave the order. Quickly, people worked with the hessian, layering it deftly backwards and forwards over the food and stones. That finished, the shovels came into action and like demons the men piled earth on top, higher and higher, into a great mound. On Nahuel's signal they stopped, just at the moment the flaming sliver in the west disappeared. The earthen oven was finished.

'The sun's last rays are trapped within our fire, all will be well!' Nahuel announced.

Four hours later, the earth was removed and the hessian peeled back, revealing a primeval feast. The night air circulated mouth-watering aromas around us. The fiery sun had worked its magic in more ways than one.

We sat, perched on rocks and crouched on the ground, much like scavenging condors ourselves. We ate off scrubbed wooden platters, one or two off cardboard, using just our hands, juices running down fingers.

The next day we had to leave. Claudio returned one of our feathers to us. 'The other had to stay,' he said, softly. I understood, but was relieved we were to have a feather back with us. It was our talisman, after all.

Yet again, we reluctantly drove away from Patagonia. It was important to return Claudio to his village in Argentina, and we desperately wanted to continue our journey northwards. Glancing back, I took one last look at the dark feathers, waving in the wind on their tri-coloured string.

The journey back was uneventful in comparison to the previous week. We were able to talk more easily than on the trip down. Nahuel had kept the *wara* and Claudio was relaxed, even jovial. He talked about everything: life, birds, his village and his ecological group. We, too, talked about our lives and family, birds, and the environmental groups we had worked with at home. We had so much in common.

By not planning too far ahead we were learning that every day became ripe for encounters, a rollercoaster of accidental events. One such example was meeting Claudio. He had fallen into our life for only a few weeks but during that time we had become close, and from him we had learnt a very different way of viewing the natural world. For Claudio all nature, including ourselves, was sacred.

Claudio was also something *more*: less tangible, mysterious, like the Green Man of our ancient forests.

Back at Claudio's house in Belen we sat around the table drinking *maté* for hours. We should have gone earlier but there are some people and places you never want to leave – something prevented us going; perhaps we thought it was simply too difficult to say goodbye. Eventually, we had to go.

'Where are you travelling to now?' Claudio asked.

'North, following the Andes,' we replied as we stood up regretfully, gathering our things together.

Suddenly, there was a loud rap on the door and in walked the gentle bear, Miguel, a broad smile on his face. 'Before you leave, can we go birdwatching?'

CHAPTER 10

BIRDS CHANGE LIVES

Miguel seemed desperate and we listened attentively to his plea: 'I don't know much about birds at all, but I love them. In town I've seen cardinals and doves and lots of others but I don't know their names. I've always wanted to go birdwatching and you're the first birdwatchers I've met!'

'We're heading high into the mountains tomorrow. It'll be too cold for you to camp,' I said.

'It's warm in Formosa. That's not too far. The Bañado La Estrella is supposed to be great for birds. We could go there,' Miguel countered.

Paula and I looked at each other. We'd never heard of the place. Here we were, at a crossroads of decision-making again. A journey into Formosa would take us away from the Andes, but we had heard that the surrounding Gran Chaco habitat was an important area for birds. But we had already been away from home for so long, and were still in Argentina. Would we ever get up north?

'We can do whatever we want,' said Paula. 'We can carry on following the Andes after we've helped him. This'll be fun.'

The comment surprised me. Once something was arranged, Paula was usually the last person to change plans at the drop of a hat. Perhaps our new life was affecting her too?

There was so much to do, but we did want to show Miguel the birds of his own country.

During my own childhood, it hadn't been easy being fascinated by nature. No one at my primary school had been particularly interested. So I would disappear into the woods on my own, searching for nests and listening to birds without knowing what they were. I would make one of my mother's stockings into a butterfly net to catch the delicate insects and put each one into a matchbox as my very own museum. Birds' eggs, feathers, fossils, snail shells and rocks, as well as bones washed out from owl pellets – all these were displayed in matchboxes and kept in paper bags, then stacked in shoe boxes in a roof loft, accessible by ladder from the outside and where no one visited but myself.

Later, at boarding school, no one had bothered about anything other than survival.

The following day, we met up with Miguel. He was carrying two carrier bags containing a tent, a blanket, a set of clothing and packets of biscuits. It had dawned on us that we knew next to nothing about him except he was perhaps nineteen and we were about to take him with us for a couple of weeks, introducing him as much to his own country as to birdwatching.

We headed north-east, away from the Andes. Our first destination was the Chaco national park, which was 1,100 kilometres from Belen, on the way to Bañado La Estrella. The Chaco is a paradoxical region of arid sub-tropical forests, savannahs and wetlands. The forest is predominantly low, with dense prosopis trees whose branches are barbed with great thorns. The thorns are arranged along their stems in a circular fashion, which means that as small twigs fall to the ground, they land like a caltrop – always with one of their spines facing upwards. So dense and so thorny is this forest that the *gauchos* who penetrate its depths have the entirety of their horses draped in thick, protective hide to ward off the thorns. Armoured like medieval knights, they themselves have similar hides covering their legs.

The large canopy trees are native red and white quebrachos, valued for the tannins that can be drained from the great trunks but which, when sucked dry, are felled for their hard, durable timber. There are also the pink-flowering ceiba trees with curvaceous bottle-shaped trunks covered in stumpy conical thorns. But it was the cacti that amazed us. Even those we had seen in the Monte Desert had not prepared us for the Chaco. Never had we imagined cacti as tall as trees, some twenty feet high with thick trunks and massive fleshy thorny plates – vegetative dinosaurs.

It was dusk when we drove through the entrance into a makeshift campsite. No one was around and as we opened the truck doors we were stunned by loud screaming: chorusing black howler monkeys in the trees above us. The tropical forests of northern Argentina are as far south as black howlers live. There were a dozen or so animals but only a few were howling: rows of white teeth gleaming from wide open mouths, their heads thrust skywards, the deafening sound shaking the leaves around them.

Reaching under my driver's seat I pulled out one of the pairs of binoculars we had brought from England and passed them to Miguel. He stared upwards, his cheeks glistening with tears: '*Hermoso . . . hermoso*, beautiful . . . beautiful,' he murmured. 'I've heard about these but I didn't think they'd be this loud!'

The following morning was no quieter either. First came the occasional *pop . . . pop . . . pop* as discarded seedpods landed on the camper roof above our heads, followed by the harsh calls of the perpetrators: turquoise-fronted parrots, feeding in the tops of the trees above us. Like so many parrots, they were mostly green, but this bird had a lovely yellow patch around its eye and a light turquoise flash on its forehead. They are a common species but, as they can be taught to speak a few words, we often saw them caged up and hanging outside shops and in cafés.

The parrots were much noisier than Miguel. He was a quiet person and seemed content as we pointed out the parrots. At the sight of his first woodcreeper, however, he became excited, his serious face now wearing a broad smile.

Seeing birds through binoculars for the first time meant a new world of colour and beauty was opening up for him – as it was for us, too. Like a sponge he wanted to know everything and, as we hardly knew many of the birds ourselves, there was a lot of laughter. His English was very good so we could chatter away as if he was family, something that we had been missing.

'There are many similar-looking woodcreepers in South America,' I explained, as I started the truck. 'They're brown birds, usually on trunks of trees. Look at that long decurved bill.' This was one of the most distinctive of the family: a scimitar-billed woodcreeper, its crazily long bill curving downwards, with striking creamy vanilla underparts flecked with chocolate-coloured streaks.

Through the window, Miguel kept the binoculars tight to his eyes and marvelled at it. 'I've never seen a bird like this.'

The bird wheedled out a spider. 'The anteater of the bird world,' I said, as I put the truck in gear and pulled out onto the deserted road. 'How many bird species have you seen?'

'Never counted.'

'Well, it's fun to count the species you see; that will help you to remember them. Keep a note of the birds as well, where and when you've seen them. That's birding at its simplest.'

We saw Miguel's next new bird sitting in a lone tree ahead of us, a favourite bird of ours: a roadside hawk. Slowing down, I stopped almost opposite where it was perched. The hawk has a dark hood, and its belly and breast are patterned with orange stripes.

Paula, who was sitting by her open passenger window, talked to Miguel as he watched it. 'It's a juvenile, which makes it more difficult to identify, as books don't always show their picture.'

'Oh, this one's easy,' said Miguel. 'It has condors down it.'

Startled, Paula exclaimed, 'What? What do you mean?' She looked carefully, scrutinising the bird for some abnormality.

'On the underneath,' he replied. 'The feathers are condor shadows.'

I could see what he meant, as across and down the creamy belly of the bird were golden-brown markings which resembled soaring raptors.

Impressed by his attention to detail, I wanted to know if anyone else in his family was interesting in nature.

Miguel picked up the binoculars again. 'I have no family.'

Paula and I exchanged glances.

'I'm sorry.'

'Its OK. I was adopted and have never met my real family. I have a sister, Sabrina, but we've never met. She lives in Buenos Aires. It's all a bit difficult.'

'How come?' I felt this was pushing our friendship a little, but as we were travelling together and living so closely, thought I would let him end the conversation when he wanted.

'Too much money to get there, and I'm not sure the time is right. One day, perhaps.'

There was a pause after that and, not wanting to make him feel awkward, we moved the conversation on.

Not for first time it was brought home to us how lucky we were, doing what we were doing. People we met either couldn't understand why, or asked if they could join along: 'We can fit in the back, buy our own food?' The reality for them was that Argentina had been in economic turmoil for generations and most people found life difficult. We knew Miguel's situation – it was one of the reasons we wanted to help him.

Formosa is the hottest part of the country and we were thankful for the truck's air conditioning. Paula passed round bottled water at intervals and sometimes juicy *empanadas* to keep us going. During the course of the drive, we stopped at intervals, Miguel adding Brazilian and ringed teal as well as a great egret to his growing list of birds, proudly announcing: 'Hey, that's sixty-nine species so far and it's only day one!'

By a lake we struck lucky seeing a male snail kite and a limpkin. 'Both these feed off freshwater apple snails,' I told Miguel. There must have been plenty of snails to accommodate both these birds, but they feed in different ways so are not really in competition. The kite drops from the air into shallow water and picks them up with its sharply bent bill, the ideal tool for prising out the sticky molluscs. The limpkin is a large rail-like bird that skulks among the reeds and probes in the mud for the snails. 'The limpkin's call is like a child crying,' I told Miguel.

'Ah!' His face lit up. 'I've heard of the bird, we call it the carrao. I've wondered what they look like.'

'There will be lots more with a bit of luck,' Paula said cheerfully, as we turned off onto a sand road, straight as a die and disappearing into the distance. The road, however, was sided by broad swathes of bush that had been crushed down and pushed back on either side – the dubious sign of road widening. But with the soil disturbed and the smashed branches still green, it was a magnet for small birds, and we stopped to watch a flock of red-crested finches darting about like embers in a fire. A portent, unfortunately, for shortly afterwards puffs of grey smoke caught our attention.

My heart sank and I took a deep breath: on one side of the road a digger tore at the bushes, hefting them out of the ground, while behind it a bulldozer pushed the debris on to a fire. Passing the mayhem, we continued slowly on our way, birding from the open car windows and adding great antshrike to the list. The male is startlingly black and white but the female is chestnut brown and white, while both have bright red eyes and, when stressed, will raise a short crest. Tropical parulas, black-capped warbling finches and masked yellowthroats were also added to the list.

Then more smoke billowed ominously ahead, and a man by the road waved a yellow flag, shouting, '*Suave . . . suave . . . gently . . . gently*,' as we passed. Suddenly, we were in among tractors, trucks and bulldozers. Aghast, we manoeuvred along the branch-strewn road, either side of which lay a nightmarish scene. The entire landscape was being ripped to shreds. As far as we could see were spirals of smoke, the shattered remains of trees piled high, thrusting their torn branches towards the sky. This was the deforestation of the Chaco.

The high spirits with which we had started the day evaporated. Stopping, I climbed out of the car, walked a few paces and stumbled in agony. A searing pain shot up my leg. I shouted, concerned that perhaps I had stood on a snake or a scorpion. Miguel lifted my leg. Something protruded from my sole, and whatever it was had impaled my foot, making it impossible to remove my trainer. Rushing back to the truck, Paula fetched the tool kit and gave Miguel a pair of sizable pliers with which he managed to get a grip on the article and wrench it out. Fortunately it didn't break. Out slid a vicious-looking prosopis thorn as long as his hand. Thankfully the pain subsided, to be replaced by a wet sensation of blood soaking into my sock.

Returning to the truck I sat down, had a coffee and looked around. The land was a ruin to the furthest horizon. A tanker sat over to my right, fuel for the beasts that heaved and tore the vegetation, groaning as they did so. Scavenging caracaras drifted between the clouds of smoke, picking at the dead and dying like ravens on a battlefield. My foot hurt but the ache in my heart was worse, helpless at the scene of a crime. We were the prime witnesses for the prosecution, agriculture versus nature.

We eventually reached Copo national park. It took all day despite only being a few hundred kilometres' drive, as getting into it proved the most difficult part. We thought we were on the right track but as it faded out and became overgrown with tall grass, we turned back. An hour later we found someone to ask the way and he confirmed we had been correct in the first place. Apparently the chief warden had taken down the directional signs as he didn't want visitors.

We retraced our route and soon found a pleasant place to

park up for the night. There were some buildings, including washrooms, but these had fallen into complete disrepair: broken windows, with taps and piping ripped out. If it had been on the outskirts of a city I wouldn't have been surprised, but there were no dwellings within ten kilometres and it was four-wheel access only. During our stay we saw no *guardaparques*, only one bearded young Argentinian who walked in one day with a small tent. He spent most of the day sitting cross-legged in a yoga pose, but he was interested and knowledgeable about snakes and told us this was a great place to find some of the most dangerous ones in the country.

As we slept, the heat was tempered by aromatic air that wafted through our mesh windows, scent from the pink ceiba flowers.

Exploring these strange forests and introducing Miguel to its special birds – cream-backed woodpeckers, many-coloured Chaco finches and spot-backed puffbirds – was a joy for us.

The appreciation of many birds is all about colour, but not always. If biodiversity can be measured by the number of species of birds of prey, the Chaco's forests were wonderfully rich and brought to Miguel a new dimension to birdwatching, that of the speed and acrobatics of the hunt – the fleeting view and behaviour of a bird, what birdwatchers call *jizz*.

There were hawks, with their broad wings – they are the foot soldiers. A bi-coloured hawk we watched, hidden among leaves, waiting in anticipation, was planning its attack. They rarely failed: their long yellow legs dressed in scarlet socks are deadly at the point of kill.

Falcons have narrow, sharp wings like arrows. They are the archers on the battlefield, in flight tearing down at the speed of a missile. We watched a laughing falcon, distinctively cream-coloured with black spectacled feathers round its eyes, an adaptation that probably works to deflect bright sunlight. Ours swooped low over grassland, spotted a snake in the grass, somersaulted and pounced. It missed, but they are hit and run bandits and their favourite prey, snakes, can sense an attack in an instant.

Eagles are the heavily clad knights. Everyone ogles at eagles: muscular and proud, they circle beneath the clouds. Without binoculars they are near impossible to see. Miguel spotted his first eagle that day – a black and white hawk-eagle. No doubt the bird had seen him first, their eyesight is so sharp. They ride down the thermals towards their prey – an armadillo or bird on the ground. Just like a mounted knight in armour, there's no stopping them once they have committed to the attack.

Each day we followed animal trails. The leafy canopy above us was sparse and thin, the leaves small, allowing sunlight to penetrate to the bare, hot, yellow sand, the home of great spiny-plated cacti. Between these tiptoed graceful black-legged seriemas. The dry Chaco forests were the only place we came across these long-legged birds. They were never common and when we did see one, it strode away quickly, a haughty-looking grey bird disappearing into the grey bushland, like a lawyer leaving court.

Another, even more secretive species and one named after the trees under which it lives is the quebracho crested tinamou. Tinamous are one of the ten endemic bird families to Latin America and closely related to the rheas. Whereas the greater rhea is flightless and the size of a footballer, tinamous can fly and are only the size of a football. The understated colours of these small birds' plumage are enhanced by the intricate swirling hues of coffee-coloured patterning that disguise them in the undergrowth.

After a day or so of watching, we discovered a group of trees that a family of quebracho crested tinamous frequented. We set up a hide, returning to it the next day. I stayed inside, hidden, while Paula and Miguel positioned themselves the other side of the trees and waited.

I was motionless, conscious of every movement and sound. I was a sniper with a long lens, not a gun. I was a yogi seeking inspiration. My mind was attuned to everything about me. The sun shifted, shadows changed, leaves sang gently in unison.

Paula and Miguel saw the family. Carefully, they stood up and walked forward a little, hoping to encourage the birds towards my hide. Seeing them, the birds moved away slowly through the undergrowth, meandering between the grass and fallen leaves, feeding as they walked with the jerky steps and bobbing head of an Egyptian dancer. The size of an elegant cockerel with slender curving necks, they are masters of camouflage whose cryptic plumage imitates the sun-dappled sandy forest floor. Their large, bright eyes are constantly alert, the tuft of feathers on the top of their head giving them a comical appearance.

At times like this, when I am looking through the camera lens, I feel that the birds are inside the hide with me. I wear gloves and often a close-fitting hat that I pull over my forehead; that way my light skin won't be as visible in the darkness of the hide. I can feel my heart beating, because I know this is a once-only opportunity. If the birds see a movement they will flee; if I scare them with a sound, all is lost. I try to think positively in the hope that invisible waves of calm and peace will cloak me in invisibility.

On this occasion it must have worked. The birds came to within ten metres of me, practically eyeball to eyeball. The camera shutter clicked, and the birds passed, disappearing into the bushland. I continued to stare out, hopeful they might reappear from the impenetrable Chaco, but they didn't.

A magical moment with nature, a once-in-a-lifetime vision, was over.

It was time to pack up and head for the town of Las Lomitas. From there we would head into the flooded forests by the Pilcomayo river, which acts as the border with Paraguay, the area known as the Bañado La Estrella, which Miguel was so keen to visit.

Once we left the national park, rude regimented lines of soya more regularly interrupted the native forest and we discussed for how long this unique thorny tangle of cacti and quebraco, so full of birdlife, would survive. The most famous Argentinian folk singer-songwriter of the last century had a fond eye for the neglected yet noble landscapes of his country and wrote thoughtfully: 'For those who cannot see, land is just land.' The present-day destruction of the Chaco is testament to those words.

By the time we reached the town of Las Lomitas, our total bird species seen had risen to 105. We stayed that night at a scruffy hotel and ate an unimpressive meal of cold chicken and chips. The evening was enlivened by a discussion with a strange-looking youth at a neighbouring table who worked as a Michael Jackson tribute act.

Breakfast was animated, however: chatter over the previous days had worked to cement our friendship with Miguel. We had a field guide that he was flicking through, pointing out one bird then another. 'I never realised there were so many, it's never-ending.'

I gave him a small notebook in which to jot down his sightings. 'Write down what you've seen, and make notes of anything interesting. It'll make all the difference to learning and remembering the birds when you see them next time.'

No one had taught me about birds but I had still had many more advantages than Miguel. I had been given my first pair of binoculars for my thirteenth birthday, and then there were BBC nature documentary programmes, and holidays to Scotland with my parents. People sometimes ask me why I am interested in birds. What do I see in them?

It's not sufficient to say that birds are beautiful, as beauty is subjective and personal. When I was nineteen I visited the Tate Gallery in London. Being neither knowledgeable nor overly interested in art, I wandered from room to room in a manner and frame of mind similar to walking around a posh flea market. Then I entered a room containing the Pre-Raphaelites. My eyes were drawn immediately to the far corner, where a painting hung like a lit candle – *April Love* by Arthur Hughes. I can see it now in my mind's eye, many years later. What was it that captured me? That wistful girl with auburn hair? The intensity of the colour? The hidden drama of the scene? The sorrow or the shyness? It's all in the eye of the beholder. The image lodged in my soul and I adored it instantly, a moment that changed my perception of art forever. The American painter Edward Hopper said that, 'Art cannot be described in words, it's not just a visual thing. Art is the thing that's left, after everything beyond the first moment of seeing has been stripped away.' That's what it's like when I watch birds. It brings me more than the excitement at the time. It imprints on my mind a holistic love, a feeling that remains long afterwards, sometimes for decades.

I remember the birds I see because they invoke my senses.

Smell evokes sensory memories. The pungent aroma from 20,000 nesting gannets is ingrained in my brain from my first boat trip to Bass Rock in Scotland. The essence of hyacinth from a bluebell wood carries the song of the blackcap and cuckoo through my mind.

Tactile memories can also help recall events. The feel of wet spray stinging my face reminds me of ploughing through the waves off Muckle Flugga, the northernmost point of the British Isles, watching great and Arctic skuas mercilessly chasing down auks for their hard-won food.

Unlike almost all other animals, birds surround us daily. They interact with us through their sounds – songs as well as calls. Birds talk to each other all the time; they respond to what's going on around them and they respond to us. They express love, they threaten, welcome and warn, shout in alarm and fear. When I listen to the rapturous notes from a song thrush in a dusky forest, a curlew's plaintive cry carried on the heathery wind or the love duet of a pair of tawny owls on a winter's night, I feel as though I am joining in with their conversations.

The images, smells, tastes and sounds of nature remain as nature's memory within us. The act of watching birds, of lifting binoculars to our eyes, is the equivalent of looking through a microscope, conjuring magic. The invisible becomes visible. Landscapes come alive. A single round circle eliminates the unnecessary and concentrates the eyes. A blob of a duck that you've seen every day on the lake becomes a teal, a bird whose flanks are like a da Vinci etching, its head crowned with emeralds.

At its most elemental, watching birds makes us more human.

'What are we doing today?' asked Miguel.

'Exploring the Bañado La Estrella, searching for more birds.' We also hoped to see an indigenous village and maybe visit their school.

Miguel chipped in. 'Before breakfast I was speaking to a lady in the hotel who said that there are some indigenous villages about fifty kilometres up the road. El Descanso is one. If we go, we ought to take some food for them – biscuits for the kids, rice and flour, that sort of stuff. They're very poor.'

Before we left the town of Las Lomitas we called into a small shop to buy some fresh bread for ourselves and food for the villages we hoped to visit.

In common with most shops in the town, rickety tables stacked with goods spilled out onto the dusty pavement, the shopkeeper chatting to passers-by. Paula and I pushed between gas cylinders and brooms leaning against the outside walls and into the shop itself, our eyes taking a few moments to get accustomed to the dimness. Though the shop was small, cramped and dark, it seemed an Aladdin's cave of colours. Row upon row of narrow wooden shelves lined the walls, and each shelf was filled with a rainbow of assorted goods: blue cartons of sterilised milk, red tins of fruit and yellow packets of biscuits. White packets of sugar had been mixed in between green bags of pasta, cans of oils, cleaning fluids, matches and tall plastic jars of sweets – a Mayan temple of groceries. Underneath the shelving, on the floor, were boxes of carrots, eggs in baskets and sacks of potatoes and maize. There was barely sufficient room to walk around without brushing against a pyramid of planks on crates in the middle of the shop.

Paula called to me; I turned round and knocked against a stack of boxes. The top one fell, collapsing more items beneath and more beneath that, shelves emptying their goods onto the rough-tiled floor. Embarrassed, I quickly started to replace them, only adding to the avalanche. The shelves started to rock a little and down they came. I looked behind me to the shopkeeper standing in the doorway by her counter. I was expecting stern faces and tut-tuts but she seemed quite unconcerned, as if this were normal.

We quickly picked up as many things as we could, putting them on the counter, not thinking to buy them but to tidy the floor. The store owner smiled and started to put everything into boxes behind where she stood, then hefted them onto the counter. Before we knew it, we had unwittingly bought three large boxes of goods: *maté* leaves, rice, flour, maize, biscuits, tins of tomatoes and packets of dried peas, oil, toothpaste, soap and, of course, sweets. As Paula paid, the thought occurred to me that perhaps this was a magical shop, where the goods decided for themselves what you were going to buy when you entered, the items jumping off the shelves and into your basket. The magical realism of South America was working on me.

We hurried out, leaving behind a place that looked as if a mob had run through it. As we approached the truck, Miguel gave us a broad smile and off we went.

The Pilcomayo river floods regularly. Three years before our visit, surrounding land up to thirty kilometres away had been inundated. Villages were swamped, and the people were forced to flee and rebuild their homes on higher ground. Forests where howler monkeys and toucans had lived became the domain of caiman and fish. For the mighty Algarrobo forests, the water didn't recede quickly enough and the trees died. Many parts of the Bañado La Estrella now look like a vast ghostly apparition, with bare boughs and trunks, bleached white by the sun, thrusting out of the shimmering silver water as if gasping for air. For lianas and aquatic climbing plants this was an opportunity, and they scrambled up the dying lattice of branches, cloaking the great trunks, climbing into their brittle branches in a final act of emerald-encrusted strangulation.

Where nature is concerned, death always gives way to life and so it had been for this place, as waterbirds abounded. 'Look at that dagger-sized bill!' piped up Miguel from the back seat – but then the Amazon kingfisher darted off and was lost in the greenery. Atop many of the trees and bushes perched what first appeared to me to be lady vicars addressing church councils. Standing very upright in bright red tights, they were beady-eyed and indignant, with clerical dog collars and dishevelled hair-dos. But no, they were southern screamers, goose-like birds with their high-pitched *chaa ha, chaa ha* cries.

Elegant black skimmers glided so low over the water as to be water skiing. Thick-necked jabiru storks probed the shallows. A great black hawk perched on a prominent branch and surveyed the activity beneath, waiting for its chosen moment to attack, to take a chance on a fish swimming close to the surface or even an unsuspecting jacana bird. In the roadside bushes noisy bands of scarlet-headed blackbirds chattered and jostled about, each trying to gobble up their chosen patch of berries before other birds moved in.

We had been driving and birding all day and needed a break, a walk and a coffee. Ahead of us were two small towns, Lugones and San Martin. In Lugones there was nothing, it seemed deserted. Reaching San Martin, we stopped at the first house at the edge of the town. It looked as if it might be a shop – many village shops have so little to sell that they have no window display, not even a sign; that the locals know it is a shop is sufficient, as few travellers pass through these places.

We went inside, and everything about this journey suddenly changed. Miguel's life was about to be turned upside down.

Not seeing anyone inside, Miguel called out and a man sauntered through, looking as if he had just got out of bed. He stopped, pointed to Miguel and exclaimed loudly. 'I know your face! What are you doing here?'

We were surprised, as was Miguel.

'I've seen your face before. Where are you from? What's your name?'

Miguel gave his name.

'Hmm, I don't know that. But I recognise you. I knew your family, all of them.' Then he said something in an agitated tone that made me go cold. 'Your family lived in this house, right here. Is that what you're here for? It's my house now!'

Miguel stood as if nailed to the ground, moving only his head to look at us, unsure what to do next.

The man leant forward, puzzled.

Miguel took a step backwards. 'I don't know what you're talking about.'

Unsure, the man asked, 'Do you have a sister?'

'Yes, Sabrina, but I've never met her,' Miguel replied, softly.

'Then follow me. Come, come, quick!' The man now waved excitedly at us.

The house was small, dark and untidy, the concrete floors dirty, its windows covered only by rough wooden shutters. We followed as he led Miguel into a back room and pushed open the shutters. Inside was a single iron bed, the yellowing walls blistered with old plaster and peeling paint. He pointed downwards and told Miguel to look. 'See! What does it say!'

Miguel knelt down, and we peered over his shoulder.

Scrawled in the plaster was a word.

Sabrina.

This extraordinary moment led to Miguel meeting a blood relative for the first time in his life – his aunt, who as it happened lived just up the road. With the help of albums of family photos, he was introduced to his real family. Paula and I walked around the street for a while as he and his new-found aunt hugged, arms clasped around each other.

It was a quiet drive back to our camp. We sat together and sipped *mate*, and Miguel told us the little of what he knew about himself. We already knew he was an orphan. The couple who had brought him up, Ana and Jorge, had known virtually nothing about his real parents. His real mother had fled from the hospital shortly after giving birth, as she would have lost her job as a housekeeper if she had kept her baby, the lady she worked for refusing to have a baby in the house. Ana and Jorge had been given Miguel by a nurse on the day he was born – on the same day that Ana had lost her own baby.

For years Miguel had been making inquiries about his family and had only recently discovered he had a sister called Sabrina.

'I've never had the money to take a bus to Buenos Aires to see her.'

'Hasn't she told you anything?'

'Sabrina knows next to nothing; she never even knew I existed till a few months ago. She lives in Buenos Aires and has only just discovered our mother lives there too, but our mum doesn't want to see her, and they rarely talk. The only thing she's told her is that Sabrina was born in Formosa province, but I never expected this!' Miguel looked bewildered. 'I just came here to watch birds and learn to be a birdwatcher. It's as if I was meant to come.'

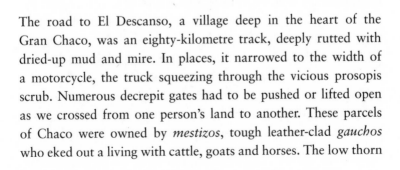

The road to El Descanso, a village deep in the heart of the Gran Chaco, was an eighty-kilometre track, deeply rutted with dried-up mud and mire. In places, it narrowed to the width of a motorcycle, the truck squeezing through the vicious prosopis scrub. Numerous decrepit gates had to be pushed or lifted open as we crossed from one person's land to another. These parcels of Chaco were owned by *mestizos*, tough leather-clad *gauchos* who eked out a living with cattle, goats and horses. The low thorn bushes were interspersed with graceful quebracho trees, speckled with long, bright red seed pods.

Suddenly we burst through the bushes, arriving at the village. The only prominent building was the school, a smart white single-storey building, surrounded by a low blue and white painted wall. Beyond closed gates, the children sat outside at tables. Dressed in their clean white lab coats, they stared at us.

We had found in the past that the best introduction to a village is through its school. School teachers are the most educated and respected people in the community and generally welcome visitors. The schools we had previously visited all had a visitors' book where the names of the local mayor, nurses, doctors and dieticians were the most common. When we told them we had stories and pictures to show on our computer, they were eager to invite us in.

The school at El Descanso was no exception and they were keen to start. First though, it was mid-morning break and we joined them for a mug of very sweet hot chocolate and a fresh doughy pastry, made in the school kitchen. The poverty of an indigenous village means that the school gives the children all of their meals, thereby encouraging the children to attend, although pressure to work at home – collecting wood or minding the goats – keeps many of them away. After the break, we talked to the children, telling them about ourselves, where we came from and about our country and culture and why we were in South America. They crowded around our laptop as we showed them pictures of the wildlife in their area. I had been working on my imitation of a howler monkey, and it seemed to go down OK. The children sat wide-eyed and eventually all the teachers, the cooks and others close by came and sat down with the children. We asked lots of questions: 'Who knows what the capital of Great Britain is?' Immediately, the adults' hands shot up, and they waved them about, trying to catch our attention. No one had ever shown them pictures of toucans, armadillos and butterflies, the animals of their backyard.

'What's this?' I asked, as up on the computer came a picture of an eagle. Up shot all the teachers' hands again – they were loving it more than the kids!

Paula and I are supporters of Leicester City and in South America football is on the same pedestal as religion, so we had pictures from the inside of the Leicester City stadium and other sports as well. Cricket was a complete mystery to them. As the afternoon passed, eyes widened and widened and the children and adults clambered over each other to get closer and closer to our computer screen. Most of the schools we visited had digital projectors. Not here, where there was no electricity anywhere near – or water, for that matter, or much else either, except nature.

Miguel was as keen as ever to join in with the discussion and explained in much better detail than we could about the importance of protecting trees and not trapping wild animals.

The villagers were of the Wichí tribe, proud, fiercely independent and very poor. Most lived in wooden shacks with corrugated tin roofs. Open doorways were large, while the walls were stockade-like rows of small, rough-cut logs. For most of the year, the temperature hovered around 40 degrees and upwards.

One of the village elders, Valoy, called into the school to see what was going on. His hand cupped his mouth and Miguel told us he had severe toothache. We gave him some painkillers and told him to take two now, two in the evening and the same tomorrow. Later in the day he came back, full of life, to say thank you and that he would take us into the Bañado La Estrella the next day to see the flooded forest for ourselves. With a bit of luck he would show us one of its special inhabitants.

As we talked to him, Miguel whispered to us that he had taken the whole packet of painkillers in one go.

We set off at midday the next day with Valoy and one other villager, Pinto, in two heavy dugout canoes. With a long pole, twice as tall as themselves, they pushed the craft through the water like a punt. Miguel was in the other boat, ahead of us, his hands clutching the sides, a very worried expression on his face.

We headed for open channels; the water was crystal clear and not very deep, aquatic plants waving with the current. Occasionally shoals of shad darted underneath us. With no oars or motors to propel us, the only sound we made came from droplets of water off the pole as it was pushed and lifted rhythmically out of the water.

Punting through the canopy of a forest was strange, in the same way as flying underwater would be. Here we were, in a boat, halfway up a tree ... nothing quite made sense. The trees were dead algarroba swathed in vines, or pompom-like caranday palms. We saw more southern screamers. We floated nearer and nearer to one until it turned towards us with a hostile look. A moment later it was off, screaming its painfully shrill call. The bird had been sitting on its nest. Floating closer, I leaned out of the boat to see five whitish eggs on a platform of sticks.

We continued, jacanas skittering away this way and that over the water hyacinths while snail kites soared overhead. Valoy and Pinto were still searching for their special creature. I was peacefully dangling my hands in the water until I suddenly saw a four-metre-long caiman cruise below us, eyeing me with its black and gold eyes. More often than not they rested half submerged, log like, but as soon as our canoe came close, a heavy whip from their tails would send the great reptiles into the depths.

Valoy pointed towards a liana-covered tree and Miguel's canoe slowed, drifting nearer and nearer. Pinto stood up, moved to the front of the canoe and passed the pole to an unsteady Miguel. The boat rocked wildly from side to side. Pinto brought his canoe to rest by the vegetation. He leaned forward, half hanging over the prow and suddenly threw himself towards the tree. Then the commotion really started.

Pinto, now prostrate on the vines, was holding on to something with only his feet hooked under the inside of the boat. Miguel was holding the pole in the water, trying to keep the boat steady and at the same time steadying himself. Instructions were being shouted one way and another, and our boat came alongside to prevent theirs from tipping over.

Miguel was pulling on Pinto's trouser belt, trying to get him back into the boat. Then we saw what was happening – he was wrestling with an enormous snake, a yellow anaconda, the second largest snake on the continent, and not venomous, but still a powerful constrictor.

Despite the tail of the snake coming out and whipping across Miguel's head, he finally managed to pull Pinto back into the boat, the monster coiled around his arm, shoulder and neck. The boat tipped to and fro more violently and Valoy got ready to fish them out. Miguel had given up with the pole and was gripping either side of the boat.

Finally, with a broad smile on his face, Pinto stood up, both hands clasping the anaconda, nearly as long as himself. This top predator of the water world was now held captive by a much more powerful predator. Pinto shook the snake free until it hung limply, its yellow underbelly strikingly patterned with dark leopard-like blotches. After a few moments, the Bañado's special snake was returned to its home.

The men pushed further into the trees. When the surface vegetation made it too difficult to move the canoes, pushing their poles on tree trunks helped them move into free water. Muscovy ducks flew in front of us and, on one occasion, we watched as a bird shot out from a hole in a tree, probably a nest site.

Through the vine-covered trees a cabin, elevated on stilts, appeared. The men steered towards it and tied up close to a short, vertical ladder leading to a platform. We were led up on to a covered balcony.

Miguel was a little unsteady on his feet and not his usual smiling self. Eager to talk, we all sat down. One of the men unwrapped a flask of hot water and a gourd and within minutes *maté* was being passed around.

Valoy turned to Miguel. 'This is where we used to come to rest when we were hunting anacondas.'

'Why did you hunt them?' we wanted to know.

'We have hunted anacondas for generations; we used to sell the skins to traders. That was an important income for the village. The skins went to New York, where they were made into handbags. The anacondas used to come and go with the seasons. Then dams were built up in Paraguay, the river changed and the anacondas started to die off. We are very poor now.'

Valoy passed the *maté* to me. I looked into his eyes, he smiled, and I noticed a resemblance between him and Miguel. I took a long suck on the *bombilla* and passed it to Paula. The five of us quietly sat, surrounded by a flooded forest. A small black bird with a snowy white head the size of a robin hopped onto the bamboo rail.

'Look, Miguel, a white-headed marsh tyrant.' The bird cocked its head one way and then the other, and flew off.

'Another new bird!' exclaimed Miguel, groping in his pocket for his notebook.

We left as the sun dipped low, partially obscured by a streaky orange sky, the flooded forest an inferno as birds came to roost. Hundreds of great egrets, white egrets, wood storks and jabiru flying overhead and weaving between the skeletal trees to settle down. Snail kites wheeled around us and Muscovy ducks sat in the branches of the palms. We drifted under a tree with a great black hawk peering down at us, and watched as a great flock of roseate spoonbills flew past, their pinkish colouring echoing the sky behind them.

When we reached land and alighted from the canoe Miguel was still unsteady on his feet. I turned to him: 'Well, how about that for a day's birding?'

He could barely speak. 'I've never been in a boat before and I can't swim, never mind the anaconda!'

Before we left the village, another visit to the school was called for. We had some posters about birds to give them, as well as the food. In the school it was mealtime; the school cook had baked trays of *medialunas*, a type of croissant, and the children were sitting around a large low table quietly eating and drinking hot chocolate.

We said our goodbyes and handed over our goods. The children crowded around us, overjoyed. The head teacher bowed his head in disbelief. 'How did you know we needed these things? The government gives so little money to our school; we have no money to buy luxuries like toothpaste and soap, there's none in the village.'

As we were about to leave, a small girl appeared. Approaching us, she held out her hands. They contained an armadillo. The teacher said that this was a present from the children for us.

Turning to the head teacher, I asked him to tell the children that this was very generous but wouldn't it be kinder to let the animal go free? The teacher spoke to the children and the girl let the animal go. As it ran off they all shrieked, and the little girl smiled at us.

We thanked the teachers and drove off, leaving behind us a crowd of white-coated children waving madly.

Several days later we dropped off Miguel back at his home. He beamed shyly at us. 'I am a birdwatcher now. We've seen over one hundred and fifty species of birds in just a few weeks. I know what to do with my life now. As for finding out about my family, it's something I never imagined possible and I still can't believe it.'

We left him on the dusty roadside, our binoculars around his neck.

We never realised that being hugged by a bear could be so pleasant.

CHAPTER 11

TICKS AND A TOUCAN

One of the joys of birdwatching for me is the surprise and mystery of being in a new environment, where every aspect of nature is unknown and ready to be discovered. The shrieks and cries, grunts and booms, buzzing and zipping from unfamiliar birds, mammals and insects excite me. To be a birdwatcher is to be an explorer.

We had left the parched and stony hillsides of Catamarca behind and were entering the southern end of a warm sub-tropical humid forest called the Yungas. These forests extend northwards as a narrow belt on the eastern flank of the Andean foothills. They stretch all the way from northern Argentina into south-western Bolivia, a unique and fragile ecological ribbon, one of a myriad of forest types succoured by the Andes.

Responding to an email from one of our nationwide support team, a member of Aves Argentinas, we had stopped off in the town of Concepción where a local camera club had asked us to show them some of our photographs and films. At that event a local forest warden told us about a nearby newly opened national park, Los Alisos, one we should visit.

To encourage visitors into the protected area, the authorities had just completed the building of a significant bridge, stretching 400 metres long and 80 metres high, arching over the Jaya river. Prior to this, vehicles had had to drive through the boulder-strewn waters below. Once over the new bridge it was only a few kilometres to the newly built visitor centre. We were the first visitors into this vast area and noisy construction work was still going on. After some deliberations we gained permission to continue deep into the hills to camp.

We followed a narrow track up the mountainside, over two streams, climbing higher and higher. In the next valley we found a level grassy area on which to camp. It was surrounded by dense forest, our altimeter reading 1,950 metres. This was a mid-level rainforest of tall glassy-leaved evergreen myrtles, laurels and cedars, which in the days to follow we grew to love.

Through the twilight of our first day in the Yungas came a series of excited, raucous, throaty coughs. Nothing was visible through the darkening void of vegetation. We slept fitfully and, just before dawn, it started again, an annoying sound. We wandered around searching for the source, but saw nothing. The next day was the same. On the third morning we traced the sound to a moving shape that stayed hidden in the trees. Our strategy on the fourth morning was to be up before dawn and walk the trails, watching and waiting. Our patience was rewarded: a black shape flew through the air and landed lightly on a mossy, bromeliad-laden branch. The creature, more serpent than bird, was surprised to see us, craning up a long neck with red pulsating throat wattle, moving its head from side to side as if to make out what we were. Perhaps the bird had never seen people before, but we knew it to be a dusky-legged guan, locally called 'el pavo del monte'. This 'turkey of the woods', with its long tail and sinuous neck, crept slowly around the tree, stretching its legs like a toad, reaching out to pluck fruits – round dark maracuja passionfruits or juicy-looking morsels reminiscent of raspberries. Also like a toad, the birds were silent except at the opening and closing of each day; the dusky-legged guans are to the Southern Yungas forests as blackbirds are to the hedgerows of a Devon village.

The trees around us were broad and deeply gnarled, their trunks riven with half-glimpsed faces and patterns. Boughs and branches wound around each other in twisted confusion. The undergrowth was a dense and tangled chaos. From everything hung long, damp curtains of moss, the whole forest dripping in a multi-layered emerald cloak of green lace. In contrast, spiky bromeliads, many a metre tall, fought for space on the branches, along with tendrils of ferns, cacti and vines.

'Never been anywhere like this. It's primeval,' I said.

'Eerie,' Paula agreed.

Birds were elusive, their calls absorbed by the luxuriant vegetation. Plush-coloured jays watched us closely. They were the size of a common magpie with black Mohican-like feathers on their head, a custard-yellow iris and flashes of blue around their face – squawking, inquisitive forest clowns.

The most vocal birds were red mitred parakeets. Flocks of fifty or more would noisily fly across the thickly forested, steep valleys. The pink-flowering ceiba trees, the national tree of Argentina, were a particular favourite for the parakeets to feed in but, unfortunately for us, once inside the trees, the birds were almost impossible to see: green on green. Like squawking gangs of youths they chased each other high in the thick canopy, hide-and-seek-playing parrots.

One afternoon, as we traced the narrowest of muddy trails, several large piles of droppings indicated a tapir had preceded us. The size of a large pig with a demeanour as gentle and an intelligence as keen, this animal, with its long delicate shrew-like snout, is a true friend of the forest; its scat is a self-contained compost holding seeds, a future forest in the making. We never saw the animal, neither did we need to. Just knowing of its presence was enough to give us a warm feeling that the forest was in good hands. Time and time again we discovered it was more enjoyable not to seek things out, to fret about what we had missed. It was better to let things just happen.

Following this philosophy, as we followed the trail, stooping low under a massive fallen giant of a tree, another glorious surprise claimed us as we stood up.

Still and silent they hung, suspended, frozen in space: a curtain of closely packed butterflies that stretched from the forest floor up into the ceilinged vaults of the forest, a wondrous array of golden-threaded chandeliers, too many to comprehend, making it difficult at first to understand what we were seeing. Accidentally I brushed against an overhanging twig, causing a snowstorm of the butterflies to swarm off and up into the trees, the remaining millions remaining transfixed. Each the size of an oak leaf, the butterflies were transparent, the veins on their wings like a spider's web, while around the edges of their fore and hind wings was a shimmer of gold as fine as a princess's circlet. There were perhaps millions. These glasswing butterflies were packed so tightly together no foliage could be seen. We had entered a magical arbour of living golden suspended filigree.

Mobile phones are used primarily 'on the go' in streets, shops and out walking. During their innovation, a significant stumbling block was how to ensure that users could see the screen in bright sunlight without glare. As scientists often do, they looked to the natural world for answers, for only nature has perfected perfection, having had four billion years to do so. To hide from predators animals use all sorts of tricks, but the family of glasswings has one of the best: a cloak of invisibility. There is no shimmer, reflection, shadow or sheen from their wings as they fly. From any direction, in any light, a predator sees straight through a glasswing to whatever is behind. The truth as to how this is achieved is made clear when looking through an electron microscope. The cellular structure of the butterfly's wing surface is like the Andes themselves: peaks, pinnacles and points which diffract, twist and then bend the light in such a confusing way that it passes through the wing with zero reflection. This paradoxical discovery helped mobile phone manufacturers to design screens. When we look at our mobile phone we are looking at a wonder of nature, the design of the screen mimicking that of the glasswing butterfly. As for the millions in front of us, they were almost certainly on migration to a secret unknown winter home deep in the forest, for the following morning they had gone. Perhaps they had sensed the violence of what was about to happen, the drop in air pressure and distant vibrations.

Living in a forest clearing is a little like living in a tin can: we didn't see the dark clouds until they were directly overhead, and were only alerted to them by a sound as if someone had thrust a can opener into the lid of the can. But not a tearing wrench, a heaving thud or an explosion that reverberates – this was an almighty and instant bone-shattering *crack* that made us automatically duck. Looking upwards, the sky was the colour of a rotting orange; one minute we were outside in the warmth, the next running for shelter as if a shower had been turned on.

As the hours passed the rain became torrential. The thunderstorm rumbled and roared above us as if the heavens were at war with the forest, ripping out its trees, shaking the ground. Normally I like thunderstorms – it's what I call real weather and makes me feel alive, invigorated – but this one had me flinching. We tried to ignore it and hunkered down in the tiny space our camper afforded to watch a favourite film on our laptop, but this was a waste of time, as the noise from the hammering rain on our aluminium roof was so deafening that listening to the film became impossible. So we read, eventually falling into a fitful and restless slumber, the sort of sleep you have when the room next door is occupied by an argumentative couple or someone playing loud rock music.

It rained constantly throughout that night and by morning it didn't look like abating any time soon. Now I was starting to worry: perhaps the seasonal rains were early? We only carried enough food for ten days and we had been there nearly a week as it was. We needed to make a decision: no one could help us and no information was available. Should we stay and risk running low on food or return across the two streams which by now might be dangerous torrents?

Paula does not panic or get fazed. Teaching in an inner-city high school for many years meant she had learnt that the best way to face adversity was with humour, so her suggestion: 'We could stay and film the torrent ducks; they'd love this,' was typical but not much help. We have complementary approaches to situations: I'm impulsive and see the big picture, whereas Paula is cautious and sees the detail. If I dare say she is pedantic she retorts that I am vague.

My approach was to strip off most of my clothes, shouting, 'We've got to get out!' and set about abandoning camp. My immediate concern was our ability to drive down the steeply forested mountain track. After that, would the streams be passable? In just trainers and underpants, rain pounding down on me, I collected all our outside gear, reloaded the back seat, lowered our sleeping compartment, fastened down the roof and removed the wheel chocks. Then, tyre by tyre, I reduced their pressure by half: I wanted as much contact with the ground as possible.

The deluge hitting the ground threw mud over me. I might as well have been working under a waterfall and was slipping and sliding all over the place. Paula moved about inside the truck and camper, stacking stuff away in boxes and cupboards, tying down loose equipment: this was going to be a bumpy ride.

I jumped back into the driver's seat. I was hot, dripping and nervous, my head pounding. Paula asked if I was OK – she knows me better than I know myself. We both knew this would put an end to our visit to Los Alisos, that we'd never get back again and the forest was wonderful. Who was to make the decision to move? Inside the truck we were safe.

I looked outside. The trees swayed and twigs flew about, the rain still lashing down. I thought about the guans and parrots; they had seen this all before. 'How do those butterflies survive this?' Paula didn't reply. 'I wonder where they've gone?' I continued.

'Stop yakking – if we're going, let's go!' Paula snapped.

We left the grassy clearing and entered the forest. It wasn't long before we started to slowly skid and slither down the muddy track, thick forest on either side. Rocks which a week before had given us leverage were now as smooth as ice, bouncing us from one side of the track to the other. Thankfully, the track levelled out as we approached the first stream, but that was now a gushing brown torrent twice as wide as a week ago.

In we careered, arcs of mud sloshing up the windows, the wipers and rain washing it away as soon as more hit.

Out the other side, the track narrowed and the slope steepened. Paula grasped her taut safety belt and shouted, 'We're sliding!'

'We're back-heavy.'

'Turn the opposite way, then!'

'I'm trying, it's no good!' I was panicky: this wasn't any old truck we were in. It was our home and everything we owned was inside. The rear tyre hit a bigger rock and straightened us up. With the wheels spinning we continued down a muddy slope, ping-ponging off rocks, slithering from side to side, all the while just managing to keep going straight.

Several more kilometres brought us to the second stream. I shuddered. It was worse than I imagined. It was much deeper than the one we had just come through. Brown waves of crashing water had engulfed the boulders, making it impossible to see which route we had previously taken across the riverbed. Getting out of the truck, I went for a closer look. 'No way across this, it's too dangerous,' I shouted back to Paula.

But as I did so I saw, with utter dismay, more water starting to pour down the track we had come. The river above us had broken through, carrying down with it branches and a slurry of rolling mud. There was no going back: our options were to go onwards or be swept away.

I looked around wildly. 'What do we do?'

'OK, stop, listen to me,' she said, in her no nonsense way. 'Get into the water, feel where the rocks are and shout their positions to me. I'll sketch a route across.'

'There isn't time!' I replied.

'All the time we have is right now. Get out!' was Paula's practical rejoinder.

I needed to locate the big submerged boulders – hitting one of those would stop the truck and, once stopped, the torrent of gushing water would tip us over.

I returned to the river, still in only my underpants. The force of the water against my legs was close to pushing me over. Feeling with feet and hands, water pouring over my head, slaloming branches scratching and snagging at me, I held up my hand when I found a big rock, Paula marking its position on a sketch map, one after the other. Still the rain pelted down.

At the other side I turned around and waded back, the water rising all the time. Once I lost my footing, the force of the water nearly sweeping me away. Exhausted and very cold I reached the truck and slumped into the driver's seat.

Paula was still calm. 'Reverse over there.' I did so. 'Now stop.' She showed me the sketch that was to be our route out.

'There's too much water, it's not passable,' I said, still shivering with cold.

'Look at me.' Paula looked straight into my eyes and spoke in clear syllables. 'We can do this. We have to.'

Down went the accelerator hard. We had to keep moving. I had to believe the impossible was possible. The first wave of foaming river swept over the front of the bonnet. Paula's hand shot out. 'That way!' For a moment I sensed we were tipping, the water pushing us. Again Paula pointed: 'Hard left!' I gripped the wheel expecting to be engulfed. Glancing upriver, the forest spewed its brown tumult. 'Look straight!' Paula yelled. A jabbing hand shot out again: 'That way, GO!' I swear we were floating. I felt us bump as we glanced off a rock, then the front wheels bit into the river bed again, I was back in control and we roared out, up and onto the far bank.

Stepping out of the truck, we looked back. The foaming river was widening all the time, the forest track above it awash. By a hair's breadth our journey had averted disaster.

Such is the power the Andes can unleash. But it is no match for the determination of an inner-city-school maths teacher.

Further sections of the Yungas forest are protected within the two national parks of Calilegua and El Rey. We wanted to see more of these forests, to get higher, but first needed to dry out our gear. Muddy clothes had to be washed and food and water needed replenishing, so we headed for the city of Jujuy.

At times like this the difficulties of overlanding in the wild came to the fore, but the kindness of people we met was overwhelming. In Calilegua national park the warden's wife offered to do our washing, while the warden made and cooked homemade pizzas. In exchange we entertained their two young toddlers. Sometimes we used village laundries to get our clothes washed. Usually this only took half a day, and when we collected it back everything was washed and neatly ironed.

While in Tucumán, Ada had told us of an expert biologist who worked at the university in Jujuy. We did manage to see her and we chatted in her office, whose walls were plastered with colourful posters of parrots and trees. She and her partner had been researching the Southern Yungas for over ten years.

'These Yungas forests are special,' she said. 'They transition between the dry thorny Chaco in the north and east and the remaining pampas grasslands in the south.' She continued to enthuse about the variety of tree species at the different elevations and told us that if we wanted to further explore the Yungas we should contact Carlos and Silvia Strelkov, who operated their own unique private reserve, Ecoportal de Piedra. 'It's where many of my students do their research.'

A NEW LIFE

PATAGONIA

TRAVELLING WILD

MAGELLANIC PENGUIN

ROCKHOPPER PENGUINS

OUR FIRST VOLCANOS

FILMING AT THE END OF THE WORLD

THE BEAGLE CHANNEL

STRAITS OF MAGELLAN

SOUTHERN BEECH FOREST, LOS GLACIARES NATIONAL PARK, ARGENTINA

MAGELLANIC WOODPECKER

MIDSUMMER'S DAY, LOS GLACIARES NATIONAL PARK

BUENOS AIRES PLATEAU, PATAGONIA

CAMPSITE ON THE PLATEAU

HOODED GREBE COURTSHIP

TANGO IN THE WIND

PART THREE

CONDOR COUNTRY

ANDEAN CONDOR

A WINGSPAN OF THREE METRES

CLAUDIO PRESENTS THE WARA

CONDOR LIBERATION, SIERRA PAILEMÁN, PATAGONIA

THE CONDOR'S FEATHER

CHILEAN FLAMINGOS OVER MAR CHIQUITA

ANDEAN FLAMINGO

ROSEATE SPOONBILL

ARMOUR PLATED FOR THE THORNY CHACO, BY THE RIVER PILCOMAYO, NORTHERN ARGENTINA

QUEBRACHO CRESTED TINAMOU

WICHI GIRL, FORMOSA

A PRESENT OF AN ARMADILLO

LAND OF THE INCA

MADRE DE DIOS RIVER, AMAZONIA

GREY-BREASTED MOUNTAIN TOUCAN

COLOMBIA

BAREFOOTED LLANERO, LOS LLANOS

BUFF-BREASTED SANDPIPER

ORINOCO GEESE

THE BIRD OLYMPICS, LOS LLANOS

FOREST ESCORT ON THE OLD ROAD TO BUENAVENTURA

WHITE-NECKED JACOBIN HUMMINGBIRD

CROWNED WOODNYMPH HUMMINGBIRD

DISASTER STRIKES ON THE CARIBBEAN COAST

VERMILION CARDINAL

WAYUU CEREMONY

SANTA MARTA SCREECH OWL

Ecoportal de Piedra lay one valley to the east of Calilegua, on the other side of the San Francisco River close to the provincial park of Las Lancitas. Here wildlife conservation pioneers Carlos and Silvia had purchased a huge swathe of land stretching from the river in the lowlands to the alpine meadows on the high tops. Theirs was a low-impact approach to managing the land: the removal of cattle; fencing off key areas to avoid disturbance; and the maintenance of the historic tracks into the mountains to enable access. They welcomed visitors wanting to explore the Southern Yungas, single-handedly building rustic cabins where they could be accommodated.

Carlos, a small dapper man with a moustache and wearing a Spanish-style wide-brimmed hat, threw open the door for us. 'It isn't locked, no need to here.' Once inside, cosiness wrapped around us. For a week or so we were to abandon our truck – almost a holiday. Our cabin had wooden floors, rafters hewn from the forest and a veranda from which we watched a family of white-barred piculets: a woodpecker the size of an English wren, their underparts finely striped in a black and white zebra pattern and, as with many woodpeckers, the male has a scarlet forehead.

Despite never having met us before, the Strelkovs insisted we eat with them. Silvia, slender and lively, did most of the talking, telling us how her missionary family had fled from China to Argentina when she was a small child at a time when the Chinese government was persecuting all religions.

During the meal on the second evening I brought out the small green feather tipped in red and laid it on the table. I had retrieved this from the slip pocket of my first red notebook from three years prior – all my notebooks were stored securely in the camper.

Carlos's eyes lit up. 'How did you get that?' We told him the story of the railway museum. 'Amazing. It's from an *Amazona tucumana*, an alder parrot. I've never found a feather like this myself.' Placing it on the rough-hewn table had an effect better than a bottle of whisky: we were friends forever.

The following evenings we enjoyed long discussions about

wildlife conservation. Then the invitation I had hoped for was given: 'Shall we search for the alder parrot?'

I needed no encouragement.

'Can you ride?'

'Yes, of course.'

Paula gave me a withering look. The last time she had seen me climb onto a horse I had ended up facing the tail.

With so many parrots stolen for a life in a cage, the alder parrot is now classified as 'near threatened'. The birds mate for life and if their partner is killed or trapped they will never pair up again. 'Kill one bird and you kill two,' sighed Carlos.

The next day we took horses laden with gear for an overnight stay in the mountain forest above 3,000 metres: saddle bags of food, water and coffee, rolls of bedding, binoculars and camera equipment – all that anyone needs. We criss-crossed the jungle, leaving the deciduous southern oaks behind, following ancient logging trails, dropping down to a stream then up again. By following precipitous ridges we avoided deep forested ravines. We rode under a colony of crested oropendolas. Their name reveals a lot: *oro* is Spanish for gold, and the birds have golden tails and bills. The *pendola* bit is from their pendulous nests, with some as long as 6 feet that look like long-necked hairy coconuts. These were what swung about over our heads.

Up from around one of the horses' feet flew a rufous-collared nightjar, the horse having just avoided stepping on the nest which contained two cream and blotchy eggs, almost impossible to see, like the bird itself due to its cryptic plumage. Like most nightjars, the rufous-collared is active in twilight, and feeds on insects.

Gradually our surroundings became darker, as if the sun had disappeared. 'How high are we?' I called to Carlos.

'Fifteeen hundred metres. Why?'

'The forest looks different.'

The high, dark green canopy closed over us – myrtles, laurels and cedars similar to Los Alisos – though being around five hundred kilometres closer to the equator, it wasn't rain that ran down my back but sweat. The temperature must have been in the mid-thirties and the sticky strap of my binoculars chafed my neck. Occasionally, a swinging liana slapped against the horse's face, making the animal jerk its head. As we walked onwards, small birds flitted in front of the horses. One that I managed to identify was the cinnamon flycatcher, because of both its habit and colour. Then there were the cacti: the first time we'd ever seen the sort that hang as long prickly belts from branches thirty feet up.

'They're called rhipsalis,' shouted Carlos. 'Take care as you pass by them.'

One miserable aspect to the ride was that as the horses pushed through the vegetation, we had to keep giving ourselves a light thrashing with a bunch of twigs in order to brush off the multitude of ticks that dropped down on us.

Suddenly, Carlos put up his hand for us to halt the horses. Carefully, he pointed to a branch on which sat a tiny metallic-green-blue hummingbird with what looked like a ball of white cotton wool on each leg. Silently, we watched as the bird made a dart into the forest air to catch an invisible flying insect.

As I sat on the horse almost eyeball to eyeball with this jewel of the dark forest, I thought of the man who first described the bird in 1828, a famous French zoologist with the incredible name of Alcide Charles Victor Marie Dessalines d'Orbigny. I suspect that he was so embarrassed by his own ridiculous name that he saw his mission in life to name animals simply: he had called this bird the blue-capped puffleg, which described it perfectly and precisely.

The gentlest of highland breezes ruffled my hair as the land became less steep. The horses seemed to lighten their step and the reins loosened in my hands. We had to dismount to carefully negotiate a narrow ridge whose sides fell away sharply, then remounted and entered yet another subtly different forest. The trees were smaller, their lower branches giving us an opportunity to see the profusion of other plants growing on them: cascades of tiny white florets from orchids; a purple and red upright flower with long spiky, fleshy leaves; and a multitude of smaller and more colourful shrubs. Cloud forests are very special, occurring in only a few high and rugged places where the topography is severe enough to affect the movement of clouds – not those high up in the sky, but clouds originating from the forest itself. A rainforest is maintained by massive amounts of normal 'vertical rain'; cloud forests are succoured by 'horizontal rain' – mist – and continually nurtured by moss, ferns and epiphytic plants that cover the trees, acting like sponges that slowly release moisture. Epiphytes are plants that derive all their needs by living on trees. They are common in sub-tropical places, such as where we were. Many of these were exquisite orchids, mostly with snow-white or flamingo-pink flowers. Heat from the morning sun evaporates the moisture released by these plants, and this forms into mist that floats amid the trees. This mist slowly rises through the branches, drifting up and up into the sky, then in late afternoon it falls again as rain. This is the daily cycle of the cloud forest, so it wasn't a surprise that at the end of the day the rain started.

Fortunately, a small open-sided stone shelter came into view and we stopped, removed the saddles and gear and let the horses graze before tying them up for the night. We unrolled our blankets and slept, the ticks having an enjoyable night feasting on our bodies.

I woke stiff and cold. It was just getting light so I ventured into the forest and found a rocky ridge overlooking the canopy. I sat, shoulders hunched, uncomfortable from the damned ticks. I react badly to ticks and for the next few days I had a headache and a fever, as well as being itchy everywhere. Hands under my chin, cupping my face, I looked down aimlessly.

A family of yellow-striped brushfinches, an endemic bird to the forests, scuttled between bushes scattering droplets of water. Rays of brilliant warming orange sunlight burst between the mossy trees and almost immediately wisps of vapour drifted between their branches, pulsing one way and disappearing, then re-emerging. A toco toucan glided below me, its top-heavy bill like a huge carrot, then another followed and another and then two more, silent streaks of black and orange birds winging through the dreamy mist.

'Michael, Michael!' A call came from Carlos up the hill. I clambered back up to our shelter.

'The horses have chewed through the rope and vanished,' Carlos said. 'It's all walking from now on.'

We hadn't gone far before the forest changed again; now it was much more open with grassy tracts, a sort of wood pasture. The dominant trees were those we had come to find, the alder and mountain pine, both indicators that we were at last in the montane forest above 3,000 metres.

Carlos turned to us, keeping his voice low. 'Keep a look out, this is where the alder parrots nest.'

Twice we saw small groups of alder parrots flying across the valley but after a long morning's search we failed to locate any active nest holes. This was the middle of their nesting season and with eggs in the nest, the birds would be trying to be as inconspicuous as possible.

Biologists from Jujuy University have found that the chicks are fed almost exclusively on the seeds of the endemic mountain pine. This tree is now known to be so important in these forests as to be termed a 'keystone' species. The term is used to identify the single most important animal or plant in a given habitat, one that holds the entire ecological web of life together. In the past, the pines have been extracted for paper manufacture so there is a scarcity of older mature trees – and it is in the pine trees snags and holes that the alder parrots prefer to nest.

This highlights a common problem with unsustainable forestry in the Southern Yungas. Forests throughout the whole altitudinal range need to be preserved because in different seasons birds move from one level to the next, and back again. In December, for instance, the alder parrot nests in the high montane forests but as the austral winter approaches, the birds descend to the lowland forests at 600 metres and roost communally from April to October.

In the Southern Yungas it is the mid-elevational myrtle and cedar forests that have fared better because they exist in steep valleys and ravines. The lower parts have been deforested because they are easy to access and close to villages, while the higher parts are highly suitable for grazing land. These alpine pastures are continually being expanded by setting fire to the forests: first extracting the pines and then burning the rest of the trees. Timber requirements always favour the larger trees, those that are upright, tall and in their prime. Few are left to reach full maturity and old age.

The great veterans that do remain hold the forest's history – and survival – within their spreading limbs. Over time, trees lose the occasional branch to a thunderstorm or gale. Rot sets in and expands the damage into crevices and cracks, homes for owls, parrots, monkeys and snakes. Insects feed off the tree, boring, drilling and chipping holes by the million. Fungi spread through the bark and penetrate the heartwood. Gradually, the trees fall and over time are sucked back into the ground from where they originated.

After a long hard trek back down the mountain we found that our horses had returned by themselves and were contentedly back in their stables at Ecoportal. We laughed. As for my ticks, Paula was able to remove all 136 of them with tweezers, but their ill-effects stayed with me for some months.

Carlos's wife, Silvia, taught English at the local high school and asked if we would talk to her class the following day. We were happy to do so.

Our talk was in two parts, the first about us, where we lived and what we did, as well as about the geography and culture of England, Wales and Scotland and a lot about sport. The second half was about wildlife and why the wildlife in Argentina was so special and important. At the end of the session, we were packing up to leave when another teacher came to ask if we could repeat it for their class too. This went on all day, and we ended up talking to the whole school.

The last class consisted of the oldest kids. They gave us a hard time and one of the wise guys asked us what a Scotsman had under his kilt.

We replied, 'Legs, of course, for dancing,' and to raucous applause from them all, we danced the Gay Gordons up and down the classroom.

PART FOUR

LAND OF THE INCA

CHAPTER 12

BIRDS OF THE INCA

In my view only one type of bird has mastered flight to perfection: they move through the air with almost supernatural speed and agility. And they have adorned themselves with the most gorgeous, extravagant plumages conceivable. The Inca considered them to be the messengers of the gods. If there was just one reason why we had come to South America it would have been to see these birds. Like children on Christmas Eve, we were nervously excited at the prospect of finding them.

Hummingbirds.

The road northwards from the city of Jujuy in northern Argentina is the Camino Real del Alto Perú (the Royal Road to Peru), now unimaginatively known as *Ruta* 9. The road enters the wide, richly cultivated valley of the Río Grande. Gradually, we gained height as it cut through the pre-puna landscape of the Andean foothills, the Humahuaca mountains, famous for their stratified patterns. Pinks come from the red clays and mudstones, white from limestone, greens from copper oxide, and in places the heavy lead content gives rise to vivid streaks of brown and purple. Time has folded and corrugated the land. Erosion from rivers, wind and water has sculpted it further into rainbows of rock from which matchstick cacti stand proud.

Approaching the village of Susques we crossed an invisible line, the Tropic of Capricorn, and, continuing to climb, drove to the Paso de Jama, the international border which would take us into Chile.

We were sad to leave Argentina for the last time, even if it meant we were entering Chile by driving over the top of the Andes. Traversing a hundred kilometres of wide open landscape considerably higher than the summit of Mont Blanc, we enjoyed looking at the arcs of smooth purple mountains, broken by occasional darker snow-capped volcanic cones that towered even higher, sulphurous steam circling upwards.

Lower slopes drifted into golden stony plains surrounding ice-fringed lakes of languid blue. A fine sprinkling of snow crystals glistened on rocks, adding sparkles to the champagne-clear air. Groups of baby-faced *vicuñas* lifted their slender necks to watch us pass.

We stopped several times and breathed in the pure air; it was a wonderful place to stand and stare and imagine all sorts of impossible things: being the only humans alive, discovering a different planet, living in a dream . . . From which we were rudely awoken when a convoy of eight droning car transporters roared by, taking vehicles from Chile's ports on the Pacific to Argentina and Uruguay.

The descent from the northern Chilean Andes is on a twisting, snake-like road, the air becoming warmer and the distant Atacama Desert in front of us gradually increasing in scale and haziness. We reached the town of San Pedro de Atacama. This old, established frontier town of single-storey stone and adobe houses grew up around a desert oasis on a plateau in the Andean foothills. After several days of journeying from Argentina we were looking forward to exploring it but our excitement was short-lived.

The old church in the main square, famed for its interior roof made of cactus, was closed for repairs. The streets were overflowing with tourists aimlessly wandering about looking lost and bored. Loud, thumping music spilling out from bars reverberated over the heads of people, and the scent of cannabis tinged the air. Walking the narrow dirt streets we were accosted on all sides by racks of T-shirts, sand-surfing boards, heaps of tat in gift shops, and menus depicting slices of pizza and ice cream sundaes. Chalked billboards were advertising trips to tourist hotspots like the nearby Tatio Geysers as well as the Uyuni salt flats of Bolivia, even to Cusco in Peru. It seemed that once tourists arrived in the town, their principal occupation was drinking, shopping and booking coaches to take them somewhere else.

Irritated by the mayhem, we left within an hour or so of arriving and looked for somewhere to camp. After a short while we found a suitable spot in a serene forest. It's certainly unusual to find a forest in the middle of a desert. The trees were tamarugo, the only ones that naturally grow on the saline soil of the Atacama, while centuries of harvesting for firewood had reduced their numbers drastically.

Our camper's pop-up roof was just low enough to fit under the short, sparsely leaved trees that held us in a cocoon of their protective spiny branches. We slept deeply; there are few places as quiet as deserts. However, trees will always attract birds and in the morning we were woken by a high-pitched chittering, as if made by a mountain beck trickling over rocks. It was the calls of tamarugo conebills, grey-brown birds the size of a chaffinch with a rust-red throat and half-rim spectacles, one of the very few breeding birds to be found in this unique forest.

For two further days we travelled along an unwavering black asphalt line of road. There were few places suitable for us to camp and one night we ended up outside a dirty roadside motel.

'That's good security,' commented Paula, as two police cars drew in behind us. It turned out they were escorting a truck full of dynamite, which arrived and parked next to us.

'Hmm. Perhaps not so good after all.'

We were travelling through a lifeless-looking expanse of rock and sand, the Atacama Desert. It's the driest place on Earth, but mouth-wateringly sublime for photography at dusk and dawn.

The low afternoon sun sends shafts of light deep into the desert's sharp serrated ridges, setting them aflame and cave-black, in alternating layers. Molten lava light bubbled up before being pulled back into the night.

Mornings were unerringly quiet and cold. With gloved hands clasping my first tea of the day, I would watch the sky's ice moon, translucent in the morning's blueness, slowly disappear as the new day's sun gave the snow-white sand its first flush of a pink gin. An hour later, and the desert would have won back its glaring blindness.

Having drunk my fill of the changeover from night to day in the desert, it was time to take Paula her tea in bed.

'We didn't see a single bird yesterday,' I said.

'I know,' she replied sleepily. 'Let's move on quickly. Our Amazon film awaits.'

We reached the Pacific coast of Chile, where the Atacama Desert meets the Pacific. On one side of us sand dunes rose up from the road as high as tower blocks, on the other was a blue refreshing ocean. Here the offshore Humboldt Current affects the landscape in a dramatic way. Hot, dry air blowing towards the Pacific from the Atacama Desert is rebuffed and pushed back by colder air off the sea. Most mornings a low-lying fog moves inland, covering the coastal strip with minute droplets of condensation. Called the *camanchaca*, this fog gives rise, in places, to a fairyland environment of spectacular round cacti, some as large as a small car.

We camped on the shore, a place rich in rock pools that abounded with starfish and small crabs. There were few land birds; offshore, however, it was a different story. Peruvian pelicans with their fish-scooping bills would flap lazily around and then, as if someone had shot them, they would flail around, wings in all directions, before flopping in a heap of feathers into the sea. Peruvian boobies, white-necked with long wings, would sweep along in longer glides, their long silver dagger bills at the ready. Seeing fish they would rise a little, convert into a missile and enter the water with barely a splash. A massive offshore pinnacle of rock was where these birds bred, along with red-legged cormorants.

We stayed a couple of days, intrigued by the birdlife we saw, then continued up the coast as far as Iquique, where we found a secluded seaside village. The road continued to a dead end by the shore, where there was what looked like a smart new bus stop, but a sign indicated it was a tsunami shelter. Beyond that was a narrow passageway through tamarisk bushes onto the beach, while on the other side was the welcome sight of a restaurant.

That evening, enjoying a very rare meal eaten out of the camper van, we undertook a bird count – a particular method for estimating bird numbers in any area. We counted for five minutes and then rested for ten, then repeated this for another hour, estimating the passage of 16,000 shearwaters one hour. It was a great way to end our short journey through northern Chile. The following day would be the border crossing into Peru.

We found crossing borders in South America much like visiting the dentist: sometimes it was straightforward, other times painful, but never a day trip to be looked forward to. Our experience of our many border crossings from Uruguay into Argentina, from Argentina into Chile and back again were routine; the crossing from Arica in northern Chile into Peru was of the painful sort, and took many hours.

Our passports were checked and stamped. The temporary import permit (TIP) – in effect the Toyota visa – was exchanged, the old one for Chile being left with the Chilean officials and a new one issued by the Peruvians. Normally there was a casual search through the back seats of the Toyota and the camper, checking for people smuggling and perishable food. Occasionally a dog was sent in to sniff out for drugs or fruit – the Chileans in particularly seemed sensitive in not allowing any fresh fruit or uncooked meat into their country. In Arica it was different.

We were told to empty everything we had, one box at a time, and put them through an X-ray machine – much to the astonishment of other travellers on coaches. Paula kept guard on the growing pile of our possessions on the Peruvian side of the border while I ran to and fro between the conveyor belt and the truck. It took two hours, but eventually we drove off into a new country towards new adventures.

We felt strangely elated to have reached Peru – especially as it had taken us over three years of travelling and we were still only halfway up the Andes. We would never have believed before we left that this might be the case. We had thought we might be home in the UK by now, job done. Nearer the truth was that we were having the time of our lives. Homesick sometimes, missing family sometimes . . . but travelling together, living close to birds in the wild . . . fantastic. And helping people protect their birds as well.

So now we were in Peru, a country with over 1,800 bird species, and we had things we wanted to do. We had a new project to move on to: a promotional film for the NGO Conservación Amazónica. But we wanted even more to watch and film the messengers of the gods: hummingbirds, as well as fulfilling one personal quest as well: to find nesting Inca terns, a very beautiful seabird.

We understood that Inca terns bred on coastal cliffs near the seaside town of Paracas and so that was the direction we headed in now: north.

Nearing the town of Arequipa we needed to stretch our legs and have a cup of coffee, so we took a narrow track leading east across the river and into farmland. No sooner had we parked than we saw a bird zip in front of us and start feeding from red fuchsia-like flowers high up on a large bush. Moving the truck forward a little I climbed up onto the camper roof, which doubled as a photographic platform, and Paula handed me the tripod and cameras.

I was almost level with the bird. It had a longish bill. Even before I used my binoculars, I felt a twinge of excitement – its fast, bee-like feeding behaviour was giving it away as a hummingbird. A moment later the bird flew even closer than I expected and settled on a twig in front of me. It was larger than I expected, dark on top, with white underparts, but as I was not used to seeing hummingbirds close up, I was in for a shock, for as it turned its head I saw its brilliant emerald gorget fanning from the bird's throat. The bird was so close, its shimmering feathers stood out like exquisite sequins. It was an Andean hillstar hummingbird.

Seeing someone standing on the top of a camper van does attract attention, so it wasn't a surprise when a car pulled up alongside us. A man leant out of the window: '*Hola*, what are you doing?' We did our best to explain, but he remained curious, asking about the condor logo on our truck. Then the man asked, 'Do you know what day it is?'

'Er, it's Saturday.'

'Yes, the first day of August. Pachamama Day!' For a moment I thought that perhaps we were doing something wrong. Maybe this was a local religious day when everyone ought to be in church and certainly not enjoying themselves. We expected some sort of admonishment.

'Today we celebrate Pachamama, Mother Earth, and give her presents! My name is Roberto Fascio and this is my son, Santiago.' He gestured to a young man in the passenger seat of the car. 'Join us for our celebrations, come for lunch! Over there's our holiday home.' The man pointed to a rather stylish adobe house up on the mountainside.

After a hearty lunch with Roberto's extended family, everyone trooped outside.

'Come on,' Santiago said, putting an arm round our shoulders. 'Now is the time for giving presents to Pachamama. Christmas Day is for our children – Pachamama Day is for our community.'

Although we had spent months in Patagonia and driven a

sacred *wara* stick over thousands of kilometres; although we had met a Mapuche chief, Nahuel, and lived on indigenous territory for a week, we still did not fully appreciate how or why the concept of Pachamama ran so deep in South American culture. I asked Santiago to explain.

'Pachamama is Mother Earth – nature. All year she gives us everything – all our food – and we take it without thanks. Today we pay her back with love and offerings. Today we complete the circle between Pachamama, who is of the Earth itself, and ourselves in the material world.'

We joined everyone, now gathered in small family groups, under the shade of a few trees up on the stony hillside. The laughter and chatter had dissipated, faces were thoughtful. One man carried a very strange object, like a hunting horn, but about four metres long. Roberto's wide-brimmed hat, which he had worn since we met him earlier in the morning, was laid to one side. He and his wife, Maria, knelt on a mat in front of a hole dug in the ground in which a small fire had been lit. The couple crossed themselves and, cupping the smoke, wafted it over themselves. Roberto then kissed his hands and scooped them into the earth, picking some up and letting it fall through his fingers. At their side were bottles of wine and dishes of food – meat and vegetables – some of which they tipped into the smoke. Words of thanks to Pachamama were spoken, for the rains that came and the crops that were harvested. Cigarettes were passed to the couple and pressed into the ground; from the back of the crowd someone blew the long horn.

Everyone remained dignified and quiet. Wisps of smoke drifted about. One by one, each family took turns to kneel in homage. Young children were lifted by mothers and set down close to where the offerings were being placed; teenagers scooped up the food, held it up to the sky then carefully sprinkled it into the hole.

Santiago looked at us. 'Now's your turn.'

Looking at each other, we hesitated. Roberto moved to our side. 'Pachamama knows you are here, she will expect an offering.'

'How does she know we are here?'

'When you stopped in the valley below,
hummingbird, the bird found you. Hummingbirds
for the condor and for Pachamama.'

Reassured, we knelt down, took a sip of wine and poured
the remainder into the hole, crumbled food and said a blessing
to Pachamama. We had plenty to thank her for: for keeping us
safe in the duststorm, for seeing us across the flooded rivers, for
the hooded grebes, her southern beech forests and its Magellenic
woodpeckers, the wind that blew, Miguel, Silvia and Carlos, and
so much more.

After we stood up, the hole was covered over, stones laid
on top and the empty bottles of wine stuck upside down in the
earth. 'These blessings and the food we left is to offer thanks to
Pachamama,' said Santiago.

With final blasts from the horn, everyone clapped, the
solemnity of the occasion fading as groups returned down the hill,
the children flitting about like butterflies.

Returning to our camper parked close to the bush with its red
flowers, we slept soundly that night.

The topography of Peru could be likened to a Neapolitan ice
cream: one side is a thin coastal strip of hot, dry desert about
fifty kilometres wide; in the middle is a thick wedge of Andean
mountains a thousand kilometres across; and the other side is the
luxuriant Amazonian jungle. This was the ancestral land of the
Inca people, and I had always thought that a culture that valued
birds' feathers as highly as gold was a worthy one.

The Inca traded feathers over long distances, from the dark
Amazonian jungles to Pacific islands; they were currency in the
same way that oil is to the Middle East. Pedro Sancho de la
Hoz was secretary to the cruel Spanish Conquistador Francisco
Pizarro. He recounted that when they opened the great storage

rooms of the last Inca Emperor, Atahualpa, they found 100,000 dried birds – exotic-plumaged macaws, hummingbirds and quetzals. Archaeologists, unearthing an ancient burial site in Peru, found a hoard of sealed ceramic jars containing ninety-six rolled-up feathered panels, the sort that would have decorated the cold stone interior of palace walls. These glorious panels, made by the Wari tribe, comprised the golden yellow and sparkling blue feathers from tens of thousands of macaws, each feather having been individually handsewn together using threads of *vicuña* hair. Many of these panels are now held by the Metropolitan Museum in New York.

We reached the town of Paracas. There was a small car park overlooking a shoreline where a few dapper sanderlings, white as snow, raced along the sand. The tide was receding, exposing small rocks covered with filaments of bright green algae. Many local people were sauntering along on the opposite side of the road, and we spotted an ice cream shop. We couldn't remember how long it had been since we'd had one, so we bought the two biggest cornets and sat on a rock to watch the waders.

A whisper of birds drifted along the shoreline – more sanderlings, accompanied by a few surfbirds. Like a flurry of snowflakes they settled close to us and we admired how wavy streaks of dark brown on the neck gave way to delicate curls on the breast with white bubbling in between; their belly a pure white with specks of light yellow giving way to sandy underparts. With their plumage like the rippling tide behind them, they were birds born from the sea.

These were the first surfbirds we had seen in South America and as it was the first week of September, it was likely that the birds we saw were new arrivals from their breeding grounds, the rocky coast of Alaska and the Yukon. We lay down on the shore with our cameras and, after a while, the birds were unconcernedly feeding at arm's length around us. Born in the Arctic wilds, the birds were unused to people.

An hour later, and delighted with the footage we had obtained, we treated ourselves to a second ice cream while I watched the birds. Captain Cook was the first person to collect this unknown bird, from the coast of Alaska in 1779. A month later, he was killed on a Hawaiian beach and the specimen, which lay in his sea chest on board HMS *Endeavour*, eventually made its way to Germany.

Paracas itself is a small and mostly new town, consisting of one or two smart hotels and restaurants and many seedy-looking hostels. The day we visited, coaches moved in and out depositing and collecting people from an impressive visitor centre.

We knew that the bird we most wanted to find, the Inca tern, nested on the cliffs but that most pairs were confined to the offshore Balastas Islands. We walked down to where we hoped to get a boat and found out that landing on the islands was not allowed, but that tourist boats cruised the seas around the islands most mornings. We watched as several of the boats departed, large twin outboards belching smoke. They roared across the waves, people cheering and waving.

This was not how we wanted to see the birds. We would have to find them for ourselves, but that would mean trusting our luck to the desert.

We approached a national park warden and asked where the best place to camp in the park was.

He gave us a strange look as if we had spent too long in the sun. 'No one can camp here! It's a desert. There's no water, no shade, no shops and no roads. Just there, down the street, you'll find hotels.' He walked off, shaking his head.

Undaunted, we reduced the pressure in our tyres down to

15psi, thereby increasing their contact area with the sand, and headed off into the desert.

After a while we stopped, and the two of us trudged with sinking feet to the top of a high sand dune. We wanted to see life – instead we saw ... sterility. On one side there were smooth, saffron dunes stretching to the horizon – hills, hollows and flatlands with a misty veil draped over them that softened every edge, every detail – simple, uniform, stripped-back, naked environment. On the other side floated a seamless sheet of turquoise, the Pacific Ocean – two complementary colours of sand and sea, the artistry of nature, while green – the giver of life – had been rubbed out.

But nature is never that simple, and life there was conjured in a different way. With the two vivid colours as the backdrop, the magic was all to do with a play, one that was performed every day, in a drama of epic proportions.

The stage was the desert and sea. The actors, both powerful and elemental, were the sun, the water and the air. Rehearsals started during mid-morning as the sun gradually moved over the stage, heating up the desert. By midday, the doors opened and the show commenced, when super-hot air rose from the ground like a spectre from centre stage. The vacuum this left was filled immediately by cold air rushing in from the wings, from the ocean. The movement of air created a wind that whipped the sand into spiralling, dancing vortices that chased each other around the stage time and time again, building in intensity until they coalesced into a tempest. All afternoon, the tempest would rage over the land, absorbing each delicate twirling vortex.

On the other side of the stage, the play reflected the marine underworld. The movement of cold air off the sea's surface stirred up the ocean, bringing nutrients and phytoplankton from deeper down to the surface. This attracted a plethora of fish such as mackerel, which bubbled up to the surface to feed. Chasing the fish came birds, flocks of black and white Guanay cormorants, white Peruvian boobies, pelicans, terns and shearwaters, albatrosses and petrels; multitudes of them swarming from their roosts and breeding cliffs. Attracted by this furore, whales, dolphins and porpoises entered the fray. The ocean became a frenzy of catching, diving, chasing and gulping. By late afternoon, the show would be over for the day.

Time had choreographed this play to perfection and everyone was the winner; everyone, that is, except for the hapless birdwatcher out in the afternoon when the birds are at their best, having to contend with pellets of sand stinging their skin. But that was the nature of Paracas; in Quechua, *paracas* means 'rainstorm of sand'.

Before we left the top of the sand dune we found a spiny gecko feeding off a windblown strand of algae – despite the fact we were a kilometre from the sea.

With the loose surface churning under our wheels, the vehicle struggling to find a grip, we drove onwards, the sand becoming deeper and softer. Keeping going is the most important part of driving in sand: stopping might mean we would never get going again.

Coming across a wide bay we got two wheels on the shingle shore and drove as far as we could, scattering small groups of waders. The end of the bay was dominated by enormous dunes as high as tower blocks. Two small, open fishing boats lay at anchor. They were painted red on the outside and blue inside, with crab pots stacked in their prows.

At the foot of the dunes appeared what looked like a wreck, as if the tempest had sucked up some hapless barque and, spinning it round and round, had cast it down in a ragged heap. Poles and wood protruded through white flapping canvas sheets, and drums, barrels, logs and crates lay scattered around. However, the presence of nets and buoys strewn on the ground suggested this might be someone's dwelling. We could see no windows or door, but a movement revealed a small dog which lifted its head, then returned to sleep. Someone did live there after all.

We parked on the shoreline some distance away. It was hot,

still and utterly silent, except for wavelets gently lapping the shingle, shells following the seawater back and forth.

One fisherman put out to sea early the next morning, his outboard engine waking us. We walked over to the wreck to see if anyone else was living there. '*Hola, hola?*' we called. An old man pushed aside some flapping material and backed out hefting a barrel of drinking water. He pushed it up against a rusty chest freezer. He was short with a crooked stoop, his unshaven face a mirror of the desert: pitted by sand, burnt by the sun and creased by the wind. His torn clothes hung on him loosely; had he lain down, you might have dismissed him as flotsam washed up on the beach.

'Hello, we're Michael and Paula, camping over there. OK?'

He bent his head towards us like a lizard, squinting his eyes as he peered at us. 'If you say so.'

'We'll only stay a few days, we're looking for birds.'

There was no response. I might as well have told him we were just there for some ice skating.

I continued: 'Have you any fish?'

He opened a cool box loaded with ice. Stacked inside were rows of glistening blue mackerel.

'Swop a few for a cold beer?'

His eyes widened and a grin revealed a gapped scattering of teeth. 'Help yourself.'

The fish were small, half the length we were used to, but glisteningly fresh – blue and purple. We took eight, exchanging them for two large cold beers from our fridge.

The old man smiled and clutched them to his chest as if we'd given him a bag of gold. I did the same with our fresh food, my mouth already watering.

Before I set out on my search for Inca terns, I launched our drone and flew it above where I intended to go along the coast, watching the film of its course on my iPad and noting the possible areas where cliffs might be suitable. I needed to find cliffs that dropped down vertically to the sea, as Inca terns like to nest directly above water. I usually flew the drone at 100–150 feet up. Paula stood by me and as I operated it she would keep sight of it with her binoculars. We were so afraid of losing it, which is easily done, and there was no buying a replacement for it. People were fascinated by it – no one had seen a drone in use. One man wanted us to film the roof of his house to show him where broken tiles were – it took us ten minutes to do that.

On this occasion the view down onto the featureless yellow and ochre landscape did show some areas which I thought might help my search. It might also have inveigled me into a trap . . .

Paula had decided to stay in camp. The previous day's driving had been hard, and a book that had been engrossing her for a week needed finishing off.

Walking up the steep dunes with a heavy pack was no easy task. I slipped back continuously and often needed to scrabble up, grabbing handfuls of sand. The featureless landscape didn't help either, as everywhere looked the same. I would fall over, roll a little, then getting up would look around – and head off in a slightly different direction. I knew there were parts of the coastline that looked promising, but finding them was proving more difficult than I'd anticipated.

As usual, the afternoon brought the windblown sand, which made my eyes smart. Much worse, though, was the lie of the land: the dunes curved like balls, directly to the cliff edge. In a few places, however, rock outcrops broke the dune surface and so, at one, I abandoned my rucksack and cautiously moved towards the cliff edge.

To my horror, after a few steps, I found myself sliding, and moved quickly onto my stomach, making my body as flat as I could, my fingers clawing deeply into the sand. I even pressed my chin down as hard, desperate to anchor myself.

My body halted. I didn't dare move, though, as I sensed still-shifting sand around me.

When climbing rock faces, I had been taught to always retain three points of contact, only moving one limb at a time. Accordingly, I carefully pulled a foot out, bent the knee upwards and dug the foot down – and down it slid. That didn't help much, but neither did I slip further. I followed suit with the next foot, lifting it up and pushing back. This time I slid down a little more again, my fingers automatically frantically digging deeper.

It was no use: I was getting nowhere and couldn't afford to make another mistake. Staying motionless, still with my head pressed desperately into the sand, all I could hear was the sea crashing somewhere behind me. All I could think of was what it was going to be like sliding over the cliff and onto the rocks beneath.

Normally, Paula and I kept together in case of emergencies. I had been so stupid to go there alone! I thought of Paula back at camp reading her book, a cold beer in her hand. I remembered our comfortable camper. Would she be able to drive back alone? Then I thought about the condor feathers. One on the shelf in Sara's house, one twisting in the hillside air in Patagonia on a cord of three threads. It was not supposed to end like this. I felt my heart beating, my fingers cold.

Hearing the slightest of sounds, I lifted my head a little and glimpsed a bird perched a metre from where I lay. Ironically, it was my first sighting of an Inca tern.

The bird just stared, then fluttered upwards and landed a little further back. *That's crazy*, I thought, but there it was – a tiny grey patch of rock where the tern was perching.

Slowly, I moved one hand up, willing my finger ends into talons, digging deep into the sand, then followed with a foot and again with my hand, till the rock was underneath me. With one last pull I had a foot braced against the rock, and only then did I attempt to sit up.

The bird sat on the rocky edge of the cliff eight metres away, beyond it a void of deep blue swirling sea. Shakily, I edged myself backwards to my rucksack and firm ground, where I remained for an hour or so, shocked and dizzy.

The tern returned many times during the afternoon, turning occasionally to look at me. Its body the colour of dark chocolate, it had scarlet legs and webbed feet. But it is the black head of this bird that is so striking – it has a large red bill as if to match its feet, while on either side of its bill is a fleshy bright lemon 'mouth'. As if that wasn't enough, an expansive white twirl of feathers between the eye and mouth flicks upwards then curves down, reminiscent of the ceremonial headwear of Inca chiefs.

I talked to the tern a lot that afternoon, thanking it for its help in saving me, saying how handsome its plumage was and what a good parent it was – it must have had a nest on the cliff beneath, as it would fly off but return after a while with a small fish in its bill, and disappear with it. I was unsure what the bird said to me but at regular intervals it would join a few others and wheel above me then over the sea and back, a rolling, joyous display.

With the sun setting further round the cliffs, the birds did one last fly-past above me, the low evening light shining though their feathers, and then wheeled off. It was my sign to leave, too.

It was dark by the time I saw the tiny, welcoming light of the camper far below. Nearer still, I caught the smell of frying mackerel.

Paula called out: 'I saw you coming. Dinner won't be long. Did you find the terns?'

'I did. And did you finish the book?'

'Yes, but it had a scary ending.'

I decided to keep quiet.

With the sapphire-blue Pacific behind us we left the coastal desert and crossed the Andean mountains towards the ages-old city of the Incas, Cusco.

It was an excruciating drive, struggling around the tightest of hairpin bends, one steep V-shaped valley after another. At the bottom of each, small jumbled villages clustered by the rivers, people bent double in the fields collecting potatoes and stacking onions. Winding upwards again through terraces of maize, potatoes and green vegetables we found ourselves on expansive, tussocky plains. Trees were sparse: centuries of deforestation had shaved the ground of its precious cover. A network of stone walls separated isolated thatched homesteads. Some were larger two-storey houses with blue-painted balconies and corrugated iron roofs. Close by each house were small enclosures with herds of long-necked cream or brown llamas and alpacas, essential to the household for their wool and milk.

The route took us through the Quechua-speaking town of Chuquinga, where we stayed the night. The narrowest of alleyways wound between small brick or adobe houses, and from one we heard soft musical notes. Turning a corner we saw two men, one with a violin and one with a local instrument – a cross between a harp and a lute the size of a double bass. Sitting on a log, the man played his harp with the huge instrument lying horizontally in front of him, one end of which was balanced on a curved wooden block. The musical notes came from six holes in the top: two dinner-plate-sized round ones, two a bit smaller and two smaller still, each edged with intricate coloured paintings. An ornately carved and decorated triangular frame held the strings. As he plucked the strings I stared upwards, beyond the ladders of mountain terraces to the snowy peaks above. The music he played was 'El Condor Pasa', known as the second national anthem of Peru. The Peruvian Daniel Alomía Robles composed it based upon a traditional Peruvian folk tune. It's now, thanks to Simon and Garfunkel, probably one of the most well-known tunes in the world.

Cusco is unlike any other city in South America, or for that matter anywhere in the world. At 3,400 metres high, it is a place where altitude sickness is common among visitors. Tucked away behind half-open ancient wooden doors are families in craft workshops working on embroidered religious tapestries, silver jewellery or weaving. The attraction of this city lies in its peace and simplicity, characterised by the most basic of materials: stone. Most of the domestic houses are whitewashed with red pantiled roofs, the remaining buildings are stone. Walking the alleyways around the central plaza with their ancient buildings, cathedrals and palaces, stone surrounds you. These comfortingly smooth blocks, as big as sacks of maize, fit tightly together without any mortar. The streets are paved with stone, cut and laid in geometric patterns. Vulgar black tarmac is banished to the outer roads. Cusco is hilly, so stone steps wind like rope around the houses. Smooth stone is always under your feet and, when tired, you can sit down and the stone is smooth and cool on your skin.

The reason most tourists visit Cusco is that the city is the jumping-off point to visit the Sacred Valley, above which lies the magnificent imperial estate of the Inca, Machu Picchu. Every day 4,500 visitors pour over the ruins of Machu Picchu and, in common with many other World Heritage Sites, tourism is becoming both a blessing and a curse. To alleviate this, Peruvian authorities are sensibly trying to spread the visitors out into the equally stunning surrounding landscape, off the Inca trail.

One of the newer trekking routes to Machu Picchu lies 100 kilometres due west, close to the mountain of Salkantay. Access to this hitherto unreachable valley is from the village of Mollepata. The route from this village to the start of the Salkantay trail is now regularly graded with stone to fill the gaping holes and storm-ripped crevices that can tip a vehicle down hundreds of metres into the gorge below. Ten years ago, access was only possible along a tenuous path on foot or by a nimble and trustworthy horse. We were able to negotiate it in our nimble and trustworthy Toyota, though it took us a day to crawl along in low gear – a day spent trying not to look down.

The road ended in a small flat area, 4,000 metres in elevation, beyond which was a large wooden hut, an encampment of flapping purple geodesic tents and what initially looked to us like the site of a massacre: a dozen or so people lay spread-eagled, unmoving; more had fallen with backs against rocks, heads down. They were trekkers, exhausted at the end of their day.

Dark cliffs like a crab's pincers held the tiny camp and overlooking it all, imposing and dominant, were the snow-covered ridges leading up to the 6,500-metre peak of Salkantay.

Early the following morning, the rattle of mess tins and the harnessing of pack ponies indicated the departure of the trekkers. Already ahead of them was a line of luminous orange shapes winding up the mountain: the organised trekking tours ensured that there were sufficient porters – either local people or ponies – to carry food and equipment, as well as the majority of personal goods. On average each young trekker carried a 5–10 kilo day sack while we, decades older, carried 20–30 kilos. Tripods and cameras are not light.

Beyond the encampment, higher up the mountainside, a huge hotel was in the process of construction and a developer's board close by outlined its sumptuous interior and range of facilities such as restaurants, swimming pools, gyms and massage parlours. It seemed peculiar to us, almost obscene, that despite the astounding world-class grandeur of the environment and the solitude wrought by nature, visitors still wanted televisions and a gym. Imagine anyone wanting a gym at an altitude of 4,000 metres! We could hardly get our breath even when only sitting down.

We left the main path taken by the trekking groups to follow a trickling stream up the mountainside. By all accounts the route that this three-day trek took to Machu Picchu was glorious, but our destination was different. The mountains and their birds called us.

Once onto grass, the walking was more comfortable but the slope steeper, and the higher we went, the slower our progress. We felt as if we had bricks tied round our ankles, and our heads were pounding, our breathing laboured. Looking back down the valley, we could just glimpse our truck with its oxygen cylinder safely stowed away on the back seat. That would have to wait until we returned.

It started to rain a little so we decided to rest for a while, crouching under the shelter of a bush that had yellow berry-like flowers. The habitat we were in was the sub-páramo, an intermediate zone of alpine grassland, above the treeline but below the true páramo. It's a habitat comparable in some ways to the puna found much further south, in Argentina. Around us were scattered small shrubs and herbs with many rocky outcrops as well as a few marshy spots. The skyline ahead was dominated by the snowy slopes of Salkantay, still many miles away and partly obscured by mist.

Many times we have found that bird activity increases following wet weather and, as the rain stopped, a small sparrow-sized bird as blue as a delphinium, a tit-like dacnis, moved through our bush, picking off tiny insects as it went. Then we sensed a sudden movement, gone before we realised what had happened. Was it a hummingbird, or something else? Walking round we could see nothing, but then it appeared again – a brown jet of a bird.

'It's a hummer!' I let out quickly.

The bird zipped from a nearby bush and away, out of sight. Then a second bird appeared, visiting the yellow flowers on the shrub we had been sitting under. Like so many hummingbirds it was mostly brown and difficult to identify, but it was a fairly large species with long pointed wings and a forked tail.

For a bird, the relationship between wing length and body weight is critical. The smaller the wing length the easier it is to hover, but hovering greatly increases energy requirements. Small hummingbirds lose heat quickly and in cold climates need to eat a lot more food. In warm and hot conditions, small hummingbirds can hover and manoeuvre quickly – hummingbirds that live by defending their food patch are called territorialists. At these higher altitudes, a different body design is called for. There are no large trees full of flowers; food is scarce and scattered over large distances, so hummingbirds need to fly from bush to bush and to do that they need longer wings and larger bodies. These hummingbirds are called trapliners.

The bird spent less than ten seconds at the yellow flowers then disappeared from view, but we'd seen enough to know it must be a trapliner.

With our cameras on tripods, we gradually moved around the steep hillside, constantly watching for the bird. Carting the heavy equipment made our headaches even worse. After a while we understood which bushes the birds preferred so we tried to position ourselves close by and wait. Strong freezing winds blew off the icy peaks above us and as fierce rain showers numbed our cheeks we hid underneath the bushes, nursing our cameras within our jackets as if they were babies. As the hummers continued their search for food around us, the wind howled and we felt helpless and fragile. Salkantay had us in its grip.

Eventually another bird came to feed close enough for us to see it properly. Its feet clung to the stem of the flowers to feed – another way to save energy. The bird didn't hover but held its wings out for balance on the swaying bush. We watched, entranced, as the magic of the bird revealed itself: the otherwise brown bird transformed into a subtle kaleidoscope of reflected shades as it pirouetted around the flower, moving from side to side as its tongue sought out the nectar. Purple-blue waves swept down its back to its tail like a rippling lake at night, while the dark wings, breast and belly became a shining suit of bronze armour. At its throat was a sparkling emerald pendant tipped with purple and blue. It was a blue-mantled thornbill hummingbird, beautiful to behold.

After a second storm and cold to the bone, we peeked out from within our bushy shelter to see a straggling line of bright orange and yellow anoraks on the far side of the valley. Heads down, they pressed on remorselessly, the trekkers and their guides barely looking up: they had a kingdom to conquer – but we had met one of its kings. Tracking, finding and filming a bird like this in such difficult terrain had been a battle of stamina and perseverance for us. Seeing this bird in its snowy kingdom was a goal achieved.

The Inca treasured gold and had storerooms filled with the alluring metal but it brought them only death and gruesome destruction. The enduring treasure and colour of these mountains lay in its sparkling hummingbirds. As gold has distorted the minds of many over time, these birds had intoxicated us with their brilliance. We had to find more, but that would mean climbing even higher. Ecuador and Colombia, we were told, had the finest high-altitude humming birds and that was where we would be heading for. In the meantime, however, the Amazon called.

CHAPTER 13

TWO WORLDS, ONE PLANET

We continued our journey east from Cusco to Puerto Maldonado in the Amazon, an exhilarating but exhausting 1,600 kilometres of driving between towering Andean peaks and across wide-open, sparsely vegetated plateaus, the Altiplano.

Circling down from the Andes, the continuous switchbacks in four-wheel drive was hard, and I wondered if condors ever felt tired and weary. The lower we went, the greater the amount of forest and the steeper the ravines, spanned by long, narrow bridges. As we approached one particular bridge a large truck came towards us from the other end and, a few seconds later, a coach overtook the truck. As we sped towards each other, I flashed and flashed again, but the coach held its ground. There was nowhere to go other than over the side into a precipitous drop. Paula was screaming and crouching low in her seat. I braked hard and the coach swerved just in time to miss us, barrelling into the narrowest of gaps that exist between life and death.

From that moment on the journey could only get better and a sign of this came moments later as two bright orange and black birds flew over the road. They were cocks-of-the-rock, legendary South American birds that partake in a dazzling 'lek', their courtship display of flouncing orange feathers, deep in the tropical forest. These birds are normally very difficult to see and so for us proved a good omen on our way to Amazonia.

These rapid highs and lows of emotion were starting to characterise our journey.

The further north we went, the number of people increased and the roads worsened: cause and effect. My brain was subject to a barrage of global information: new birds every day, new campsites, safety concerns, new foods to buy and eat, villages and towns that we couldn't find on a map. Only by immersing myself in nature could I ground my mind in the quiet reality of the miraculous events of the everyday.

We were in the fourth year of travelling, but it didn't seem like it. Physically the journey was getting tougher, but mentally I was getting stronger.

While I hankered after the wide open spaces and cool mountains of Patagonia, I had to appreciate the fact that we were on the threshold of the Amazon. We could hardly believe it. Both of us had read stories about this place, seen TV documentaries since we were children, seen the newspaper horror headlines about rainforest destruction. Now we were going right into it, to make a short film for the NGO Conservación Amazónica.

And as we sped towards our destination, we chatted to each other about Libby and Philip.

Libby Jones and Philip de Roo were two young friends of ours. They loved the cold and snowy northlands, while Paula and I loved the warmth of tropical forests; two worlds, one white and one green, linked by the molecule carbon dioxide.

We had known Libby since she was a bubbly teenager at school. Determined and adventurous, she was a girl more likely to be seen in walking boots than platform sneakers, a lover of Harry Potter rather than Britney Spears. Philip was a tall, fresh-faced professional explorer. Exploration seems an unlikely career path for anyone, except for someone like Philip. He had made a number of long-distance skiing expeditions across the northlands. He had walked around the entire border of the Netherlands to highlight environmental concerns, talking to everyone from politicians to disadvantaged schoolchildren. When Philip proposed the ambitious idea to take the future king of the Netherlands, Willem-Alexander, across the Greenland ice cap, it was his humour, good company and meticulous attention to detail that enabled the crossing to succeed.

Before we left for South America, Libby and Philip called round to our home in England. It was a cold wintery day with snowflakes caressing the windows: they were happy – we huddled around our wood-burning stove. In front of us the floor was covered with maps and charts, names like Resolute Bay, Svalbard, Bathurst Island, Nasca and Amazonia catching the eye like diamonds.

Libby had recently returned from the Antarctic and had a voyage planned to the Arctic in a few months' time. Her task was to understand the effects of carbon dioxide and its impact on the oceanic environment. A doctoral scientist working at the Institute of Marine Research in Norway, her research papers were widely cited and contributed to the global pool of knowledge used by the International Panel for Climate Change.

'I'm planning something very different,' Philip said, spreading out another map. 'My friend Marc Cornelissen and I will walk 400 kilometres across the Canadian Arctic, measuring the thinning of the Arctic ice as we go. The more the "whiteness" disappears,' he continued, 'the quicker the ice melts, seas will rise and ocean currents change. In a nutshell, this is climate change.' Philip sat back on his heels. 'It'll take a year or so to plan.'

The staff of Conservación Amazónica in Puerto Maldonado was expecting us. We were there to make a film for them about Los Amigos, their conservation concession deep in Amazonia. They wanted a promotional film to encourage travellers to visit this biodiversity hotspot. Finding a local wi-fi spot, we checked our emails on our phones; it would be weeks before we would be able to check them again. One was from Richard wishing us good luck, another was from Libby and Philip telling us that Philip and Marc would shortly be starting their Arctic trek, and one was from Paula's brother to say our house was OK, together with photographs of correspondence from the Inland Revenue. A smartphone is to the modern adventurer what a compass has been to explorers in ages past – but taxes have united everyone in misery across the centuries.

Our hosts found us a safe place to store our campervan and the following day they put us aboard a long, open-sided wooden boat painted orange and green, the *Valentino*, the boat that would speed us along the Madre de Dios river. With difficulty, slithering up and down the bank, we loaded our fourteen boxes of photographic and personal gear. They were stored in the very rear of the boat alongside twenty or so crates of beer; if we were marooned, we clearly weren't going to die of thirst.

A dozen local people then quickly boarded the boat and, almost immediately, the skipper started the engine. With one hand on the throttle and a bare foot steering the tiller, the craft moved into the turbid water.

The woman behind us had a cardboard box on her knee. Opening it, she pulled out two parrot chicks – more were inside. The birds were only a week or so old, featherless, with bulging, open eyes. She had bought them in town and I was relieved to see that these birds at least were going back into the forest; even as pets, they would smell the trees and hear the sounds of other parrots – they wouldn't be shut in a crate and shipped across the world.

For the first hour of the journey, the river banks were about the length of a football stadium apart and at regular intervals we passed one environmental disaster after another: dozens of conveyors tipping sand onto conical mounds. Illegal gold diggers at work, the mercury they used to separate the gold poisoning and discolouring the pools of standing water around where they worked.

Moving to the prow I sat facing the wind. To the bewilderment of some people in the boat, Paula filmed me as I introduced our film. I gazed across the water to the forest. My thoughts turned for some reason to Philip in the Arctic. Here we were zipping over warm water in a green land that was witnessing environmental challenges, deforestation, road building, gold mining and the persecution of indigenous peoples. Yet so far away, at the other end of the world, Philip was zipping over frozen water in a white land, but one that was also witnessing environmental damage; changes that could also affect us all.

The Madre de Dios narrowed and, as the river meandered through the forest, wide sandbanks appeared. A troupe of small monkeys moved through the trees and birds called raucously. As a small landing stage appeared, an umbrella of greenery closed over us, closing us off from remnants of blue sky, and we entered an utterly green world: 1,500 square kilometres of lowland Amazonian forest managed by the NGO Conservación Amazónica.

It was midday when we stepped off the boat, absorbed in the forest. I was surprised. I had expected my senses to be assaulted by sounds and smells, to feel danger lurking in the vegetation, around every tree, on every leaf. It was not like that at all: the forest was still, tranquil, quiet. I could have been in a concert hall listening to Beethoven, only here I was enveloped by the music from the hot, humid air and the gentle hum of insects. There were discordant sounds, of course: a scampering squirrel monkey, a distant macaw, but these were like coughs and sneezes from a concert audience. The music of the forest slows you down and by slowing down, you see its tiny treasures: stick insects, butterflies, sunlight illuminating the veins on a leaf.

Henry Walter Bates, one of my heroes, was a Victorian naturalist. He spent eleven years in the Amazon and collected over 8,000 species unknown to science. In one of his books he describes a typical working day in the Amazon.

'*I rise with the dawn and take a cup of coffee, and then sallied forth after the birds. At 10am breakfasted, and then devoted the hours from ten till three to entomology. The evening was preoccupied with sorting, labelling and preserving my specimens.*'

Our daily timetable was very similar, but with more showers. We would rise around 4 a.m. and have breakfast. We would film in the forest till midday, then return to our cabin, shower and have lunch. Then it was a couple of hours in the lab reviewing footage, another shower, 3 p.m. back in the forest, 6 p.m. return to the cabin for a shower, then dinner and bed by 8 p.m.

We would be in Los Amigos for a couple of weeks. Every day we would go into the forest hoping to find something to film. Time precluded the use of hides, so to start with we concentrated on getting to know where the birds and animals were, their territories and their feeding spots. We needed to get to know our way around quickly, and knowing that a tropical forest is essentially like a massive food court helped.

The forest floor is scavenged over by partridge-like tinamous and trumpeters, which look like long-legged ducks. Dead and curled-up leaves are flipped and turned over by inconspicuous foliage-gleaners and gnatwrens, which for their diminutive size have ridiculously long bills that they use like an expert gardener would his fork, searching for insects. These birds spend their whole lives mining this source of food because, unlike temperate forests, leaves in a tropical forest fall to the ground every day.

Another forest food store are the vines and lianas that drape between the trees or twist like coiling snakes around the broadest of trunks and thinnest of branches. These are a favourite haunt of the warbler-sized pygmy antwrens and the larger fasciated antshrikes. Both these birds have finely etched feathers of alternating black and white. Avian zebras!

Another food store is to be found in the nectar of flowering plants, such as the multitudes of heliconias, frequented by hummingbirds. Hermit hummingbirds, with their particularly long curved bills, are especially attracted to these plants.

Seeing trumpeters in the darkness of the forest is difficult. One morning, the two of us were walking along a narrow trail, tripods on our shoulders, cameras at the ready. Quietness is essential; we rarely talk out loud in the field. The first consideration of every living thing in the forest is to avoid being eaten and that means spotting or hearing trouble before trouble finds you. Ahead of us the path veered to the right so we carried on, stopping every ten paces, placing the tripod down, watching, then moving on. We saw a movement, a black shape, gone, back again, and another – was it a bird or a mammal? Paula gently lowered the tripod legs down to the ground and started filming. The shapes returned, one walked towards us, then another and another: long legged, black with white wings. A family of pale-winged trumpeters. Paula managed to get the ten seconds of film we needed before the birds melted back into the undergrowth. Great! This was our first footage that might contribute to the film. Pale-winged trumpeters are not rare but are difficult to see, as they feed only in the dense thickets of the forest floor on fallen fruit.

The natural history of this great forest revolves around the association of the trees with the animals. At home we are used to walking in woodlands where there aren't many species of trees – oak, beech and pine predominate. Not so in the Amazon, which has more tree species than exist in the entire northern hemisphere. There is little wind inside the forest and no space on the ground immediately beneath the trees for seeds to germinate, so Amazonian trees rely upon animals and not the wind or cross pollination to spread their seeds. When a parrot or an agouti – a large rodent, looking like a cross between a hare and a rat – takes a seed or a fruit, it may carry it miles before leaving it on the ground inside its droppings. This is happening a thousand times a day, with seeds being spread over a wide area.

The same tree whose fruit was being eaten by the trumpeters will, at a different time of the year, be visited by blue-headed parrots, which perch on the topmost branches and take its ripening seed pods. (Knowing what this tree looked like, we found another a few days later and filmed the parrots doing just that.) In a temperate forest this would be unknown, but not here in the Amazon where many different trees of the same type have the ability to blossom, seed and fruit at different times of the year, and in different parts of the forest. The animals therefore have to travel widely in the forest to eat, spreading the seeds even more widely, while at the same time the animals increase their ability to meet their own species and all the advantages that brings.

Open areas are created when the lightning bolts produced by violent tropical storms smash giant trees to pieces. This sudden, light-filled space gives an opportunity for other plants, such as bamboo, to move in. Andrew Kratter, an ornithologist from Louisiana State University, found there were nineteen species of birds that live only in Amazonian bamboo thickets. And it was by spending time close to these thickets that we came across the beautiful white-bearded emperor tamarin monkey, one of eleven species of primate that live in the Los Amigos forests – a staggeringly high number. These little primates are dark grey with black faces, about the size of a small domestic cat. They have long white wispy moustaches hanging down to their shoulders.

We tracked down a troupe to one area of bamboo, which they seemed to favour around the middle of the day. Finding them was difficult enough; filming them even more so, as the monkeys were so small and the forest so tangled and vast. Paula and I would station ourselves 50 metres apart, ready to signal to each other when we saw one, relying on noticing their pure white moustaches – beacons in the greenery.

Birding for the first time in a tropical forest can easily be disappointing for birdwatchers. It is possible to walk for an hour among pristine forest without seeing a single bird. Songs echo through the trees and calls can emanate from dense thickets, but seeing the birds can be notoriously difficult. It takes time to 'tune in' to any habitat. Mammals are even harder to see.

One day, as the first rays of dawn streaked through the lianas, Paula and I were sitting, silent and watchful for anything that moved. I have learnt to sit as if meditating in a forest, motionless. But while the aim of traditional meditation is to clear and empty your mind of thoughts, we have to do the opposite. Like a true hunter or the hunted, our senses must be on full alert, checking twigs and logs, movements of leaves, following shadows and the slightest of sounds. My mind was so absorbed at first that I didn't feel Paula's first nudge to my arm, or the second. I finally registered the more insistent third dig. What had she seen? I slowly turned my head and felt the hairs on the back of my neck prickle.

Not ten metres away, an animal the size of a cheetah had materialised and was looking straight at us. The creature had large flaming eyes, while its pale yellow coat was covered in open blotches of black.

An ocelot.

The three of us, all predators, looked at each other, all startled into silence. The seconds passed and then the cat, almost casually, sprang unbelievably high into the air and was soundlessly absorbed by the forest, yellow into green.

My mind often replays that scene over and over again in slow motion, fearful of forgetting it, but just as you can never forget your first love, so the eyes of the ocelot will always haunt me.

Tropical forests are dangerous in ways unimaginable in a temperate forest. Snakes abound and are difficult to see and don't move until you are almost on them. We were far from medical help so a bite could have been fatal. Ants do not pose that level of threat, except there are billions of millions of ants and very few snakes. The most fearsome ant is the bullet ant, which is black and between three and five centimetres long. This was definitely a critter worth avoiding: its bite, we understood, was similar in feel to having a finger cut off. Bullet ants were everywhere and we constantly encountered them throughout the forest, nearly putting our hands on them as we touched trees or branches; twice we even had them climbing up our tripods.

In the Los Amigos forest there are over 40 different ant species, but the two species of army ant were the ones we wanted to find as they have a fascinating association with tropical rainforest birds.

An army ant colony may number several million and, like most social ants, comprise workers and warriors. They live in a tight mass above ground and have two main life stages. For several weeks the colony will remain in one location as the queen lays eggs. As soon as the eggs start to hatch into larvae, the ants move in search of food. The colony goes on the rampage and, like an army, they spread out in columns and ravage the forest in their search for other ants, insects, spiders, even small mammals and frogs – anything that cannot escape quickly enough.

While the army ants are on their feeding frenzy, many species of bird will follow them. The birds do not feed off the ants, as their formic acid makes then distasteful to almost all animals; instead, they are watchful for the multitude of insects that are escaping the ants and nab them. There are about nineteen antbird species that are solely dependent upon this method of finding food, like the hairy-crested antbird and the rufous-tailed forest-gleaner. However, many other species will team up with them occasionally, often creating a flock numbering a hundred individuals of perhaps twenty species.

Mixed feeding flocks are integral to understanding birds and birding in tropical forests. And it's because many of the forest birds join these flocks and these range over such wide areas that it's possible to walk in the forest and not see many birds; however, when a mixed feeding flock crosses your path, everything is revealed in an explosion of activity and colour. It's what birdwatchers and biologists are always hoping to encounter.

Mixed feeding flocks of birds stay together and work together in order to find food. Some flocks will operate low down in the understory, some in the canopy. Helping them will be sentinels.

These birds will keep a lookout for rival gangs, raptors that can attack the flock while they are busy feeding, or a snake on the ground ready to attack. Their loud alarm calls will send the foraging flock into cover. The sentinel, however, has been seen to double-cross the flock by emitting a false alarm, then darting in and grabbing a tasty morsel for itself.

After the excitement of watching mixed feeding flocks with their brightly coloured tanagers, their antshrikes, antwrens and antthrushes, I was left in wonder as to how these forests are so different from even the finest and most diverse temperate ones. From extensive field work done here in Los Amigos and the nearby biological station in the Manú national park, scientists have shown that the differences are considerable. One of their surprising findings is that there are a similar number of actual birds per square kilometre in both; however, there is a much higher number of species in the Amazon, though these may be represented by only a single pair.

Another difference is the higher number of families of large birds, such as toucans, parrots and jacamars. And with so many different species covering a wide range of sizes, so the predators follow suit. There are many more species of hawks, eagles and falcons, though again they are sparsely distributed. One such predator is the legendary harpy eagle. Distributed from Central America down as far as northern Argentina, it's very rarely seen as each pair requires hundreds of square kilometres of primary forest as a territory. Birdwatchers will travel halfway round the world to see a harpy eagle, the second biggest eagle on the planet, with talons as big as those of a grizzly bear.

Nowhere in Los Amigos was far from the Madre de Dios river, which has its own birds, like the sand-coloured nighthawks that breed on exposed islands and sand banks. These pale, pointed-winged birds would skim the water for insects, often till late into the night. Close to the river was an isolated oxbow lake where we came across a leaky canoe. We quietly paddled past palm trees with their attendant Amazonian macaws eating fruits and dropping the stones *plop, plop, plop* as we paddled underneath. A floating log had a resting group of nighthawks lined up like flat tweed caps on a shelf.

There are so many stories to tell about the rainforest and the animals that live there, but our film could only capture one or two. We were fortunate to enlist the services of the conservation officer at Los Amigos, a young woman called Arianna Basto. Arianna was not fazed when we asked her to speak in English without a script in front of a camera. Knowledgeable and full of smiles, she was happy to repeat filming takes, all the things that help to make our work easier.

Each day we acquired more footage, until we were happy we had as much as we needed to complete the film. Our final day was declared a 'day off' and we walked the forest one last time, unencumbered by heavy equipment, an opportunity to meet the forest on its own terms.

We rose before dawn as the red howler monkeys roared their greeting to the disappearing moon. Stepping into the green world, we followed a trail along the high terrace overlooking the river. A log made a convenient seat to watch the darkness disappear and listen for the world to awaken. Blue and yellow macaws flew past, a rude interruption for a silhouetted white-throated jacamar that was perched silently on a nearby branch, also waiting and watching. The forest stretched as far as our imagination would allow – greenery to the end of our world. The jacamar moved slightly, its arrow-pointed bill lit by the glow of the morning sunrise, an orange glow that slowly lifted the forest canopy out of the mist. The forest was stirring. A screaming piha let out its distinctive call – a high-pitched wolf whistle – then stopped. Chaos and noise are never as tense as quietness. The forest rustled; the forest always rustles with something, creating curiosity by day but gooseflesh at night. With a tiny movement, out crept a magnificent rhinoceros beetle onto a large flat leaf. He was six centimetres long, black with a shining metallic purple cloak. He stood, a noble warrior with a pointed spear curving backwards from his head, a strong shield on his back. Slowly, using one hairy front leg and then the other, the beetle brushed his head, wiping away the glistening dew. A moment later he threw back the purple elytra cloak, stretched out two bat-like wings and, sounding like a miniature helicopter, circled upwards into the forest and away.

Shortly after dawn, we loaded all our equipment on board the boat and started the long journey back to Puerto Maldonado, the macaws shrieking their goodbye. After an hour downriver and fast asleep, I was woken by a smell in my nostrils. Smoke was drifting over the river and across the boat, a thick choking smoke. Unconcerned, the passengers slumped in their seats, scarves over their heads and faces. Along one bank and as far inland as I could see, the trees were on fire, tall black plumes interlaced with flashes of orange rising high into the air, vandalising the perfect blueness of the sky. The forest screamed at the cracking, whooshing, sizzling and crashing thuds, a hideous firework display of gigantic proportions. The boat sped up but the flaming forest seemingly kept pace and the boat was showered with a multitude of splinters; the forest was falling on us. Tiny, lifeless embers and ash landing on our clothes and heads, we coughed and choked as we breathed. I thought I might carry this forest with me forever, in my ears and hair, lodged in my very flesh.

The immediate horror subsided as I forced myself to think back to the magnificent rhinoceros beetle we had met earlier, the warrior with his pointed spear. But were his ashes now rising into the sky along with butterfly, orchid, snake and monkey ashes? Did those ashes perhaps contain the genetic fingerprint of animals that had never been seen, never been named?

In the 1980s the biologist Terry Erwin, using an insecticidal fogging machine, worked out the number of arthropod species (insects, spiders and crustaceans) in the tropical forests of the Amazon. His research led to him predict that there were thirty million different arthropod species worldwide. Thirty *million*. So much beauty and life in this green world. It's no wonder that most of us cannot grapple with the meaning and wonder of biodiversity.

The villagers who were burning the forest as we sped by in our boat would have no knowledge of this, nor understand the consequence of their actions. Would their forest fire mean that on the other side of the world my house would get flooded? Would their forest fire exterminate a species of plant that might lead to a cure for dementia?

We were a little subdued when the boat pulled alongside the muddy bank at Puerto Maldonado. People milled everywhere; dogs barked and chased chickens, boys on mopeds went this way and that. White sacks of maize were stacked by one boat, a pile of newly cut logs by another, and amidst all this a woman with a lovely voice sang her wares for sale: 'Tomatoes, tomatoes, lovely tomatoes' – a sound that has echoed across this continent for 5,000 years.

Back in the town our truck was waiting for us, and we repacked all the equipment inside, tighter than sardines in a tin.

In the hotel we were able to relax for the first time in a couple of weeks. The following morning we would depart and cross the Andes for the umpteenth time but this evening was a time to relax. First of all we needed to eat. We found a table at a pavement café. During the meal what looked like a carnival float drove by, a truck pulling a trailer with a speedboat. The boat was full of teenagers: girls in bikinis, boys in bright bermuda shorts. Singing to loud music, they waved drinks in the air, jumping up and down and shouting to passers-by. While we enjoyed our meal the speedboat made three circuits of the town, everyone having a great time. Cheered up by their crazy antics, we headed back to the air-conditioned hotel to a comfortable double bed that wasn't in sweltering heat and humidity; a time to check emails and messages from family and friends, post a few photos on Instagram and upload a blog.

The news we were to read was devastating – news that you first think is both unbelievable and yet wholly believable; news you don't want to hear, news that felt like we should run down to the boat and go back to the forest, and hide in our green world.

Despairing, we scrolled through messages that had accumulated over the previous days:

'Philip de Roo is missing in the Arctic.'

'Their daily communications have ceased.'

'Bad weather has precluded a search being started.'

'A search plane has spotted a dog on the ice and one sledge.'

'Better weather has enabled a search party to leave Resolute in northern Canada.'

'A helicopter has managed to land nearby and retrieve a dog.'

'A rescue party has arrived at Marc and Philip's last known position and retrieved Philip's sledge and the body of Marc. There was no sign of Philip.'

'Philip De Roo is missing, presumed dead.'

We sat down and quietly wept.

Above us all as we sleep and go about our daily work, a bright yellow object, the size of a mountain tent, orbits the Earth. This is the European Space Agency's CryoSat satellite, using radar to measure the thickness of polar ice. NASA aircraft also fly regularly at low level over the Arctic ice sheets taking measurements. Smaller aircraft using skis are able to land teams directly onto the pack ice to take even more detailed measurements of the snow thickness, as well as the ice.

There are many areas that planes cannot land – these can only be reached by foot and that is what Marc and Philip were undertaking. These are the dangerous lengths that scientists will go to in order to understand the nature and effects of climate change.

The last post from Marc and Philip on Twitter says: 'Skiing in shorts: Tropical day in the Arctic.'

In the audio stream, Marc jokes that he's skiing in his

underwear because the heat is so intense and says, 'Too warm, actually.'

He talks about seeing unusually thin ice up ahead. What is believed to have happened is that Marc's sledge suddenly went through the ice. Judging by the condition of Philip's sledge and equipment, it seems he attempted a rescue and in so doing also fell into the icy water. Philip's body has never been found: he was absorbed into the white world forever, to stay with his beloved ice.

As for Libby, she continues her work at both ends of the world, traversing the two polar oceans, her work a massive contribution to understanding the role of carbon dioxide in the oceans. When not working on the ice in minus 30 degrees, she dives the freezing waters or runs the mountains behind her home in Tromso, alone – and yet not alone.

CHAPTER 14

CHIMBORAZO

When setting out for South America, we were naive.

We both love mountains, as they take us closer to the domain of birds. With closed eyes, we can hold out our arms, feel the gusting wind and imagine flight. At the dizzying height of 1,200 metres, Paula and I have edged across icy hummocks of the Scottish Cairngorms to track snow buntings, only to see them tossed away from us, like snowflakes, by the wind. Walking the Cairngorms is no stroll in the park – sudden changes in the weather lead to many deaths, but these are never due to altitude sickness.

During our first week in South America, an eminent professor of geology in Tucumán, Guillermo Aceñolaza, had provided us with a large cylinder of oxygen longer than my 600mm lens and ten times heavier. We were already well overladen in our truck and this had seemed a little over the top to us but we had accepted the geologist's help and thanked him for his concern, secretly thinking that we would never need the stuff.

We knew we wanted to film some iconic hummingbirds, those that were high-altitude specialists. We knew their heart had to work at ten times the rate of a top competitive athlete, but strangely we had never thought how we might be affected on a mountain top. Our complacency was astounding.

In 1799 the Prussian scientist, naturalist and polymath Alexander von Humboldt – he of the penguin fame – travelled to South America and for five years explored from Mexico to Peru. Like every explorer he had a bucket-list of places he wanted to visit and the foremost of these was the Chimborazo volcano in what is now Ecuador, which he reached in 1802. In late June of that year Humboldt, his companions and porters with mules started the ascent. At 4,114 metres they had to leave the animals behind: it was too cold, they were haemorrhaging blood from their nostrils and as a result the mules were behaving stubbornly. At 4,754 metres, the porters refused to continue and they also turned back. Despite suffering from altitude sickness – their eyes were bloodshot and their gums bleeding – Humboldt and his companions continued, taking countless barometric and other measurements as they went. The explorers reached 5,917 metres, higher than any human had climbed before, but could go no further, their progress to the summit being blocked by a treacherous crevasse. Turning around and looking at the landscape before him, Humboldt suddenly had his 'Eureka' moment – the whole of nature suddenly made sense, how it was formed, how it worked.

It was with some disbelief when we first saw Chimborazo, the highest peak in Ecuador, one October afternoon. Heading from the south and having passed through the town of Cuenca, the road followed a series of Andean ridges and eventually came to a flat area with a stupendous view. Needing to rest, we stopped, made coffee and had a short walk. Beneath us lay a plain where secluded villages lay hidden in groves of trees, while in the distance beyond, more mountains shimmered in a cloudy haze that reached into a perfectly blue sky.

The anomaly in this scene was a triangular patch of pure white.

'Surely that's not Chimborazo,' Paula said. 'We're too far away.'

After consulting the map, we realised it was Chimborazo, over a hundred kilometres away. Once down the mountains we lost the volcano in the haze, with villages and forests hiding it for the rest of the day's drive.

There was nowhere obvious to camp for the night so we pushed on, eventually reaching the gate of the Chimborazo national park where a notice said that the park closed at 5 p.m. We had arrived just in time, and drove through the gates quickly, parking in a deserted parking lot. The wardens closed the gate and drove off, locking us in for the night.

We were safe and secure, though peering through the windscreen in the half-light of dusk the vastness of the volcano soared above us like a brooding behemoth. Getting out of the truck, we started to shiver, having difficulty believing that we were only 200 kilometres from the equator.

Winter comes every night on the high tops of the páramo. Feeling dizzy and unbelievably cold we peered at our altimeter: it was a worrying 4,200 metres.

Getting ready for the night at the end of a long day's driving is always tiring. We need to clear equipment out of the camper – the photographic hide, a mountain tent, cameras used during the day, food bought en route – and this is stowed in the two front seats of the car. Next, we need to unclip the camper top and crawl inside to push it up. The kettle is put on to make tea. Then we rearrange the interior and bedding, unpack computers to download images and footage from the day and then think about supper. Doing this at 4,200 metres at was exhausting, and throbbing headaches were the result. We tried to cook some food. After an hour the rice remained uncooked as the water couldn't get hot enough: the air pressure at that altitude meant that the water boiled at too low a temperature to cook the rice. Instead, we went to bed having eaten cold tomatoes and bread, and most of that we left.

We needed the oxygen in the truck but were too tired to fetch it – it was buried under equipment and it was dark and freezing outside. And the more I thought about retrieving the oxygen the more confused I became. Was the mountain weaving a dangerous web of ambivalence around me? I staggered out of the van, unearthed the 15-kilo cylinder and carried into the camper. Once inside, we switched off the gas heating: naked flames and oxygen cylinders don't go together. Paula and I then took it in turns to fit the face mask on and breathe deeply.

The heating stayed off during the night to enable us to take oxygen regularly. Though we were warm in our down sleeping bags, our heads pounded, we could feel our hearts beating too fast, we felt nauseous and sleep was fitful.

At night, high-altitude hummingbirds enter a state of torpor, their metabolism slowing as their heart rate plummets. We wished we could do the same.

Unable to sleep any longer I went outside. It was four o'clock and the temperature read minus ten degrees, but the strong wind blowing off the volcano meant it felt like minus twenty. Everything was white, each blade of grass an icicle, stones looking like snowballs. By the truck stood three large black upright birds looking at me like priests at a funeral. With their breasts finely streaked in white I thought they had been in a snowstorm. They were carunculated caracaras – the first I had seen. I ought to have been more excited.

As the wind bit my cheeks, I returned to the van and crawled back into my sleeping bag and tried again to sleep. By mid-morning we were both awake but still feeling ill and very grumpy, and to make matters worse the oxygen was almost empty. If we were to find any hummingbirds we would have to move fast, but that was the one thing we couldn't do. Somehow, we managed to sort out the truck and in the warmth of the car huddled together with the last of the oxygen.

Eventually, we drove further up the volcano. There was a road that went to a mountaineering hostel at 4,876 metres, close to the height of Everest base camp. The nearest we had been to this height before was on the trail of puna flamingos at Lake Pujsa in Chile, close to the Paso de Jama several months ago. This new height was definitely a record one for us, and the small car park at the top we understood to be the highest in the world.

At the hostel we could get hot coffee and shelter. A few climbers sat on a bench looking tired and dispirited, their chatter broken by long pauses and gasps.

We couldn't help but marvel at the stamina and endurance of Humboldt two centuries before. We had technical clothing, two merino wool base layers, quilted windproof trousers with waterproof ones on top, thick windproof top layers, military gloves as used in the Arctic, neck scarves and balaclavas. We might die through lack of oxygen, but we weren't going to get hypothermia. Anyway, we had a hummingbird to find.

Carrying cameras on tripods we moved slowly, twenty paces at a time then stopping to get our breath and scan. The mountainside was cut by steep gullies full of a chaotic jumble of rocks. Between the gullies were extensive slopes covered in ochre soil mixed in with small tennis-ball-sized greyish rocks. Vegetation was scarce – there were two sorts as far as I could see: bright green cushions of werneria that hugged the ground, and a dark green shrub half a metre high that had erect, prickly leaved stems topped with bright orange flowers – the chuquiraga. Tongues of snow lay between the sporadic bushes. Thicker, more permanent snow licked down towards us from the volcano's mist-shrouded summit. It was a bitterly cold, dreadful universe of rolling mists swirling around us. We moved glacially, not wanting to trip on a bone-breaking rock.

My oxygen-depleted brain played Russian roulette tricks on me: 'Carry on, risk it!' but then the next moment instilling in me the fear of falling into a crevasse. We stumbled wearily on, cold and grumpy. Where were the birds?

Then, seemingly conjured from the ether, a will-o'-the wisp of light flashed by, then vanished. Then again, from nowhere, but this time we knew it to be the hummingbird as it flew across us at lightning speed, then another, both disappearing into the thin air. Mystified as to where the birds had gone, this happened again before we pinned the elusive birds down to a small area, but still couldn't see them. Standing 30 metres apart we waited and watched. A bird flew out from behind one of the boulders and we went to look for ourselves; as I peeked over the boulder, another darted away. On my hands and knees I crept behind it, in case there were more. Touching the rock, it was warm. This particular rock was angled such that it collected and held the sun's rays, and the hummingbirds knew this was a good place to be. We retreated, waiting for the birds' return.

Our patience was rewarded when, twenty minutes later, one alighted on a tangerine chuquiraga bush above the rock and fed on its flowers. Snowflakes drifted in the air as the bird probed its bill into a floret, withdrawing it and delving in deeper again, like a child with a straw, sucking out every drop of nectar. Then in flew the other and did the same. We never saw the bird hovering: it fed perching on a twig or even from the ground, reaching up to a lower flower.

The Chimborazo hillstar is so small, if it settled on your finger you would hardly feel the bird was there – it's just a tiny bundle of feathers, the size of a pansy flower. The male often appears dull but lit by the sun he shimmers, dazzling the eye that beholds him, a prince adorned in a purple headdress with an emerald-encrusted throat.

After feeding, the birds darted behind the rock. Huddling on the ground, the birds pressed themselves into the rock face. We watched as their bodies, pulsing from heartbeats, appeared to be frozen. As dark clouds skittered by the wind allowed the sun to shine, its bright light turning the bird's head iceberg blue, its belly as white as snow.

In such a vicious environment we couldn't help but marvel and wonder which came first: the birds or the flowers.

Humboldt, in his writings about the inter-relationships between plants and animals, formulated many ideas about what he called 'this puzzle of life'. But it took another person, Charles Darwin, to solve the puzzle, one hundred years later. Darwin carried Humboldt's writings and observations with him on HMS *Beagle* and they were to be a huge help in Darwin formulating his ground-breaking theories on evolution. It was evolutionary adaptation and the survival of the fittest over aeons of time that gave the Chimborazo hummingbird and the chuquiraga plant the ability to survive and evolve together in harmony.

Humboldt and his companions suffered badly from altitude sickness and severe frostbite during their aborted ascent of the great volcano. During his weeks of recovery he pondered the sights he had seen from Chimborazo, his 'Eureka' moment. He developed the ideas of that moment into a painting of the Chimborazo volcano, called his *Naturgemalde*. In this simple picture he showed the principles of how everything in nature was interconnected; how the climate, soil and altitude affected the plants and where they grew, which in turn dictated the distribution of animals. In that moment, when Alexander von Humboldt gazed out from near the summit of Chimborazo, across the magical Ecuadorian landscape, the discipline of biogeography was born, and out of that the whole of modern ecological thinking. Chimborazo was to Humboldt what the Galapagos was to be for Darwin.

As the sun sank towards the Pacific and a clear sky, we had to leave, our oxygen cylinder exhausted, our bodies tired but spirits high. Behind us, the volcano sulked behind dark clouds, knowing we had discovered its secret: a love story between a hummingbird and a flower.

PART FIVE

COLOMBIA

CHAPTER 15

COFFEE COUNTRY

It was 2018. After nearly four years of trail-following, mountain-climbing, feather-finding, film-making and self-searching, we were nearing that Elysian Field for birdwatchers, Colombia.

The country is a cross between Switzerland and Mongolia. The western half of the nation, stretching inland for 700 kilometres, is split by the three towering mountainous talons, or cordilleras. The Western, Central and Eastern Andean mountain ranges, adorned with dense tropical forests. These three talons emerge from a great claw, a volcano-dotted Andean massif in Ecuador. Between the talons are two wide valleys, through which flow the Cauca and Magdalena rivers. It's in these fertile valleys that the majority of the population lives, in great bustling cities like Cali, Medellín and Bogotá.

The eastern half of the country beyond the Andes resembles the Mongolian steppe. There are no towns of any significant size and roads are few and far between. This is the Llanos, the second largest savannah in South America. The northern portion of the Llanos is seasonally flooded by rivers streaming off the Andes. Further south, the savannahs become higher and drier, before being absorbed into the steaming, succulent Amazon rainforest. In the far north of the country lies the isolated and ancient Sierra Nevada mountain range and beyond that the arid deserts of Guajira, bordering the Caribbean Sea.

Of all the places in South America, nowhere evokes so many disturbing emotions as does Colombia, where anarchy seems to have been its master forever. So that spring morning, as we swept out of the quiet wooded hills of Ecuador into the border with Colombia, what met our eyes was no surprise – an ants' nest of threatening-looking yet orderly activity. Heavily armed, black-uniformed soldiers were positioned at strategic intervals, waving batons to direct buses and trucks. Straggling lines of tired-looking people were trundling about with worn suitcases and bags tied onto makeshift carts and trolleys, all heading for an enormous mushroom-shaped shelter.

Clutching our passports, we were inexorably sucked in but then saw the reassuring tell-tale pale blue signature of the UNHCR (United Nations High Commissioner for Refugees) emblazoned across the roof. People were sent in different directions, all the while being careful to step over bundles of children huddling close to gaunt-faced parents. Despite the tension, the overall atmosphere was of an exhausted quietness.

These were refugees, good people, families like us. They were fleeing the terror, insecurity and political madness of Venezuela. Since the death of the maverick and charismatic leader Hugo Chavez in 2013, the country has descended into a perpetual and ever-deepening economic crisis. Medical supplies are almost non-existent, and food prices are beyond most people's reach. Money is worthless. According to the UN in 2020, 5 million people left the country, spreading across Latin America.

Colombians are well used to crises such as this. It has experienced its own 50 years of drug-fuelled civil war, suffering at the hands of the rural-based FARC guerrillas and their opposing right-wing paramilitaries. The country has 4 million of its own people internally displaced, the implosion of Venezuela adding to the numbers. Colombia, and to a lesser extent Ecuador to the south, was on the brink of a refugee catastrophe.

During the long-running Colombian civil war, people living in the big cities had experienced less inconvenience and direct threat than those in rural areas. For those in the countryside it was very different. Few people were able to leave their villages without permission from the armed faction operating in their area. Work outside their village stopped, even forestry ceased. Few people travelled anywhere unannounced and survived. We met a number of people who had never ventured outside the confines of their own small village.

Thankfully, since 2016, a hesitant peace process has descended over Colombia. The hopelessly corrupt police and army have been reined in and the countryside is starting to open up. In many outlying areas, though, great care was still needed. Travelling wild in South America as we were used to, alone in the forests, close to rivers and as far from people as we could get, was going to be foolhardy, and plenty of people told us so. Operating and filming in Colombia was going to be completely different to the way we had worked up till now.

The long drives through northern Peru and Ecuador and the climb up Chimborazo had taken its toll. We knew we were tiring more quickly than when we had left the UK years before. A coded remark had developed between us: 'We're getting on OK, aren't we?' The further into our journey we went, the more we used it. The phrase became as much an endearment as a question, a verbal hug. Of course we were getting on fine, but we never took each other for granted and everyone needs a hug.

Driving in Colombia was tough, too. The narrow mountain road from the Colombian border to Cali was the worst. Hundreds of kilometres of dust, diggers and cranes. One night I even dreamt of driving along the M25, everyone smiling, waving to us as we went by.

Here, men waving big red flags would halt the traffic dozens of times. These standstills were never less than thirty minutes, and sometimes up to an hour, as it would take that long for the oncoming traffic to pass and leave the road clear. We would look across gorges to see the cars and lorries, snaking round bend after bend, the road clinging to the mountainside like a belayed rope.

The real reason for the stress of these stops was the pig-headed impatience of the drivers, for as soon as we were brought to a halt, there was a hooting, screaming dash of trucks and coaches to fill any void on the road whatsoever. What ensued was swearing, fist shaking, honking and downright dangerous driving. Worse still, we had to join in, as it was survival of the fittest.

While waiting in the queuing traffic, however, drivers would exit their cars and approach us, pointing to the large black condor images on our truck. How many condors were we transporting? We evaded the question but intimated we were working for protection agencies, and out from the sun visor I would pull our feather. Time and time again the reaction of those watching was of delight, even awe, and children were held up to stroke its vanes.

Then we'd hear the roar of engines starting, and everyone would vanish, and off we would go into the chaos. But very often after these encounters, drivers recognised us. While the sound of scraping metal echoed along canyon walls one side and rocks spilled down vertiginous slopes the other, the person about to force us off the road into a muddy chasm would suddenly give us a thumbs-up, smile and wave us through. We seemed to travel with a protective halo around us.

Despite this, our nerves were in tatters, and the journey made us take a decision: we needed a holiday.

Once in Cali we drove round looking for a safe place to leave the truck. We eventually stumbled across a Spanish-style building, the Hotel Colina de San Antonio. With a pantiled roof, shutters and small balconies, it looked inviting, but what caught our attention most was at the end of the building: heavy-duty steel gates, guarded by a security man, led to an underground garage.

The hotel's interior patio had an elegant three-tiered fountain surrounded by flowers. It was quiet. Splashing water and fragrant air enticed us to sit down on a sofa and ask if we could speak to the owner. We sat with her, drinking coffee, introducing ourselves, explaining what we were doing and that we would like to leave our precious truck in her underground garage for a few weeks.

Seeing the condors emblazoned across the truck she threw up her arms: '*Que chévere!* How fantastic!' Condors were her favourite birds.

The deal was done: in exchange for leaving our truck, we would give her a dozen large prints of our best South American bird photographs for her to hang in the bedrooms.

The following day we flew to see Richard in Canada for a month's much-needed rest.

It was May, a perfect time to be in Ottawa. The snow had finally disappeared a few weeks before, the famous tulip festival was on, but the icing on the cake was that the bird migration was well underway. Dozens of species we had been seeing in Chile, Peru and Ecuador in recent months were now filling the skies above our heads. We heard them at night, invisible legions heading for the great boreal forests.

One morning I was having a cup of coffee in our son's garden. Below me, masked by waving branches and a lime haze of newness, flowed the Rideau River. The water was flowing fast, pushed by snow melt from a land of ten thousand lakes where wood duck drift along their shores. There is no more beautiful duck anywhere, with its red eye and an emerald helmet swept back, like one of Genghis Khan's warriors.

Suddenly, like an aural arrow, came a shrill cascade of notes, not unpleasant, but sufficient to make me quickly open my eyes. On a low branch, in front of me, perched a small bird – a warbler. Blueish-grey on top, a hoop of yellow round its dark eye, a daffodil-yellow tunic and a necklace of dripping obsidian. A medieval princess of a bird, a Canada warbler – the first I had ever seen.

Our vacation came to an end, and we returned to Colombia. The truck was safe, the owner of the hotel loved the photographs and we stayed for a few nights.

We had never had to operate from within a major city before. It was a shock that neither of us liked and one that I was hesitant about, concerned that my fears of crowded places might return. But they didn't; I was at ease with myself. It felt as though the continent's majestic nature had recaptured my spirit, and I felt I could achieve anything.

We had left the land of tango to come to the land of salsa. Cali is a city in the south-west of the country with nearly two and a half million inhabitants, many poor and nearly all of whom seem to own a motorbike. The roads are jammed with them. When stopping at traffic lights they surround you like bees around a honeypot, dozens in front, each side and behind. At the flick of a changing colour, they're off, swerving and twisting between each other, the drivers polishing the sides of cars with their dresses and jackets as they pass. The biggest public health issue in the city is the crazily high level of road traffic fatalities.

Driving up the steep and narrow streets of the San Antonio district of Cali took us into an old, chic part of the city. Here it was quieter, with views over the houses below and a cool breeze wafting between the brightly painted colonial-style buildings. At night, jazz emanated from corner bars. Our destination was the office of Calidris, the BirdLife International partner in Colombia. We were to meet with them to discuss how we could support their work with our film-making.

In Colombia, Calidris helps to protect its 1,800 species of birds. No one knows the precise number of breeding species; this is one country in the world where species new to science are regularly discovered.

While the membership of Britain's RSPB is over a million people, the membership of Calidris is sixty-eight. As in all the other South American countries we had passed through, the conservation requirements versus available resources in Colombia were massively unbalanced. We had set up a meeting with Calidris to see what we could do to help.

Their offices were a quaint townhouse in a small, leafy square at the bottom of one of the hills in San Antonio. We parked our Toyota truck immediately opposite. At one end of the street we noticed a smart-looking bakery. We had to go. Paula loves croissants and couldn't remember the last time she had had one. Once inside the shop, we thought we had arrived in heaven. The sweet aroma of pastry was mingled with the earthier smell of ground coffee. We bought as much as we could carry: bread, biscuits, *empanadas*, some violently coloured cakes and, of course, croissants. As we walked out of the shop, Paula was already nibbling.

As I collected our computers from the truck I noticed crouching against a nearby tree a poor man, a beggar, a shipwrecked casualty of a broken society. His trousers were filthy, his shirt tattered and torn, and he was surrounded by a flotsam of plastic bags, bottles and blankets. He was looking at us with candid interest.

I pointed to our truck, then to the Calidris offices and gave him a thumbs-up. He looked blank, so I walked over to him and handed over the larger of our bags of goodies and pointed back to our precious vehicle. At that, he nodded and smiled.

In a downstairs room open to the garden we met with some of Calidris's conservation staff: Diana, Jeissen and Kendra. They told us about the many projects they were engaged in: conservation programmes on the Pacific coast to alleviate the loss of mangroves, encouraging sustainable coffee plantations, monitoring endangered bird populations, protecting forests used by wintering North American birds, educating farmers in the Llanos grasslands, training workshops and census work on remote mountain ridges where rare endemic birds were thought to occur. Considering we were in the most bird-rich country on the planet, the question of what sort of film to make was more

difficult than we imagined. We said we would love to work in the
Llanos but they laughed and said it was a metre deep in water at
that time of the year. The conversation always seemed to come
back to one theme: local people and the peace process.

Colombia was starting to open up to tourism, and eco-tourism
in particular. People in the countryside had been subdued, silenced
and isolated by generations of civil war. They had been separated
from the reality of the outside world, one where people travelled
to the seaside for holidays, where gap-year kids sought adventure
outside suburbia, where being green was hip. This was a new way
of thinking for Colombians. The peace process had lifted the lid
off the pressure cooker of their society; employment, the hoped-
for dividend of peace, was proving hard to find. Many rural folk
were drifting from their villages into shanty towns surrounding
the big cities.

'Engaging with people is key to protecting Colombia's nature,'
said Diana, as she passed some papers across the desk to us. 'Here
are the names of some people and communities we work with.
Visit some of them – they're tuned into the local scene and can
keep you safe. Don't make films about us. Make films about them
and how they're making bird-friendly places. That sort of film
would be great.'

I must have looked a little puzzled, because Diana continued,
'A bird-friendly place is simply a place that's good for birds
and people. Even here in Colombia it's not easy to find the two
together.'

It had never occurred to us before that these two issues were
associated in the way that Diana meant: the safe protection of
birds as well as people. The environmental movement emerging
in Colombia seemed to be a fusion of the culture of birds with the
culture of peace.

Leaving the offices, we noticed that the beggar had gone. We
put our computers and papers back into the vehicle but, as we
jumped in to head off, heard a shrill cascade of notes. Sitting on
a low branch, above where the beggar had been, was a small

bird, blueish-grey on top, a hoop of yellow round its dark eye, a daffodil-yellow tunic and a necklace of dripping obsidian. A princess of a bird, a Canada warbler.

Tragically, the Canadian warbler's numbers are fast declining as it winters in the narrow altitudinal belt of Colombia's Andean forests – the area where coffee plantations are expanding rapidly.

As we scanned the names on Diana's list, one leapt out: 'Bosque Colibri, Café de los Suenos'.

I turned to Paula. 'I know what our next film should be about. Coffee.'

The mountains behind Cali rise over 4,000 metres to the Farallones de Cali national park and form part of the western part of the three parallel Andean mountain chains that run up the country. Leaving the outskirts of the city the roads twist and turn along the contours of the mountains. There are steep drops one side, with makeshift homes balancing on tall, rough-hewn poles. The other side has high banks of shifting earth and stones that regularly fall into the road. We passed through village after village, each with scrappy-looking tyre repair shops, grocery stores advertised by boxes of food spilling into the dusty road, and cafés perched on top of rickety viewing platforms. Eventually the road descended into a stony track and dropped into a forested ravine at the bottom of which was a tumbling mountain stream. Waiting for us by a wide, steel-shuttered gate was Andres, the owner of 'Bosque Colibri', an exciting environmental project and coffee plantation run by himself and his partner, Paola.

Once through the padlocked gate we negotiated a steep track through the forest, at long last halting on a small patch of level ground, within an arm's length of a small house. The building seemed to grow out of the forest, its shallow pitched roof held by sturdy tree trunks and bamboo canes as wide as a man's arm. The lower parts of the external walls were only a metre high;

above that, the windows and doors were almost entirely open to the warm air that drifted through the living space. From within appeared a smiling Paola, slender, with vivid clothes, hair streaked with silver and arms outstretched like a tropical butterfly.

'*Venga, venga,* come in, come in,' she called. Pointing us to the floor, we sat down cross-legged on large cushions around a low circular table.

Both were in their mid-thirties: Andres, serious with a round face, brown eyes and close-trimmed beard, a graphic designer; Paola, a psychologist. Their consuming passion was to produce coffee that did no harm to the Earth. Coffee that encouraged birds to their land and had an aroma of a sun-kissed forest at dawn.

Andres's work meant he had good internet access at Bosque Colibri so it was a great time to be back in contact with people. Ada from Tucumán asked for some of our photos for a book she was writing on the birds of a nearby lake. A Spanish TV company wanted permission to use the courtship footage of the hooded grebes. We even picked up a WhatsApp message from Miguel in Argentina. He told us he was now working as a bird guide in the Ibera Marshes. We were thrilled to hear he had landed his dream job.

Andres, donning his favourite straw hat, beckoned to us. 'Let's show you around.' We walked a short distance from the house, into the open, overlooking a steep valley.

In flat lands, the eye only sees what is directly in front – not so in this topsy-turvy world of mountains. Here the steep valley sides, facing all directions, displayed whatever the land held, like clothes on a washing line. There were dark, square blocks of mango trees; triangular plantations of tall, pale eucalyptus; and lines of bananas with their long pointed leaves. Coffee dominated, though. Some hillsides were rows of polka dots of young bushes, while many were densely clothed in a blur of established coffee bushes with squiggly, worm-like picking paths winding among the greenery. Then there were bare brown areas where nothing grew, and dark ominous streaks: eroded channels dropping to the rivers below.

Waves of hills and mountains stretched into the distance, but I could see no native forest. Andres told us that ten years before, nearly all the coffee had been grown under the shade of native trees – but not anymore. He passed his hands across the distant hillside. 'Those farmers have removed their trees. Their harvest is bigger than ours but their costs are much higher. On these steep slopes, heavy rain leaches the soil of the nutrients and if there are no large trees to hold the soil together, it washes away. They have to dress the ground with artificial fertilizer and spray insecticide; we never need to do that. Here the birds eat the harmful insects.'

As we walked around his 15 hectares of land there were birds everywhere. A wide-eyed Andean motmot flew above us, a magpie-sized bird whose colours blended between the soft greenery of newly opened beech leaves and the striking blue of a jay. Its two long, deeper blue central tail feathers looked like extended tennis rackets.

There were the large, turkey-sized Andean guans and so many colourful tanagers as to send us dizzy. These birds were all resident breeding species but there were migrants as well, birds from North American. Flycatchers and vireos, birds that many would dismiss as dull but that are in fact every shade of green and grey and buff, birds that bring trees from Mississippi to Maine alive in the springtime. And warblers, the tiny-winged denizens of North American backyards.

'Do you see many Canada warblers?' I asked.

'You mean the *reinita de Canadá*, the little Canadian princess? Yes, in December and January. A few even remain all year, but don't breed.'

The Canada warbler was discovered by the French zoologist Jacques Brisson in 1760 and is one of the few birds in the world named after the country in which it was found. They are known to mate for life, which is unusual for most birds, and even more uncommon in songbirds. Their breeding season is one of the briefest of any of the warblers. They arrive in the aspen forests of North America in late May and nest low down in the tangle of winter-torn forests. They live in swampy land with a well-developed shrub layer and a tall over-storey of mature trees. They sing a lot, not just in the lead-up to the breeding season but throughout the remainder of the year. The birds leave Canada in early July.

For the 200 years after Brisson named the bird, no one really knew where the birds disappeared to during the northern winter. Eventually the location was found to be the eastern slopes of the Andes mountains, predominantly in Colombia. The area that was particularly favoured by them was the elevation between 1,000 and 2,000 metres – which is precisely the altitude for the ideal cultivation of coffee. Historically, when coffee was grown under the shade of mature trees this was not a problem for the bird, but fast-forward to today and the onset of industrial-scale coffee production, and you can see that our 'little Canadian princess' faces big challenges.

In the Americas the Canada warbler is now a rapidly declining species, along with the bobolink, Baltimore oriole and cerulean warbler. The list is a long and lengthening one. All these have undergone a catastrophic 75 per cent decline over the last 30 years. The reasons for this decline are many and varied: fragmentation of habitat in their breeding area, loss of insect food caused by agrochemicals, a loss of coastal habitats on their migration routes, and habitat destruction in their South American non-breeding areas.

The total population of this little songster is estimated at between 2 and 3 million and considering that its wintering range is five times smaller than its breeding range, what happens in South America is crucially important. Between 1993 and 2009, Conservation International undertook an exhaustive study to determine the 'anthropological footprint' (e.g. deforestation, road building, lighting, oil and gas installations) in areas occupied by Canada warblers. They found that in its breeding range in North America there was a 1 per cent increase in the footprint, whereas in the coffee-growing areas, where the songster spends the majority of its life, there was a species-threatening 23 per cent increase in the footprint.

Life is tough for the Canada warbler and could get tougher, as urbanisation across all countries, as well as rising wealth in India and China, is accelerating global demand for coffee.

We stayed ten days with Andres and Paula. A partly open-roofed washroom in their house was situated at the back, one wall being the natural cliff face of the mountain. During an evening storm I showered in the most natural of ways, heavy rain ricocheting off the rock face mixing with that from the shower head. Splashed soap suds landed among leaf-carrying ants and cascading ferns. Drawn by the cooling rain, a saucer-sized tarantula spider slowly walked across the rock, black and hairy with purple on its legs, an arm's length away. There was nothing I could do except wait and watch where it disappeared to.

This was definitely not the time to get soap in my eyes.

We had been living together with nature for years now, in a way we had previously never believed we could. Claudio had said we were part of nature and now we felt like it. Why should I worry if a tarantula decided to have a shower with me? They were harmless. I should thank Pachamama for showing the handsome creature to me. Watching the large spider walk, using four legs independent of the other four, was as hypnotic as watching a concert pianist's fingers dance, though I doubted many people would pay for the privilege.

We slept in our truck, parked beneath a mango tree. As we lay in our sleeping bags, we listened to night monkeys as they crept about the branches above us. These shy primates have white faces and large round eyes like a bush baby and would suck the juice out of the mangos, dropping the skin and stones onto the top of our van.

Each day as we woke, pale-eyed thrushes and house wrens would be singing. By breakfast the familiar, rapid song of the Canada warbler would take over the chorus and later, as we walked the hillside of coffee bushes, we disturbed a fashion show of tanagers from the bushes ahead of us.

Andres and Paola had perfected the production of sustainable artisanal coffee at Bosque Colibri. Each day, Horacio, their worker, gathered the reddening beans, gently turning each twig in his search for the thumb-sized gems. Bay-headed and scrub tanagers followed him, the same as a robin might follow me in our garden, diving into the foliage as he went from bush to bush. Straw baskets of beans were then taken to be scarified in running water, the thin red skins peeling off between slow-moving rollers. The white beans, washed and slimy, were then carefully laid out on wire trays inside an opaque-roofed drying shed. Every few days they were turned until dry, with any beans showing sign of damage discarded.

Coffee production is highly water intensive. The water used was pumped from the tumbling stream in the valley beneath. The stream flowed from forested mountains, where the rare Cauca guan lived, and from much higher still, from the misty páramo, home to the even rarer spectacled bear of Paddington fame. The skin off the beans contains toxins so this contaminated water is not returned to the ground or pumped back to the river, as is the case with the larger intensive farms. Instead, Andres feeds the contaminated water into a series of narrow ditches which zigzag down his land. Each of the ditches is planted with dense aquatic plants, the long roots of which absorb the toxins from the water, these ditches ending in a large settlement pond. The pond water is fit to drink, not only by humans but also by toucans and parrots that regularly swoop down in the heat of the day. As for the red skins, they are put to compost and returned to the ground. The only part of the coffee production that Andres and Paola do not undertake is the roasting. For that they travel into Cali with sacks full of the organic beans. When the roasted beans come back to their forest home, they are packaged by hand, ready for sale.

One morning, we accompanied Andres and Paola to another project of theirs, the 'Market of the Mountains'. At this market, village people from the whole vicinity gathered to sell their homemade produce: honey and wine, vegetables of every colour, cheese, wooden toys, flowers and hand-knitted clothes. Chiva buses – one of the local open-sided, rickety and crazily decorated buses – arrived with people from outlying communities. As soon as one stopped, the passengers shot off in all directions. Children ran about the village square, pulling their parents from one stall to another, eager to buy treats. Couples walked, arms around waists. Two cafés were open in the village, and friends sat at makeshift benches in the street, donkeys tethered close by. A man played a drum, a woman walking behind playing a flute. The local school threw open its doors to everyone. Children and local groups sang and danced on a makeshift stage, a teenager sold balloons. The market only operated once a month; Andres and a few friends had started it two years before when, at last, the roads became safe for people to leave their villages and travel. It has now become more than just a farmers' market; it has evolved into helping to make that indefinable element that flows through a region, a community culture, a culture of peace, a 'bird-friendly' place.

For Andres and Paola, their coffee had been the start of this process; no wonder they named their conservation brand 'Café de los Suenos', 'Coffee of Dreams'.

The day we were due to leave Bosque Colibre, we took one last walk through the plantation. A bird flew out from a coffee bush and settled on a low branch in front of us, a warbler with a daffodil-yellow tunic and a shimmering obsidian necklace, the *reinita de Canadá*, the little Canadian princess.

CHAPTER 16

THE OLD ROAD TO BUENAVENTURA

Kendra was a lively, businesslike Californian girl, full of smiles, who worked for Calidris, the BirdLife partner in Colombia. After a stint in the Peace Corps, she came to Colombia knowing little about birds but with a heart full of enthusiasm and energy. We spent a week with her as she masterminded one of her bird-guide workshops.

The course was held a short way from Cali, in the western cordillera, at a small community called Chicoral. The idea was to engage local people with the concept of eco-tourism, taking advantage of the resurgence in birdwatching in the country since the peace process had enabled safer travel. We wanted to see what effect this was having on people's lives, and Kendra wanted us to film the event.

Those attending had come from far and wide, many travelling nine hours over the mountains on a chiva. The people attending were aged from sixteen to sixty, men and women galvanised by the desire to support themselves by some aspect of environmental work. They listened and joined together in activities from bird identification to environmental law, food hygiene to first aid, figuring out how to put together a business plan and learning English at the same time. We met Ana Melina, a young woman who was operating a small environmental group called Dapa Viva. There was Dora, who had started to run a roadside café with a balcony for birders, and Daniel, a man in his fifties, who had an encyclopaedic knowledge of medicinal plants. Another person we connected with was Freddy, a small, wiry man who wanted to be a bird guide. By our Global North standards these were mainly poor people, but their expectations were high and their hearts huge. Hope brought the group together: to improve their family's economic wellbeing, to support their community, and to protect the environment – the three pillars of global sustainability.

Our presence at the small event in rural Colombia surprised many of the attendees, especially as we were making a film. We told them that what they were doing was important and our film would encourage others to attend future courses. Freddy took a particular interest in what we were doing; he was a youngish man but with a deeply weathered face. He was insistent in asking us to visit him at his home: 'Please come to my house. You're very welcome.' Freddy repeated the invitation the next day, proud of being able to practise his English. He told us a little about the great forests around where he lived and his genial manner endeared him to us. We accepted his invitation. 'I live down the old road. Kendra will give you directions.' She did, but cautioned us to take care and only camp with people we knew.

If you need to get from the city of Cali to the coastal port of Buenaventura on the Pacific coast there is a new, fast road over the mountains. There is also an old road, if you can call it a road – many would call it a track. A track that follows a foolhardy route through the forest, and around rocks the size of houses. This region experiences very high rainfall. Water surprises you as it erupts from the greenery, cascading down the steep slopes or clawing away the roadside in its attempt to reach the river below. There are no villages as such, just the occasional scattering of tin-roofed timber dwellings along the route.

We knew when we were getting close to these homes, as signs of makeshift bathing spots appeared: on the mossy rocks, specks of white caught our eye – tablets of soap – and underneath roadside cascades, sacks draped over a bamboo pole gave privacy around a pool.

The forest challenged the road to exist at all, an affront to its mastery of the land. Lianas swung idly overhead like ropes off a buccaneering ship; aerial runways for monkeys. Towering trees, held firm by angular buttresses, spread their creeping roots over the little bit of clear ground otherwise known as the road. Afternoon rain prompted slurries of mud and rocks to pour across the track like chocolate custard.

These natural hazards were to be expected; it was the unexpected that gnawed at the back of our minds: people. This isolated, almost unused route was the way to the coast – and the route to transport drugs. In the recent past, the small communities had either joined the criminal gangs or kept their heads down and tried to survive. Things were a little better when we were there, and we were undaunted as we knew we could camp at Dora's and Freddy's along the way.

After two hours of driving a twisting uphill section, we came to our first 'safe house': Doña Dora's café. It was on the brow of a hill and had just sufficient room to pull off the road and park close to the building. At 1,600 metres high, it was an ideal place for drivers to stop, rest and take in the expansive view that overlooked the top of the tropical cloud forest. After Doña Dora had attended Kendra's bird-guide course she had decided to put out multiple hummingbird feeders and to build a covered lookout at treetop height on top of her home. It was a shrewd move, as groups of birders as well as many locals started stopping off for a coffee and an *arepa* – a maize biscuit that looks like a cork coaster and tastes like . . . a cork coaster – and to watch a mesmeric display of hummingbirds such as empress brilliants, and crowned woodnymphs, and white-necked jacobins.

From the treetop platform there was also always the possibility of seeing one of Doña Dora's specialities of the house: the toucan barbet. Scientists will correctly say that this bird originates from the family of toucans, a distinctive group with colossal bills (and a penchant for Guinness). I prefer to think of them as coming from a primary school art class, as only there could a bird so ridiculously coloured have originated. The size of a jay, the toucan barbet has a bill like the pectoral fin of an orca, capable of cracking the toughest of tropical nuts. This clown of a bird has throat and cheeks of nuthatch blue, fading to scarlet on its breast and orange on its flanks, a chestnut back and a black hat with a white feather in it. Paula stayed on the ground floor and had the good fortune to see the barbet, but I missed it.

We stayed two days at Doña Dora's and then moved on fifty kilometres down the valley to meet up with Freddy. He was hoping to earn a living by being a bird guide and we were to be his first customers.

We didn't think that the old road could deteriorate further but it did – rarely could we drive more than twenty kilometres per hour. Roads such as this one would have originated as paths for hunters with mules, whose needs would have kept them close to water courses, streams and rivers. Over time these horse trails became the established route to the Pacific coast and were widened for carts and the driving of cattle. They were never meant for motorised vehicles and we met none, only motorbikes swerving and twisting around the rocks and rain-washed ruts, their pillion passengers swaying in unison with the driver.

The old road led us deep into the western slopes of the Occidental range of the Andes, dominated by the Farallones de Cali national park soaring up to 4,000 metres, an area known as the Tumbes-Chocó-Magdalena biogeographic region. This is one of only thirty-six global biodiversity hotspots. This hotspot encompasses the coastal lowlands and mountainous western-facing forests from central Ecuador northwards to Panama, including the Galapagos Islands. Incredibly, nearly one tenth of all the bird species in the world occur in this small area.

Tragically, however, the Ecuadorian forests are down to a critical 2 per cent of their original cover, while only 65 per cent of the forests still remain in Panama. It is only in the central section, the moist broadleaf forest through which we were travelling, that the forests are largely intact due in no small measure to the civil war that had been raging in Colombia for the past fifty years.

Freddy lived with his mother in a small, rickety wooden shack with a corrugated roof. Next door lived his sister. The two wooden huts perched precariously on the side of a steep valley. We parked on the road immediately outside. Chickens abounded. To one side were a series of small wire racks on which a few handfuls of homegrown coffee beans were drying. The elevation was 450 metres, considerably lower and so hotter and more humid than up where Doña Dora's café was. Opposite his house, on the other side of the road, against the hillside, a rivulet streaming down the hill fed a concrete tank and, from an overflow at the end of the tank, the water continued its journey down into a roadside ditch. In this homemade pool large freshwater fish were cruising up and down: food for the cooking pot. Chained up by the entrance was a ferocious-looking dog, which snarled as we arrived, its look pinning me to the road. Freddy unchained its leash and led the dog into a room, closed the door, then beckoned us through. I watched the closed door carefully; my leg was only just recovering from a nasty dog bite a few weeks before.

We talked about his local birds; he had travelled little in his life, not even to the coast at the far end of the road. 'Too dangerous. We've been prisoners along this road all our lives,' he said with a sigh. I thought how lucky I had been to live in a peaceful country. Past events in my life, traumatic at the time, would have seemed trivial to him.

Edging around cardboard boxes of pots and pans stacked on the earth floor, we found ourselves at the back of the house on a short rickety veranda, not wide enough for two people to pass. With hands on the wooden rail, we gazed at the view.

The house was poor, as basic as a bucket, but the view was magnificent. I'd never seen a better one. The land dropped sharply from the back of the house then curved upwards, expanding outwards like an exploding galaxy, an unending green arboreal ocean as far as the eye could see. Either side rose rolling waves of hills, shadows indicating hidden leafy troughs and sunshine highlighting surfy crests. Beyond that, further still, holding back the bright blue sky, were dark ridges, a tsunami of lofty mountainous cliffs and peaks. I had never imagined that a forest of such dimensions might exist. This was not the 'Hundred Acre Wood' I was used to, an innocent place to wander in a carefree manner, visiting Owl's house and chatting to Heffalumps. There seemed so much forest, worlds within worlds, that it humbled me into fear: fear of entering and getting lost. Could this be Tolkien's Mirkwood, full of dragons, dwarfs and elves, a place where strange things happen? Thrusting above the canopy I could see giant Colombian mahogany and quindío wax palms towering like ships' masts above the trees beneath.

I can understand why most people have no love for the creepy crawly things of life: the minutiae of beetles, moths, slugs and snails have as much relevance to many as tide tables have to landlubbers. Trees are a different matter; they are an integral part of the human psyche, the biggest single living entities on the planet. There are few living things that watch over us as trees do. I have never met anyone who didn't like trees. People love them for so many reasons: to lean against when weary, for shade on a hot day, or for memories when they climbed towards the sky as children. Trees are essential for millions of people as fuel for cooking and for keeping them warm.

Then, to cap it all, came a bird, sweeping close by us without warning, a sleek black and white bird: a swallow-tailed kite. I followed it with my eyes, as I would a yacht on the ocean. On and on the bird flew. Minutes passed and beneath this aerial mariner nothing changed – just wave after wave of gentle greenery.

As the kite disappeared out of our view, Freddy turned to us. 'The kites have just started to arrive in the last week.'

'They're one of our favourite birds.'

'Yes, yes,' said Freddy. 'The other day I saw a flock of seventy in the valley, swooping low over the trees, picking off fruit.' Then, with an excited jump, he exclaimed that we should go into the forest. Picking up a pair of old binoculars he crossed the road and entered the great forest with no more thought than I would have on stepping from my front door into the garden.

We hurried after him, from the light into the dark, from the heat to the cool; from a feeling of space and security to one of enclosure and the unknown. After all, this was one of the largest remaining areas of primary forest in Western Colombia, the Anchicaya valley, part of the Protected Forest Reserve of the Pacific.

Being photographers and film-makers has its disadvantages when it comes to moving about in tropical rainforests where it's hot and humid and the undergrowth is tangled and dense. We both try to carry our equipment on tripods so they are 'jaguar ready' – operational at a moment's notice. They are heavy and unwieldy, which means that we have to stop at regular intervals, an opportunity to watch for birds. Well, that's our excuse.

Freddy knew this forest very well and moved through it at a fast rate; this was his home patch. We were much slower, there was so much to look at. A flickering of shadows passed above the canopy and a group of birds settled together on a branch.

'Paula! Look! Toucans!' They jockeyed for position on the branch and looked around. In striped yellow and maroon blazers the toucans were waving their great bills like cigarette holders, the epitome of three Edwardian boating gentlemen on an outing. They delicately plucked fruits, tossing them in the air like golden guineas and pocketing them in their greedy throats, then disappeared through the crowded leaves.

The route Freddy took us must have been known to him alone, for it was hardly visible; a bent leaf here or a flattened twig in some mud there being the only signs of anyone having come this way before. I couldn't help but dwell on how different this was to the forests I was used to. At home it would be impossible to get lost in a forest, as road noise surrounds us. Here it would be so easy. You could momentarily follow a butterfly and be swallowed up by the vastness. The routine we developed was to walk for ten minutes or so and then stay still, waiting and watching. Sometimes I closed my eyes, smelling the forest, especially the wafting sweet and musty fragrance from orchids. They cascaded from the crevices in trees, cocooned in moss and decaying leaves, yellow, white or red, sometimes fused together in a nebula of swirls and streaks. Some had tiny flowers smaller than the nail on my little finger; others were as big as my hand, flowers as faces, eyes peering down at us, shaped as little people or fluttering birds. The orchids had petals for moths, bees or hummingbirds to land on and trumpet-like tubes, straight or curved, inviting them to drink their nectar. Continuing to push through the greenery, there were leaves of every shade and shape: simple and compound, long and short, pointed and round, often ribbed with deep veins providing their own guttering system.

A shaft of light shone through a bright green palm leaf illuminating a small black blob on the underside. Turning the leaf over, a group of tiny wasps were busy constructing their black hexagonal cells. A few flew menacingly towards me, and I backed away quickly. Tropical wasps are not to be messed with. Low down on the side of a rotting stump sprouted a fountain of spiky purple bromeliad shafts, tough, serrated and as long as my arm, each of these leaves directing water to the centre, where it became a secret pool. Looking into one of these worlds within a world, something sat within a swirl of striking colours. It was a frog in pyjamas, small enough to fit in an eggcup, a Lehmann's poison frog, with orange and black striped legs, black feet and tiny pure white toes. As I bent one of the slender leaves back to have a closer look, the frog jumped and so did I, its dangerous colours sending a shiver down my spine. Other people are clearly not so bothered: this tiny animal has been so heavily collected for the pet trade that the species hovers on the precipice of oblivion, critically endangered.

We continued our walk; I was always at the back, Paula in the middle and Freddy taking the lead. The girth of the trees was so vast as to hide the others from my view even though we were only thirty metres or so apart.

I felt its eyes on me before I saw the animal. Turning slowly, my eyes met another pair looking straight at me – a young black howler monkey. How the others hadn't seen it mystified me, they'd walked so close. The animal's soft reddish coat indicated it to be a young female. Unusually for a monkey she never moved; perhaps we were the first people she had ever seen.

After a moment the animal stood up and stretched upwards to grab a long white seed pod off the tree above. Under her throat was a great bulge as if she had swallowed a pineapple. This was the enlarged hyoid bone that enables howlers to live up to their name and howl, very loudly. Her chest was hairless – I could see her ribs and sternum – and she reminded me of a young child reaching up to take an ice lolly from an ice cream van. Looking upwards, I realised why she was so unconcerned about my presence. Above her, lying in the crook of a branch, was a male howler. Twice as big as the youngster, the male lounged on his back as if he were on a beach. His long tail was wrapped round the tree; his head was to one side, watching me intently.

I turned to go; the female just sat, holding her food. Walking a few paces I looked back. She had gone, melted behind great leaves, off to find another lolly.

An hour later, a short thunderous tropical storm had us pinned down under a cliff overhang. After the rain ceased and as we were shaking out our wet clothes, four men appeared from nowhere. Who on earth were they? What were they doing? Camouflaged, each held a sub-machine gun and was arrayed with pockets bulging with radios, transmitters, torches and knives.

I could feel my heart beating and Paula took my hand.

The men were talking loudly to Freddy but Paula couldn't follow what they were saying.

'Look at their badges,' she whispered. The embroidered badges on their right shoulders were a tricolour of yellow, blue and red, the Colombian national flag. The FARC insignia is the same, except it has an obvious white panel in the middle with two crossed rifles. Here it's crucial to know your flags.

We were unaware that they had been watching us for some while. They were more interested in our binoculars than in what we were doing. We showed them various birds in the trees and they laughed at us when we snatched the binoculars back off them to focus on some beautiful blue and white cerulean warblers, rare migrants from North America. Eventually the soldiers disappeared into the forest.

'There's a big hydro dam down the valley and guerrillas have been seen in the area,' Freddy remarked, a little concerned. 'They say we should go back, and definitely no photography.' Evidently Freddy knew the way, for 20 minutes later we found ourselves tumbling down a bank into the dust of the old road.

All tropical forests are dangerous, but for us this was the first time the distinct danger had come from man.

Surrounded by a breeze, the humid headiness of the forest left behind, our eyes gradually re-accustomed to the brightness. It took a few moments to realise where we had been and what we had seen. We had been in one of the most abundant of natural places, a place dense with flowering plants, trees of every shape and size, sounds of every pitch: at times it was a flute, a violin and then a drum. The forest which the old road struggled to penetrate was full to overflowing with pulsating life. It was a perfect place to me, there were no straight paths, no fences, no signs saying which way to go and which way not to go, no rows of identical trees, of plastic tree guards and wooden seats with plaques, no information boards telling us what to see. The forest had no official way in or way out and there were no ice cream vans, even for the howlers. This was nature as it should be, as we should experience it, wild and awaiting discovery, dangerous even.

With a bounce in my step I walked on, kicking stones for the fun of it and disturbing another cerulean warbler from a roadside tree.

That day walking in the Pacific coastal rainforest had confirmed what had been dawning on me for some time: the Andes were becoming a second home to me and, like the land we had left behind at home, here I felt comfortable and at ease.

I was learning to understand the ways in which nature and man lived together in those great mountains, learnings wrought from the joy and pain of travelling slowly for years and from meeting so many people who valued nature.

In the last few years we had walked under the canopy of so many different trees, each in its own leafy universe. There had been the windy southern beech woods overshadowed by glaciers that echoed to the *toc-t-toc* of the Magellanic woodpecker. A little further north we had sloshed into the dark drippiness of the cold Valdivian rainforest under whose elephantine alerce trees lives an elf, the chucao. We'd sweated through the humid Yungas, its laurel forest draped in lianas home to a multitude of glasswings, and paddled between Amazonian palms upon whose spear-like shafts danced harlequin-dressed macaws. Birds such as these had once been dreams. Now albatrosses, condors, flamingos and parrots were living memories deep within me. I could instantly recall the times I had spent in their company. When I saw distant specks in the heavens – condors – I greeted them as I would friends. Entering what were once unknown lands, the puna and páramo, I now heard familiar calls and songs. Seeing a moving shape or a silhouette, I would sometimes know what it was and this made me happy, for I knew that slivers of my soul now rested on those volcanic plateaus, the guanacos' plains and in the condor skies.

The three of us chatted late into the night. Freddy told us of his past life, confined to his village, growing a little coffee, keeping his head down. Others he knew grew coca or caught frogs, birds and even butterflies for the wild pet trade. We asked him how much he would charge us for the few days we had been with him. He named a small amount and so we paid him double. I handed over to him my bird field guide to keep, containing the bird names in Spanish, English and Latin. We hoped he would fulfil his dream of becoming a bird guide. After all, he had one of the world's most bird-rich local patches, a global biodiversity hotspot, twenty metres from his front door. To have someone like him on the spot and known to Calidris was really important.

We settled down to sleep, cocooned in the quiet forest. Although we were on the edge of the road, there was no traffic, and we heard no people. No one travelled at night unless they were up to no good.

When the time came to say goodbye to Freddy, he clasped our hands, reluctant for us to leave. 'Thank you, thank you for spending time with me. I've got to go to a community meeting now and I'll tell them all about you. Lots of people have seen you and your truck parked outside for a few days. It has caused quite a stir. I need to tell them what we've been doing. Most of the people that live here take the forest for granted. Strangers here usually spell trouble.'

'Then tell them we came to marvel at the forest. To see its birds. If they look after the forest, people may pay to visit.'

'One day,' he answered, 'birdwatching may be more lucrative than growing coca!'

CHAPTER 17

SEARCHING FOR BUFFY

Spending six weeks of our time in the flat eastern grasslands of Colombia, the Llanos, looking for a small brown shorebird, might seem strange to some. However, few people had as much time as we had and travelling slowly for the last few years had taught us that rewards can come from the strangest of places.

Carlos and Yanira, two Calidris biologists, had just rung us. They were going into the Llanos as the floods had receded. Could we join them and make a film about a threatened bird, the buff-breasted sandpiper?

The request to make a film about this bird came out of the blue, and was a pleasant surprise. But why weren't we searching for the scarlet macaw, the Ferrari of the bird world? Why weren't we seeking out shimmering hummingbirds, the Copacabana beach posers of the bird world?

Instead, we were to track down the fearless astronaut of the bird world, one that orbits the skies on its annual migration, yet is almost never seen. Despite being tracked by scientists, the bird disappears for months at a time into the misty unknown. Buffy the astronaut lives a precarious existence, close to extinction and seldom seen by anyone. So a search for such an enigmatic bird shouldn't have seemed strange at all.

Few birds breed further north in the Arctic than buff-breasted sandpipers. They live in that ribbon of land where vegetation gives way to ice, separating a possible place to live from the impossible.

Stopping-off points, places to rest and feed during their long journeys, are critical for all migratory birds. Buffies like short grass prairies and it is thought that for millions of years they followed in the trail of the vast herds of bison that moved back and forth across the great North American continent. Around the time the 'west was being won' and wagon trains were heading west across the central states of the USA, vast flocks of buffies were shot. Newspaper reports from the time talk of the prairie skies turning black as these birds passed through. There were so many that the annual July shorebird hunt attracted hundreds of professional shooters. Buffies became 'fast food' and were shipped in their tens of thousands to the emerging cities on the east coast, to Chicago and New York, along with passenger pigeons and Eskimo curlews, protein for a burgeoning immigrant population. By the end of the nineteenth century the bison had gone and the industrial agricultural revolution of the twentieth century then changed the vast native grasslands forever.

Now, in the twenty-first century, another threat is making life difficult for Buffy. The Arctic is warming up and as the shrub vegetation moves northward so the rising sea is flowing southward and engulfing it. That thin ribbon of land where buffies nest is shrinking fast. Their population is now less than 50,000 individuals, equating to fewer than 20,000 breeding pairs spread across the whole of Arctic Canada, Alaska and Arctic Russia. There are so few buffies remaining that finding them, especially on migration, is a needle-in-a-haystack challenge. Landscapes are changing so rapidly that one year the birds may nest in one area and next year in another. On migration the same is true. What is known is that buffies leave Canada and migrate down the central flyway passing through states such as Kansas and Oklahoma to the Texas coast. They are known to arrive in Colombia in August, but they move south quickly. Every year a few are seen in the Beni Savanna grasslands of central Bolivia and weeks later on the southern Brazilian and Uruguayan coasts. Some stay in Brazil and Uruguay for the whole of the austral summer while others move south into the Argentinian pampas.

Buffies, like many other birds, spend the biggest proportion of their lives on the move, driven ever onwards in the push to seek food and find a mate. They are not Canadian, American, Brazilian or Colombian – they are birds of the world. Their return journey is a similar route, the majority of the population being absorbed in the vastness of the South American continent, nobody knowing quite where they are. Like a sprinkling of salt onto snow, they are almost impossible to find.

Paula and I had crossed the Andes many times and found the drive from Cali in the western cordillera of Colombia to Yopal in the Llanos to be the toughest. Three massive mountain ranges, the Occidental, the Central and the Oriental, need to be navigated up and down, as well as crossing the intervening valleys of the Cauca and Magdalena, both crammed with busy towns and cities such as the chaotic capital, Bogotá. One infamous stretch of road known as 'La Linea' consists of unending hairpin bends separated by twisting, narrow intervening sections. Long lines of articulated trucks chug up the steep inclines; all you can hear is the screeching of air brakes, all you can smell is diesel.

The antics of local people made the journey scary as well as boring. Men in hi-vis jackets wandered in the middle of hairpin bends to help guide the long articulated trucks round, acting as self-imposed traffic police. In actuality they were a hazard, as they would then run along tapping on windows begging for money. Cyclists hung onto the back of trucks, waiting for an opportunity to race past, weaving to avoid oncoming traffic. More dangerous and frightening still were the teenagers using the steep mountainous roads and slow-moving traffic as a slalom racing course for skate boarding. Faster than a falcon, they plummeted down, twisting between the traffic, turning and somersaulting as they went, even sliding underneath the larger trucks. Shrines to the dead were common. And if that wasn't unnerving enough, we came across several elaborate roadside memorials to civil war massacres, occasions when all the passengers of buses had been shot and left at the roadside.

Understandably, we were very picky about where to camp.

Paula reluctantly shared the driving but the journey still took us two exhausting twelve-hour days. We sighed with relief on reaching the pleasant town of Yopal, at the foot of the Oriental range, the easternmost Andean foothills. This was the gateway for us to enter another new world, the extensive savanna that stretched for 600 kilometres to the border with Venezuela.

Paula and I sat happily at a pavement café drinking aroma-filled local coffee and eating mango ice cream in the comfortable knowledge that the starry skies above us held migrating birds. We wondered if we were nearing the end of our long journey. In our new life we'd travelled from one end of the continent nearly to the other. For well over a thousand glorious days we had bathed in nature, lived in the wildest of places, and for all that time had been accompanied by the soundtrack and company of birds.

It was late when Carlos and Yanira arrived. The couple had worked in the Llanos for many years and had identified a number of grasslands that were highly suitable for buffies. Thankfully, many of the sites were owned by *llaneros*, local landowners, who were keen to preserve their distinct culture as well as protect the birds. The biologists' aim for this trip was to renew acquaintances and revisit these sites, looking for buffies as well as other key bird species that might help gain protected status for the land.

Carlos bought another round of coffees and ice cream and said how excited he was about the film. He wanted it to feature some of the ranchers we were going to visit so that they could promote the importance of preserving their native grasslands.

'The *llanero* culture is dying out. Their grasslands are disappearing, the birds are in trouble,' he said.

The four of us sat in silence. How many times I wondered, had I heard the phrase 'loss of habitat' cited for falls in bird numbers? The world is changing so rapidly, the phrase is losing all relevance. The word 'loss' indicates an accident, a mislaying, a forgetting of where something is. Yet in most cases it is *wilful* destruction – where rivers are dammed, wetlands drained or forests felled, taking away the home of resident birds and migratory ones too, like the buffies.

'Big companies buy up the *llaneros*' land, burning and ploughing the native grasslands. All the wildlife that depends upon it disappears.' Carlos went on to tell us the land was then fenced off and divided into small lots. Chemicals are added to the land to boost the growth of 'designer' grass. The number of cattle put onto the land is tripled, they are artificially fed, artificially inseminated and hormones injected into the cattle to boost their development. 'Only big money can do that. International conglomerates are importing tractors and combine harvesters bigger than our houses. Families are losing their livelihoods. Cafés are replacing campfires. You don't hear these people rounding up their cattle by singing to them, like they do here.'

Again no one spoke; we all were thinking of what lay ahead: Carlos hoping against hope to discover buffies, while we wondered if we could make a film in the few weeks we had.

The next morning, over breakfast, Carlos introduced us to a *llanero* rancher, Don Hernando. Paula smiled: she knew his weather-beaten face framed by his Stetson would look good in the film.

'When you've finished eating, you can follow me to my *hato*.'

'*Hato?*' I queried, looking puzzled.

'It's what we call a big farm round here. Over 10,000 hectares. Like an *estancia* in Argentina.'

* * *

The journey took seven hours. The equivalent time in Great Britain would have taken us from Edinburgh to London, during which time we would have probably passed 150,000 other vehicles. On our trip we saw none – only two motorbikes and a surprised-looking rider on horseback.

The lack of traffic was not surprising, as there were no roads, but also a blessing because the visibility most of the time was near to zero. Clouds of soft grey dust billowed up over our windscreen from the vehicle in front. Our window wipers were clogging, even the side windows were obscured. It was as if we were driving through the aftermath of a volcanic eruption. Crevices and ruts required us to swerve wildly from one side to another; hours of tightly gripping the steering wheel made my fingers numb.

Approaching a ridge of sand, we descended towards a wide brown river. For most of us brought up in the shadows of motorways and the complex but orderly road junctions of Great Britain, rivers are something that are crossed on graceful bridges designed by civil engineers. In this spaghetti western land, bridges are only for people to use – narrow struts of wood on wobbly timbers stuck in the mud and watery silt beneath. Horses and vehicles simply drive through the water, manoeuvring around sand bars and anything else that may have floated downstream and got stuck.

I got out of the truck ready to wade across the river, to test the depth of the water and gauge the firmness of the riverbed. As I took the first step into the swirling brown waters Don Hernando shouted out, 'Stop! There's electric eels!'

Rivers in the Llanos are not for the faint-hearted; their sluggish nature seduces the unwary. There are in fact two elements of danger to look out for, the first being lines of bubbles from electric eels. We had heard of them growing up to 6 feet long, rarely lethal to people but capable of emitting a painful shock, enough to disable a horse and throw its rider. The second threat in many Llanos rivers is stingrays. They are large, venomous, flying-saucer-like fish that hide on the river bed or glide just below the surface, barely noticeable except for tiny tips of their pulsating rays that occasionally break the surface. There are over 2,000 reported cases of stingray casualties in Colombia each year. The excruciating pain of a sting from their tail lasts a few months and occasionally the loss of a foot or hand ensues.

Perhaps this wasn't a river that I was going to wade through to test its depth! On the far side I could see vehicle tracks – aiming for those would have to do. What happened in between we would trust to luck.

Every so often Carlos would signal us to stop in order to scan the horizon for birds. This meant leaving the cosseted environment of our air-conditioned truck to experience the shock of meeting a blast of super-hot air as we opened the door. We logged the outside temperature as 41 degrees. Within a few minutes our shirts would be stuck to our backs as a wet carapace, and we struggled to breathe. A quick look through binoculars would suffice, before we hurriedly got back in the truck and continued our way through the dust.

Arriving at *Hato* Sinai, Don Hernando installed us in his high-powered ATV and took off with us hanging on for dear life, stopping at regular intervals to scan for buffies. The land was flat with smudges of green indicating woodland on the distant horizon; humped cattle were dotted over much of the landscape like sacred stones, with tall white jabiru storks walking like supercilious druids among them.

The Llanos comprises almost half of the land surface of Colombia and can itself be divided in two, separated by the great Orinoco river. The east is made up of a rolling low plateau which has been extensively converted into oil palm plantations. The western part, where we were, is known as the 'flooded savanna' and it is as strange a place as you would find anywhere. From May to October tumultuous waters streaming off the Andes flood half the area with up to a metre of water, making it South America's Okavango. During this time fish swim over the land and marshes rejuvenate. Electric eels, giant anacondas and stingrays threaten the only means of transport: horseback. Horses are indispensable: to get children to school, for the transport of provisions, and for moving the cattle to higher ground and into gallery forests.

For the other half of the year, the water recedes to the rivers and for a short and wonderful spring period the landscape is reminiscent of a baize-covered snooker table; then the summer sun bakes the ground and freshwater turtles lay their eggs on the riverbanks to keep them cool. The Llanos is a land of extremes.

One tree that is superbly adapted to these conditions is the moriche palm, a tree so important for the Llanos that it is a keystone species. Every so often Carlos would shout for us to stop and he would jump out and clamber up their trunks, searching crevices and holes for nesting Orinoco geese. The moriche has so many uses it is locally called the 'tree of life'. For many indigenous people in the fringes of the Colombian Amazon it is a vital part of their diet. The edible fruits, rich in vitamin C, are sold in local markets and can be made into a popular drink, jam or dessert, or even dried and ground up into a type of carbohydrate-rich flour. The bark is used for weaving and basket making and the palm leaves for thatching and making mats.

Many of the forest animals depend on the tree, too. Monkeys and capybaras feed on the fruit, parrots nest in the tops of the palms, while the rare Orinoco goose nests only in the palm.

It was February when we entered the Llanos: everything was dry except for extensive swamps and natural lakes called *esteros*. After many hours of unsuccessfully checking the grasslands for buffies, Don Hernando took us to the biggest of his *esteros*. It was huge, 50 hectares in extent, and surrounded by reed beds and marsh of at least the same surface area. Along the inflow of a small river were horned screamers and many grazing capybara. Further into the water were hundreds of white-faced and black-bellied whistling duck, but what took our attention were the dozens of roseate spoonbills. They walked sedately through the water, sweeping their partly open bills from side to side. Their bill is packed full of sensors: once a beetle or tiny fish is located there is no escape – the bill is snapped shut.

Carlos was off, walking way out into the surrounding grassland looking for buffies, while Paula was filming close to the marsh edge. I stayed where I was, just looking and thinking about the scene in front of me. As we were approaching the end of the dry season, many smaller marshes had dried up, and birds from the surrounding land knew that this place would still have water – a sparkling magnet that drew them in.

Taking my eyes off the roseate spoonbills, I became aware of the vast numbers of barn swallows that were flying and feeding, almost at ground level. I had been standing still for so long, some of the birds were catching ants, right at my feet.

By then it was getting dark and the rest of the team was heading back to join me and move on. Slowly we made our way back around the marsh, the sun dipping below the horizon. As we were leaving, something caught my eye – wisps in the sky. A brief look through binoculars and I shouted to the others to stop.

The whole western sky from the reedy horizon to over our heads was full of circling and swooping specks, coalescing into shapes forming and reforming patterns. Swallows! It was almost impossible to estimate the numbers, but there must have been up to a quarter of a million. We had never seen so many birds at one time – they must have been using the marsh as a roosting stop-off point on their way northwards to North America.

I stood transfixed, grinning from ear to ear. What a sight! We stayed as mass after mass of birds dropped into the far reeds and darkness absorbed the rest.

The owner of the neighbouring *hato* Flor Amarillo, Don Francisco, appeared with his son at the wheel of their truck early the next morning. There had been no sign of buffies on Don Hernando's *hato*. So like a baton in a relay race, we were handed over and guided further into the dusty land to Don Francisco's ranch. Our convoy followed faint tracks through the parched, golden grass savannah, its horizons broken only by shimmering palm forests.

From a distance Francisco's buildings were barely discernible from the landscape, as discreet as a nest in a hedge. Each was built of pale, rough earthen blocks, connected to the next by an open-sided corrugated-iron-roofed passageway. As ever, there were doorways but few doors, and windows were merely openings. These were buildings designed to capture the still air and move it around, forcing it through porches, along passages, between rooms. Draughts were a sought-after pleasure: wherever the air eddied, there was a chair. People slept in hammocks strung under porches or inside open rooms where we saw up to eight hammocks swinging to and fro in the semi-darkness, reminiscent of the sleeping quarters of a seventeenth-century galleon. The place smelt of leather, chickens and dust.

Within a fenced cultivated enclosure, tall green plantains remained safe – a *llanero* cookbook would be slim, and could be sub-titled: 'A Hundred and One Uses for Mashed, Fried, Sliced, Cubed, Boiled and Beaten Plantains'. Suspended from overhead beams hung strips of parched meat. An imposing mature mango tree dropped juicy fruit onto the ground like a grandmother dispensing sweets. What wasn't collected in the day was eagerly gobbled up overnight by wild pigs.

I wasn't surprised to locate a clever arrangement of black drums, wires and switches tucked away in an outbuilding. An ingenious homemade solar energy system serviced a huge rusty fridge reserved solely for beer. With villages distant, self-sufficiency was a requirement.

Adjacent to the main building, a sturdy open-sided barn housed everything necessary for the daily work of ranching. This was an armoury of supple leather ready for dispensing to a force of weather-beaten riders. In the same way as a fire station is at a state of constant preparedness, so it was here. There were rows of coiled rope, straps, stirrups, whips and ties, belts, boots and hats. Saddles sat astride a smooth log, from each hanging the much-cherished braided hide lassos. Colourful blankets had been draped from rafters. Arranged like rifles were a dozen metre-long branding irons, ready to grab and go. All these were the items used in the daily life of a working *llanero*, as much as smartphones, earpieces and laptops were a part of ours – the difference being that everything a *llanero* owned and used he had made himself; our belongings were usually made in the Far East and shipped across the globe.

Beyond the buildings a group of horses grazed in a paddock; you could have played a tune on their ribs. Further on, in all directions, a flat ochre plain was studded with white cattle. It was this sea of sparse dry grass that we scoured day after day for buffies, a bird so small that four of them would have fitted inside a Stetson hat. We walked back and forth over the plains, at intervals stopping and, with eyes pressed up to a telescope, interrogated the land with precision until our eyes hurt. All of Carlos's and Yanira's experience indicated that buffies need short grass in which to find the necessary invertebrate life they feed on. Their favourite ones are found in the dung of herbivores. Regular grazing with the right stocking levels maintains the sward at around 6 cm in height, perfect for the birds.

Paula and I decided to leave the confines of the ranch and camp out for a few days on our own. There was a gallery forest a few kilometres away; the river supposedly had a giant anaconda as well as plenty of birdlife, and we wanted to try out our photographic hide.

We had a couple of hours before it would be dark so, leaving the ranch behind us, our truck was soon careering over the bumpy grasslands in the direction Don Francisco had indicated. Eventually we found a suitable level area of grassland a short walk from where an opening led into the forest and down to the river.

By now it was almost dark and I needed to erect the hide. Paula sorted out the truck while I found a suitable spot. As I walked across the grassland with more gear for the hide, something made me stop and look into the forest. Something was looking at me. I could feel it. In the gap leading to the river was a shape barely discernible to my eyes. A big cat sat watching me, a pale sandy-coloured puma. The animal and I were only 30 metres apart, immobile yet alert, sizing one another up – or I should say the cat was sizing me up.

My mind raced, filled with images of travellers savaged by wild cats. And then, in the blink of an eye, the cat disappeared. In a nanosecond, my momentary feeling of fear changed into one of delight and wonder.

I finished setting up the hide overlooking the river, camouflaging it as much as possible with brash and returning to our truck. Once inside, Paula removed several dozen pinhead-sized ticks that had found me in the forest. These proceeded to cause me anguish during the night. It's funny how the smallest animals can produce the biggest discomfort – I had survived an encounter with a puma, only to be savaged by a bunch of tiny ticks.

The next morning some dark clouds were drifting in from the south and a refreshingly cool breeze accompanied us on our dawn walk. Above us the riverine forest leaves rattled, masking our approach so we were able to sort ourselves out in the hide without disturbing the wildlife. Once settled we slowly untied the flaps.

A little bit like sitting in a theatre as the curtain rises, we had no idea what might be revealed.

Forest surrounded us on all sides. The hide was pitched on a level piece of ground halfway down a steep, sandy riverbank. Below us ran a sluggish, turbid river about 30 yards wide, mist circling up off the water. On the opposite side a sandbank marooned by the river curved round and out of sight. On the sand lay a sleeping spectacled caiman, similar to a small crocodile.

Trees arched from either side, not quite touching over the river beneath. Bright rays from the rising sun shot through the forest momentarily turning the river, sand banks and trees the colour of a golden eagle's head.

The forest remained quiet. We sat for fifteen minutes in complete silence, waiting. Our senses told us that as we watched, we were probably also being watched. As expected, we didn't have long to wait for the action to start.

A spectral shape flew low, following the curve of the river towards us. Two oar-like beats and a glide, that's all it took for the great black hawk to come level with us. From above came raucous cries from four yellow-headed caracaras. These are best described as lazy forest falcons. They sit around and do nothing most of the day, and then swagger about looking for some other bird to mug. My least favourite of all birds. They must have arrived after we entered the hide. The birds flew straight at the hawk, one pecking its head before pulling away. The hawk was completely taken by surprise.

Pandemonium then ensued from trees on the opposite bank, an explosion of feathers. A dozen or so boat-billed herons and hoatzins erupted from the trees and flapped about in an ungainly fashion before resettling. Two more strange birds you could not imagine: the herons were medium-sized with an enormous shovel-shaped bill and a wild feathered headdress that would have made a South Sea chieftain jealous. As for the hoatzins, they were the urchins of the forest, ragged and raucous with feathers askew. They seldom fly. But they smell, oh, they smell, because they only eat tough tropical leaves, which take several days to pass through their gut, much like a cow.

The ruckus died down but the spell had been broken; gold had returned to green, and the forest was awake. An immature rufescent tiger heron appeared, gracefully walking along the sandbank as if she owned the place, a Victorian lady in a red fox stole, pearls draped around her neck. For a moment the water seethed with bubbles from electric eels and then we spotted the anaconda, immobile and coiled around a fallen tree half in the river. A bit too close to us for comfort.

Our hide can accommodate the two of us but with two tripods and big lenses there is little room to spare. We sit on small stools, talking only when necessary and then in whispers. Our movements are slow and if one of us sees something, a tug on the other's clothing is sufficient to attract attention. Eyes can easily close, however . . . a tug on the sleeve . . . but I miss a green kingfisher as it darts along the river.

I nudged Paula. 'Oriole blackbirds on the right.' I had spotted on the sand opposite a bouquet of winged sunflowers landing. The sparkling yellow and black magpie-sized birds walked across towards the murky river.

The spectacled caiman opened its eyes and watched as this flurry of colour reached the water, then shuffled a little closer and closed its eyes again, pretending not to be there.

The orioles dipped their pointed black bills and drank, the caiman reopened its eyes and shuffled closer still. Were the birds to be the caiman's lunchtime snack?

With shaking wings and dipping heads the orioles tossed water droplets into the air, shattering their golden reflections in the river. The activity made the caiman watch with interest. One more shuffle of its legs would secure a snack but in the blink of its eye the birds were gone, sunbeams drawn back into the darkness.

The midday heat was oppressive; 90 per cent humidity and temperatures in excess of 40 degrees were making us sleepy. When you are intent on focusing cameras and waiting for the right moment, it's easy to forget what else is going on at the same time.

A Colombian forest is a dangerous place. Snakes seek shade in the middle of the day and have been known to slither in with us. Large, aggressive wasps can fly through the observation holes in the canvas. Where was the puma? Was the monster anaconda on the move? These were the things we silently worried over but rarely mentioned to each other at the time. Too many good things were happening.

Hours passed. A low harsh call and flying like an arrow along the river came a streak of iridescent green and white, an Amazon kingfisher, which alighted on a branch overhanging the water not far from us.

Hearing a few heavy raindrops on the hide roof, I started to pack up and carry our equipment away, one bag at a time. On my final trip I froze in astonishment. Paula was standing motionless by her tripod, filming the anaconda as it approached her.

Giant anacondas are an apex predator, capable of devouring a wild pig by a slow, squeezing death and suffocation; children have occasionally met a similar fate. This snake was a monster, 15 metres long and as thick as a football. It slithered forward. I shouted for Paula to retreat; she held her ground for a few more seconds before backing off, leaving the camera running.

'What the heck were you doing?' I exclaimed.

'To good an opportunity to miss!' she gasped out.

The snake continued, slithering its scaly olive-green torpedo of a body between the legs of Paula's tripod. Menacingly silent, it appeared to flow over the leaves and branches, its small eyes fixed on us. Then, thankfully, the huge reptile slowly disappeared down a hole hardly big enough for a rabbit. We retrieved the camera, giving the hole a wide berth, and raced back to our truck. We hurriedly left the shelter of the trees and drove out far into the Llanos, further than we thought an anaconda would ever go, and camped on the wide open grasslands for the night. Every day the grass dried a little more, its fresh green appearance of a few weeks ago now turning to autumnal straw.

In the morning we looked out of the fly-screened window by our bed and to our delight saw Buffy probing about in the grass. By a stroke of luck we had chosen to camp overnight where the birds decided to rest for the day. Carefully opening the door, we saw another and another, eventually counting twenty-nine.

After weeks of searching, we had found our first buffies.

Buffy is a wader so has longish yellow legs and a medium-long, black, slightly curved bill. The cheeks, throat, breast and belly are a soft fawn colour with orange-tinged flanks. The fawn top of its head is speckled with flecks of black. The back feathers, its scapulars, are really distinctive, like overlapping leaves of milk chocolate with dark chocolate central streaks edged in matching fawn. Like many birds, they migrate at night and spend the day feeding and resting. The ones we watched were feeding madly, probing the ground and pulling out worms, moving on quickly and repeating the frenzy. Having flown hundreds of miles overnight for many consecutive nights, now was the time to replenish fat reserves and build themselves up for the long-haul flight over the Caribbean and the Gulf of Mexico to the Texas coast. The birds had no time to waste.

Our flock suddenly took flight and disappeared over the horizon. We circled around the area in our truck but no more were obvious.

We needed to get back and report to Carlos. Our impossible mission now seemed more likely to succeed. Buffies were around and their passage through the Llanos was underway. All we needed was more luck, to be at the right place at the right time. Locating birds the size of a can of soft drink, that only stay a day or so before flying on, in an area the size of Belgium, was never going to be easy.

Don Francisco wished us well: 'Thanks for visiting us, we see few visitors, except the birds. You're welcome back anytime; we are all sons of the savanna.' That last phrase resonated with us: it emphasised the love these people had for their land. It was to be the title of our film.

Important Bird Areas (IBAs) are special and are recognised as globally invaluable for the birdlife they hold. For an area to be designated thus it must fulfil rigorous biological criteria. The extensive moriche palm forests that support the breeding population of Orinoco geese have enabled the Chaviripa and the El Rubi *hatos* to become an Important Bird Area. The *hatos* were owned by the two Hernandez brothers, Carlos Alexis and German. They were our next destination. Whether or not we would find more buffies remained to be seen.

This particular IBA was massive and it would have taken us weeks to find our way around. Fortunately, Carlos and Yanira had visited before. This trip was a little special, though: not only were we here to find buffies but Carlos had also brought with him the completed agreement that qualified the area as an IBA.

Even to our eyes the landscape, with its mosaic of subtly different grass lengths, was more diverse than we had seen before at the previous *hatos*. There was more water: marshes, pools, sultry streams, each was surrounded by radiating bands of plants from squelchy green to spiky brittle yellow. There were no straight lines, no fences as far as our eyes could see, the skyline broken by islands of moriche palms.

It was around midday that we came across our first big flock of buffies, fifty-seven of them pressed to a tussock, huddling like leaves blown together by the wind. Carlos leant on the bonnet of the truck, binoculars to eyes, and sighed with relief. 'At last, here they are. We've come so far to find them.'

'Not as far as they have come,' I replied. 'Maybe they've found us.'

We were thrilled that so small a sighting could bring us so much joy; one page in the life story of a very small bird. The day was a particularly hot one, around 38°C, so the birds were probably conserving energy having consumed sufficient food during the morning. On the other hand, they might have been doing something quite different: perhaps communicating with each other. No doubt there were other flocks of buffies nearby, and our birds would know where they were, having flown with them in previous days. They would have shared the sort of information critical for long-distance travellers: the weather, the atmospheric conditions, the best time to depart and move on and the prime places to find food. The dangers of long journeys are extreme; pooling knowledge brings a clear advantage. We underestimate the intelligence of birds. Migration for most animals is an act of joint co-operation, not a singular bold undertaking. Maintaining kinship bonds and forming relationships beyond their immediate mate, within the larger group, is behaviour that we don't usually associate with birds, but I am sure it happens.

As the afternoon wore on, the buffies spread out. They didn't seem overly afraid of us; most northerly breeding waders aren't, as they see so few people. Slowly and slower still, I belly-crept towards the birds and then lay down flat with my camera. The buffies were now feeding constantly, probing the ground for insects, pattering on a few metres and starting again. Slowly they came closer – too close for focusing. They surrounded me, one looking at me tipping its head one way, then the other, an arm's length between us. Clearly I was no threat. I listened for something but the silence was complete. The void between us was unfathomable except for an invisible thread of thought.

The buffies' actions were determined by the need for food, the pull of cosmic forces, the wind and the weather; mine by thought and emotion, a desire for understanding. I closed my eyes, only then realising how tired I was. Like the birds around me, I had been travelling, searching, and here we were at last, together. I could feel my eyelids fluttering against my will to keep them open. I fell asleep.

Thoughts drifted like clouds: our oak woods at home, butterflies and badgers, these endless dusty roads, friends and family unseen for so long. Then I felt something on my hand. Was it a bird, or a breeze blowing across it? With an involuntary twitch, my eyes opened.

The birds, unconcerned by the madness of men, still fed all around me. A deep happy liquid of peace coursed through my body, a thread reconnecting me to nature.

Our time searching for Buffy came to an end. We were leaving the Chaviripa *hato* when a *llanero* rode in. It's common for these men to be out for weeks at a time with the cattle as they roam across the savanna. A *llanero* life is governed by the rhythms of nature. He rode barefoot, not unusual for the older men. His face was caked with dirt and as he dropped out of the saddle he laughed and spat on the ground. I swear he was chewing dust. He told us that he had seen numerous egrets heading in the direction we were taking and suggested we watch the skies for more.

Towards the late afternoon we spotted a large flock of herons flying low and to the west. We headed after them, leaving the track, and drove cross-country through tall grasses, water glistening in the distance. A little further on we stopped and walked through the shoulder-high reeds and sedge, peeling back the final curtain of leaves to reveal the lake. I sat down in the reeds to look through my binoculars.

For weeks I had noticed the disappearance of water birds as their marshes dried out. Carlos told us that the birds eventually congregate at the remaining *esteros* where there is water and food. As these too vanish, the birds move away, pushed by the seasonal heat towards the Amazon basin and the great Orinoco river, all part of the annual cycle of events in the Llanos.

I scanned the scene in front of me, the air softened by a moody haze. The lagoon was surrounded by forest, veiled in mist. This appeared as a dark mixture of greys and deep greens, indistinct layers of trees disappearing into the distance. I felt as if I was on the very edge of a massive Olympic stadium, probably a kilometre across. Within lay a sheet of seamless steel-grey water, lightly streaked with flat, grassy, emerald islands.

There were thousands of birds.

The scene was difficult to make sense of, there was so much happening. My mind conjured up whimsical thoughts that this was an annual gathering, maybe an end-of-season competition between the various families of birds, each here to impress the others with their athletic skills. Black skimmers glided close to the top of the water, their lower bill so deep it must have been touching the muddy bottom, their top bill riding the lagoon's surface. Every so often the two mandibles would snap shut on a morsel and the bird would momentarily flick upwards as if jumping a hurdle.

The large-billed terns practised the ten-metre high dive, plummeting vertically into the water to retrieve fish with their yellow, dagger-like bills.

Ibis and egrets engaged in a massed rugby scrummage for food, a confusion of grappling, pulling and pecking until one, often an egret, broke loose from the sprawling birds and ran off with its ball of goodies.

The spoonbills played a gentler game of curling, graciously sweeping under the water with their spoons as if passing fish between each other.

The South American stilts tended to keep themselves apart from the fray. As gymnasts, they moved slowly across the still mat of the water, lifting one slender leg then the other, culminating in lowering their long neck downwards to collect a titbit.

Between the various games, on the open stretches of water, the sedate rowers were lying in wait. The caimans gliding, oh, so slowly, ready for the starting gun. Officiating over it all stood the tall, serious-looking jabirus. Often they grouped together as if discussing a breach of protocol. Then one would wander through the melee and jab down suddenly, making the other birds jump.

Looking at the birds in this way, I could understand what was going on: they were all desperate to feed.

I could only hazard a guess as to the number of individuals. To help my estimations, I launched our drone and flew it high over the *estero*. My jaw dropped at what I was seeing. Seething lines of brilliant-white cattle, great and snowy egrets; grey coloured cocoi herons; scarlet ibis; roseate spoonbills; wood storks; bare-faced, green and sharp-tailed ibis; flotillas of Orinoco geese; whistling ducks; and a multitude of birds too small to identify. I could see that the stadium held in excess of 10,000 water birds. The Colombian Waterbird Olympics!

Paula nudged me, then again harder, 'Michael, Michael! What are you doing?'

'Me? I'm watching the Olympics.'

'What! Are you crazy? It's time to go.'

We returned to the truck, my mind full of the great natural spectacle. Our last day in the Llanos had been a triumph.

CHAPTER 18

JOURNEY'S END

I woke shivering several times in the narrow hospital bed, pulling up to my chin the coat that Paula had left draped over me. Next, I was pushing it off as it clung to my skin, as wet as if I'd stepped out of a sauna. Turning one way I saw pools of blood on the floor. Dragging the coat back, I closed my eyes, willing myself to sleep to escape the uncontrollable shaking and the chattering teeth. As I drifted off, I recalled a tawny bird with piercing eyes, and then my exhausted limbs were slipping, falling away. Yet the day had started so well.

Two weeks before, we had driven north from Cali following the River Cauca, which eventually led us to the far north of Colombia and the fabled Santa Marta mountains. There was the last of South America's flamingo species to find: the Caribbean or rosy flamingo. After that we had no plans. We were used to taking every day as it came now.

The shambolic system of ring roads around Medellín was complicated by heavy traffic and a lack of signs, but it was the people who were the real shock: thousands of weary families, many with young children. It was more evidence of the Venezuelan refugee problem. At traffic lights Venezuelan teenagers would entertain the stationary traffic in exchange for a little money. Often as not this was juggling balls, but occasionally more enterprising teams would race into action as soon as the traffic stopped. Sometimes a trampoline was pulled in front of the cars, with a person somersaulting high into the air. More adventurous gangs would launch a rope across the road between lamp posts, a sylph of a girl tiptoeing across as her partner rapped on car windows for a little cash, the performance not being as dangerous as collecting the money as the traffic roared off.

For us, a worry that never went away was where to safely spend the night. With our truck containing irreplaceable cameras and film equipment, we took no risks. In Argentina, Chile, Peru and Ecuador we had been happy to camp wild in the backwaters of forests and river valleys, but we'd been strictly advised against doing that in Colombia. The few campsites that existed were in tourist areas, places we avoided. If it was just our personal security that bothered us, most hotels would have sufficed. But most hotels did not have lockable secure car parking.

We discovered an exotic solution. Love motels. These motels were on the outskirts of most towns and cities, discreetly signed with suggestive names such as 'The Aphrodite' or 'Kama Sutra Suites'. Speaking through an intercom outside their secure gates you could book a room by the hour. Our booking often caused surprise: 'Oh! You want the whole night.'

It was getting dark on the outskirts of Medellín and we were desperately hunting for a place to stay. A neon sign, 'KISS MOTEL', caught our eye. Having paid by card and been issued a room number we drove around the high walls that isolated each apartment. Approaching our number, the garage shutter door opened and then closed behind us. Inside, a staircase led from the garage to a plush, immaculate apartment. We were secure, the truck safe and we had access to everything we needed in the camper. The room had the best-equipped mini-bar I had ever come across. It even boasted a huge mirror. I'll leave you to guess where it was.

After a good night's sleep, we departed the motel never having seen a receptionist, a cleaner or a manager. In fact, we never saw anyone, but of course that's the whole idea.

It was the Sierra Nevada de Santa Marta we were heading for, a small isolated triangular-shaped block of mountains at the northernmost tip of this vast continent. If the formidable Andes is the spine that supports the body of South America, then the Santa Marta mountains is the tip of its nose. Geologically, these mountains are no part of the Andes at all: they are millions of years older in origin, and this is one of the reasons why they are so important for biodiversity.

In 2013 a team of biologists, working at the prestigious French Centre for Ecology, undertook a study of our world's 173,000 nature reserves. They were keen to understand which of these was most threatened by human activities but at the same time the most important in biological richness. The team narrowed the total down to 138 sites that were 'exceptional and irreplaceable'. They were the most inspiring landscapes, containing unique and endemic wildlife, and yet the most severely threatened on our planet. These were shortlisted down to ten, with the top spot given to the Santa Marta mountains, a Pleistocene refuge of animal and plant life many times richer than the Galapagos Islands.

Unfortunately, the natural environment of the Santa Marta mountains needs to be on a life support system. If these mountains were a patient in a global hospital, they would be in a critical care ward being looked after twenty-four hours a day by the finest doctors and nurses; instead, neither the majority of people that live there nor the provincial government care sufficiently to make a real difference. The reasons are clear enough to see. Violence, drugs, corruption and poor governance have ground the inhabitants, particularly the indigenous ones, into poverty. Tourism is helping to bring some much-needed employment but this is only exacerbating encroachment of uncontrolled urban development into pristine natural habitats.

We stayed a night in the village of Minca; the mayor had been gunned down days before we arrived. Coaches were disgorging scores of backpackers for a few days' trekking before returning them to the club land of Barranquilla. We walked the deforested lower slopes, many of which were being used for the growing of coca and cannabis. To combat the illegal growing of these crops, the authorities would aerial-spray them countless times with noxious herbicides, further reducing the valuable insect life – with disastrous effects on the biodiversity.

Birds we expected to be common were absent. Higher up, extensive coffee plantations had fragmented the vast, warm, wet forests of endemic trees into pockets: only 15 per cent of the original tree cover remains. An unexpected delight was the appearance of a party of keel-billed toucans high up on a bromeliad-covered bough. Like treetop clowns with their massive bills, half banana-yellow, half jet-black, they were teasing a red howler monkey, the monkey looking on with scornful disdain.

We had heard so much about the Santa Marta mountains, we knew we had to go. The special páramo habitat found only above 3,000 metres drew us upwards. We set off up the mountain at 3 a.m., the darkness obscuring the narrowness of the track and the perilous gap between our spinning wheels and the drop into oblivion.

It was still dark when we stopped, reaching a point where amazingly there was some level ground. All about were huge round boulders and spine-chillingly deep canyons. With a strong, warm wind on our faces, the wax palms leaning, their huge latticed leaves clattering together, we carefully edged along the rocky slab towards the precipice, waiting for dawn. Wispy clouds edged upwards from the forest beneath. We weren't just standing on a rocky ledge, we were on the wing tip of a plane; I stretched out my arms like a bird.

Every day for billions of years the sun had cast dawn's rays across that land but none could have been as fantastic as that morning, our morning. One after another, the dark ridge of each sierra appeared through the diaphanous pinkish-orange haze, peaks floating beneath us like yachts becalmed on an ocean. The moments turned to minutes, whose passing flicked the switches of colour: the clouds from orange to yellow, the mountain ridges from black to purple, the trees to a dappled tapestry of greens.

As the sun woke the trees so it woke the birds. The Santa Marta brushfinch reminded us of great tits from home. Crimson-mantled woodpeckers were sporting the plumage of the Colombian flag, and blue and yellow lacrimose mountain tanagers flew between the trees accompanied by iridescent blue and green swallow tanagers. A Vivienne Westwood fashion show of outlandish, vibrantly coloured costumes flitted around us. Beneath where we stood a party of Santa Marta parakeets flew by, a species on the edge of survival as most of their nesting palms have been felled.

I should have been feeling energised, the mountain breeze brightening my senses. Instead, my legs felt wobbly, my head was hot and clammy, and tiredness was sweeping through my body. We had come so far. *Perhaps too far*, I thought. I retreated to some bushes and was violently sick. What was the matter with me?

Slowly, we walked the mountain paths; for me, one energy-sapping step after another, the forest becoming denser as we descended. Then I sensed something watching me. My fevered body urged me to forget about it: *Don't stop. Leave it. The sooner you leave the sooner you can go to bed.* It was no good, I *did* sense something.

To my right a steep wooded hillside towered above me, the trees strung with lianas. In my delirious state I thought I saw a flash of colour. Was it a bird? Upright and looking down at me was a white-tipped quetzal, scarlet-bellied and draped in a sparkling jade cloak with a long apple-green tail, one of the four sacred birds of the Americas.

Then from the silence of the forest I heard a soft call: an owl. The quetzal turned its head in the direction of the sound. The battle between my body and mind resumed: *Ignore it. Forget it. Go back.* But I knew all owls were special. This was a mantra I had grown up to believe was one of life's truths. *No, it's just another owl, you've seen plenty before. The hillside is far too steep.*

I refused to give in. This was no ordinary hillside, this was one in the Santa Marta mountains. Any owl here would be worth the effort.

So with a rucksack containing 10 kg of camera gear, I continued, as Paula returned to the truck. Peering up, the quetzal still looking down at me, I clambered bit by bit over slippery rocks. The really steep parts were only possible by pulling myself up using overhanging branches and smaller tree trunks. I slipped back nearly as much as I moved forward, falling and rolling once till a rock jarred me to a stop. Up and up – twice I heard the owl call. I had its direction and, using more energy that I felt I had, I moved forward some more till I saw the back of the bird. Then on again, circling wide and around to a position on the forested, almost vertical slope, so that I was level with it.

Wedged between sapling trees, panting and with sweat dripping down my back, I stayed for as long as I dared. The owl, a rare Santa Marta screech owl, not discovered until 2017, was unperturbed. Tawny-brown, flecked with dark streaks on its breast and white flecks on its wings, the thrush-sized bird hardly moved, except for its piercing eyes which held me fixed.

But I wanted so badly to sleep. I closed my eyes. My head started to spin and my stomach felt like it was twisting into a knot. I shuffled my legs and a sapling cracked; lurching forward, I grabbed a liana. Too late. Down I slipped and slid, over rocks, ferns and grass, then with a grunt the camera and lens cracked on my head. The pain was nothing compared to the relief that the equipment was undamaged.

I returned to the bottom of the hillside. Back in the truck, ecstatic at finding the screech owl, I fell into a feverish sleep. My dreams were vivid: my childlike self out collecting butterflies, my teenage eyes meeting those of Paula at our local reservoir seeking out black terns. I was weightless, high in the sky, looking down upon us climbing mountains, crossing deserts and struggling against a ferocious wind.

At some point in the night I woke, wet through from the tossing and turning. I struggled to get up but, like Gulliver, couldn't move. A plastic tube dripping a liquid into my hand pinned me down.

I was in hospital in Riohacha in the grip of dengue fever, a mosquito-borne viral disease.

Lying in hospital fosters a sense of introspection. I recalled my last stay in a hospital ward, in Cape Town. I had come a long way since then. More than once I thought how charmed we had been to avoid accidents and illness during our travels. At the outset of our journey I had been anxious, unsure if I was really capable of the undertaking. Up to now, Paula's bad back in El Chaltén and then a thorn through my foot in Formosa had been two of our minor emergencies. There had also been the time on the border of Argentina and Bolivia when we had thought Paula was having heart problems. It had necessitated a hectic night-time race over the mountains to a hospital in Abra Pampa. The supposed heart attack had turned out to be heartburn. That's what the doctor told us, although conversation had been difficult as his consulting room had a wide-screen television loudly showing international motor racing, which he had been closely following.

Considering the years of travelling and the wild places we had been living in, we had been more than just lucky.

A couple of days later I left hospital, still exhausted. In truth we were both weary from journeying for so long. The temperature didn't help either, hovering around 40 degrees, day and night. Nagging at the back of our minds was a realisation that as the Caribbean Ocean neared, so our road north was ending. Where to next? We found out that we couldn't travel east: Venezuela had just closed its borders to foreigners. We couldn't travel north into Panama, as the Darien Gap jungles prevented that. We considered turning around to retrace our route south, renewing acquaintances, watching condors soar, visiting places we had been unable to reach. After all, that was the life of so many birds: ever travelling.

Paula leaned towards me, a little agitated. 'We need to stop, rest up for a few days.' So, attracted by a road sign with a flamingo on it, we rented a cabin, the size and condition of an allotment shed, for a few days. Flamingos were distinctly absent but we read, slept and drank ice-cold Pepsi. I had found in the past that doing nothing, similar to walking in woodland, was a good remedy for a sick mind.

The finger of land at the top of Colombia, the Guajira peninsula, curves towards the western part of Venezuela. From its tip, the rocky finger points to the tourist islands of Aruba, Bonaire and Curaçao. Their powdery white beaches caressed by pristine seas lure people from around the world to float in the warmth and watch dolly mixture fish pass beneath them. Super-yachts, a playground for the rich, move their swimming pools across the sea. Turning from the sea and looking inland to the peninsula, a very different reality exists.

Our first indication that something was not as we expected occurred when we arrived at a tiny village, a cluster of shacks on a beach. Boats were being hauled out of the water – above them hovered magnificent frigate birds, which dropped down into the surf to pick up scraps from the fishermen's catch. On first glance it was a pleasant sight, very Caribbean: boats, birds and a blue sea, perfect for the front cover of a travel magazine. One boat was already high on the beach and a man and two children were removing the fish and carrying them by their gills to some women who sat on the sand, cleaning them. A closer inspection revealed all were in ancient clothes – more holes and patches than fabric. Men's and boys' shorts were held up with string; one young girl had a coffee bean sack for a skirt. For such smelly tasks, old clothes might be expected, but their demeanour told us more. Matted, tangled hair hung over shadowed faces, eyes dark, expressions gaunt, lips deeply chapped, the occasional ugly ulcer on a leg or arm. Their movements were resigned and laboured, none of them so much as glancing at us.

According to UNICEF, the people of the desert lands of Guajira, the indigenous Wayuu, are among the poorest in Latin America, second only to the inhabitants of Haiti.

The Wayuu villages were small, the houses made of handmade mud bricks. No roads led to them, just sandy tracks through cacti and thorny bushes. There was no sanitation and no drinking water readily available. Every day we watched as women and children wheeled carts and barrows to a nearby pond to collect their water, the liquid as brown as a robin's back.

Seldom did we see boys and men in the villages, perhaps not surprising as it is the Wayuu women who control the organisation of their community. Wayuu society is matrilineal, with children taking their mother's last name, not their father's. The wife's role in the family is senior to that of her husband; she is the one who commands respect and is responsible for the education of her children. Wondering why the women all wore scarlet, we approached one who sat in the shade of a tree. She was older than the others, swathed top to toe in thin red material, only her round face visible. Ochre colouring outlined a spiral on each cheek, down the bridge of her nose, and lines radiated downwards from her serious-looking mouth. Tentatively, we sat down by this formidable-looking person as Paula asked, 'Why are you all in red? Why is red so important?'

'Blood,' she answered, and looked Paula directly in the eye, then smiled. 'When a girl first becomes a women she can wear red, not before. Red brings the village good fortune, the red bird brings us luck.'

Interested, I asked, 'What bird? What luck?'

The woman looked around, pointing to some trees: 'Nature is everything, the good and the bad.'

I got out my field guide and moved closer, handing the book to the woman, hoping that she would find the bird she was talking about. Eventually, after much flicking through the pages, she showed us the bird. It was one we had seen several days before, a vermilion cardinal. A bird endemic to that narrow desert peninsula and nearby Venezuela, the male of this bird is the brightest red imaginable, a bird on fire, with a crest of flaming feathers. It seemed that vermilion cardinals were known to seek shelter in the village in the days leading up to severe storms and hurricanes: with the arrival of the birds, the people would pull their boats high out of the water, huts and belongings were tied down, and children kept indoors.

'The bird is sacred,' the woman said. 'They bring us luck and choose our husbands.' And with that she giggled and laughed out loud.

'They choose your husbands?'

'Yes. Come tomorrow. There's to be a ceremony.'

The next day, we were ushered into the village, a collection of whitewashed mud huts with corrugated roofs, colourful washing hanging on bushes like ceremonial flags. I sat cross-legged in the sand, Paula stood close by, filming.

Six barefoot women casually emerged from a hut, chatting quietly as they approached us. Each woman wore a voluminous scarlet dress with a large hood to cover her head, spirals of ochre paint decorating her cheeks. The women slowly circled together, a drum beating out their steps. From another hut a young man wearing a bright red loincloth appeared and moved into the circle.

Paula caught my eye and nodded a little way away, telling me to look. Two young girls in blue dresses were crouching behind a tree watching, eyes wide.

The drum beats increased in volume and rhythm, the dancers' bare feet sending sand into the air. All but one of the women moved away. The man, head bowed, offered the lone woman an imaginary morsel of food from an outstretched hand; they both circled around each other, the man continuing to offer food, the woman pecking at his hand, mimicking the blood-red bird. The women returned. They circled faster, opening their arms, hands joining, the fiery red material coalescing into a swirling inferno surrounding the man, who now fell to the ground. We could feel the ground vibrating. The women shrieked.

The man had passed the test. The blood-red bird had decided he was fit to be a husband.

As the woman had told us the previous day, nature was all they had. So the Wayuu villagers had made the vermilion cardinal, through their 'Blood-Red Dance', central to their lives, affirming their menfolk, and keeping everyone safe from natural disaster. The latter belief had no doubt saved more lives for the community than their government had ever done.

There was another red bird for us to find, the Caribbean flamingo, called by some the rosy flamingo as it's the most colourful of the six species. True to its name, this bird is found around the Caribbean Sea and its many islands, although more recently it has spread to Florida in the United States.

In previous years our search for flamingos had taken us into the remotest of landscapes. We'd endured freezing nights on plains echoing with cracking ice, we'd tiptoed across caustic salinas and squelched through marsh-fringed lakes. Now we were on the Caribbean coast, a place with a reputation for sun-kissed sandy coves, parasols and bars, languid swimming pools, and palm trees wafting in the breeze.

We found none of these, though to be truthful we weren't looking for them.

Our travels did not revolve around cocktail bars, though if we could have filmed our elusive birds while drinking a cold beer, we wouldn't have minded. In retrospect, finding a bar might have been a sensible decision, for this last search was going to be far from tranquil, taking us into unexpectedly hostile lands and near disaster.

After many days of searching we hadn't located any of the birds and were advised to take a guide, who would hopefully show us where they might be found. A local guide, Fernando, was suggested as we would be traversing unpaved marshy coastlands, venturing through indigenous land and villages seldom visited by outsiders.

Arriving in Fernando's village, we watched him as he came out of a small house and started to jog towards our distinctive truck. We had cleared a space in the back seat for him and Paula started to chat. He pointed out the direction for us to take and we soon found ourselves weaving between sand dunes, through shallow lagoons and over saltmarsh. It quickly became apparent that he was overly fascinated by the car. Bemused by the array of dials and knobs, he was asking Paula what each did.

It was shortly before we ran into a problem that I realised Fernando had never been in a motor vehicle before. He was used to getting about on his bicycle, not a three-tonne truck. We were unnervingly close to the sea, skirting between marshy pools.

'Which way now?' I asked Paula. To be charitable, I think that there was confusion between two very similar Spanish words: *derecho* which means 'straight on' and *derecha* meaning 'turn right'. The result was that within seconds we were going through wet sand on the very edge of the sea. I hesitated – a fatal error.

We were stuck, wheels spinning, churning up sand and spray. Frantically, I jumped out of the car, hoping it was not as bad as I thought, only to find water over my ankles. The rear of the vehicle tilting backwards – we were sinking. By the time Paula jumped out, the water was almost at the top of the rear wheels.

'Quick! Get everything out. Save as much as we can!' I shouted. Fernando looked distraught and had no idea what to do. He just stood and watched.

Then, blessedly, some small children appeared. I called them over, miming with hand movements that they were to carry some stuff. Opening the back doors I handed out boxes of clothes and camera equipment. Together we all ran through the water to a nearby sand dune and left it on top. The children took tripods, bags of food, computers, more boxes, sleeping bags and ferried them to the same spot. I didn't check to see if any were running off with our possessions; I trusted them. Paula was busy with her camera, filming what was going on, recording the disaster for the insurance company.

I was desperate to unlock the safe. It was behind the driver's seat, set in the floor. With water up to my knees, I thrust the key into the lock. The key wouldn't turn. I gritted my teeth and told myself to slow down. The key turned. I grabbed all our money, credit cards, passports and vehicle import permits, stuffing them safely in a bag, nothing except us was more important than these.

Sea water was now seeping into the back of the truck. After 100,000 kilometres and four years of travelling, it was tragic to see how it was all going to end – the truck swept out to sea. Surprisingly, we were calm; panicking was no use. We accepted our grim fate.

I heard the *put put put* of a motorbike, which arrived from nowhere. Paula ran over to the driver. He was a local warden for the area and had a mobile phone with which he said he would summon help.

I looked back at the unfolding drama. The truck was now tipping at an alarming angle and the incoming tide was washing inside. I grabbed a pile of heavy-duty bags, ones we had brought out with us years before and hardly used. I had a shovel and we started to shovel the bags full of sand, and the children tried to make a dam to stop the worst of the advancing tide hitting the front of our vehicle and so flush out more sand from around the wheels. It was a vain endeavour but at least it made me feel better.

And then, to our heartfelt relief, a massive Ram truck turned up and we were able to attach our substantial tow rope to it. Our truck submerging by the minute, I didn't dare open the door, as I wouldn't get it closed again, so I crawled through the driver's window, which had been left open. As I did so, the sun visor fell open and the condor's feather dropped down. Without thinking, I kissed it then laid the long brown scimitar on the passenger seat, put the car into neutral and released the brake.

The Ram driver signalled he was about to move. Nothing happened at first: wheels spun and sea water rocketed backwards. The Ram driver signalled again. I started the engine, pushed it into drive and with wheels whining and several sudden jerks, our truck edged free.

The Ram driver roared onto an area of hard stones, Paula and the children waved their hands and clapped. We were safe. I couldn't believe what had happened

We paid our saviour the equivalent of £30, the best value ever, and gave him our remaining supplies of beer. The children helped us reload all our belongings, a great day's fun for them as they fooled around. I loved them all – we had lost nothing, and gave them all our remaining loose change and biscuits. They ran off the way they had come, laughing and splashing along the shoreline.

Paula and I looked at each other.

'Do we carry on or turn back?'

'Onwards!' Paula cried. 'We've not come this far to turn back!'

Fernando apologised and looked downcast, but I knew it had been my fault – I had been the driver, after all. We just smiled and offered him some sweets: we all needed a sugar rush. Off along the shoreline we continued, turning inland a little and, reassuringly, onto a gravel track.

In a bushy area, just after a bend, two women manned a heavy chain barricading the road. 'Don't worry,' said our guide. 'They want payment to pass. They'll be happy with food. It's better than money out here.'

I laughed. 'No problem. An hour ago I didn't think we'd have anything.'

Paula rummaged through our bags of recently purchased

groceries. These were very poor people and it was likely their children that had helped us earlier. The women held out their hands after dropping the chain onto the sandy track and we passed them cereals, rice and sugar.

There were three more of these grocery hold-ups before the end of the day. We raided our camper cupboards for tins of vegetables, packets of rice and flour, boxes of oats, even packets of crisps.

Beyond the barricade we came to some salinas. Three men in T-shirts and shorts were standing up to their knees in the evaporation lagoons, shovelling the salt into sparkling pyramids. And then, in another larger lagoon behind, we saw a medley of slow-motion crimson Caribbean flamingos.

With thin stately legs, a body of feathers like a shoal of jumping salmon in the breeze, and their impossibly curvy necks dipping into the water, the flamingos moved as graceful as ballerinas, refreshing our tired eyes.

'We've made it,' I said to Paula. 'We've saved the best till last.' We sat in the afternoon sun and watched. This was the soul-nourishing Caribbean we had imagined for so long, a mirage that had drawn us so far.

'On the 7th of May 1832, while sailing from Indian Key, one of the numerous islets that skirt the south-eastern coast of the Peninsula of Florida, I for the first time saw a flock of pink Flamingos.'

So wrote John James Audubon, who had set forth in 1820 to travel through North America to paint its birds. Over the next 20 years he painted 495 species and of these paintings, none is more celebrated than that of the Caribbean flamingo. The painting showed people across North America and Europe for the first time the majesty and grace of a crimson bird with unbelievably long slender legs, a bird with an upside-down bill.

In 2018 a copy of his book was sold for $13.6 million, one of the highest prices ever paid for a book. The page that the book was open at during the auction was of the Caribbean flamingo at Indian Key.

Two children from nearby shacks ran towards us, their pockets jingling with the coins we had given them earlier.

'*Venga, venga,*' they beckoned. One took Paula's hand, tugging her to her feet and leading us up and over sand dunes towards the sea.

Dusk was approaching, the sea calm, and there in serried ranks along the shoreline thousands of waders fed madly, the breeze carrying to us their indistinct chattering.

'They're talking to us,' Paula said.

Approaching slowly, we reached the water's lapping edge. The birds were moving closer all the time, oblivious to our presence – some were now feeding right around our feet. There were greater yellowlegs with their high-pitched three- or four-note trill; lesser yellowlegs with their single sharp lower notes; and a hundred or so Wilson's phalaropes in full breeding plumage, growling like old men at a bar, low, almost duck-like. We now understood the birds as we would friends.

'They know we're here,' Paula continued.

These birds were on the cusp of returning to their breeding grounds in the far north, migrant shorebirds waiting for the right time to cross the Caribbean, heading for the United States and Canada. Navigating at night, they would skim the frothy wave tops during storms or rise 3,000 metres high, taking advantage of the trade winds.

As the sun's fiery sphere sunk into the sea we stood surrounded by the birds. Travelling the Andes, birds of every size and colour had followed us. Now we were in their company again.

I pulled out my red notebook and there pressed between the

pages was the feather, deep red and gently fading to pale salmon, like the evening sky. Nearly five years before, we had been given it, in a railway station of all places. I held open the book; the feather floated out from the pages holding my memories. Carried on the wind, it drifted a short way and was lost among the hectic birds.

Then, as if a hunting peregrine falcon had swept across the sky, the entire flock of birds went silent and with a thunder of wings took off. Circling around, gaining height over the beach, over our heads, the birds taking final bearings before heading across the sea. With them may have been our feather, trying to rediscover a previous life.

With slimy green seaweed and wet sand wrapped tightly round the shafts and cylinders, the sills and frames under the truck, we needed to get the Toyota pressure cleaned quickly. Leaving the hot breezy wasteland of Guajira we drove into the even hotter and much more humid city of Cartagena.

Nothing had prepared us for the startling change of scene. It's a city within a city. On one side mangroves have been replaced by marinas, around which, emerging like Neptune's tridents from the sea, are towering, sleek steel and glass apartment blocks. On the other side, behind massive stone fortifications, the old town, holding a dark history, once being the Caribbean's market place in misery: slavery. Cartagena has a superb natural harbour able in times past to hold a hundred Spanish galleons, and so it became a strategic naval port for controlling the Caribbean seas.

We walked the ramparts of the well-preserved walls overlooking the sea until we had to seek the shade of the narrow streets where red pantile-roofed three-storey houses crowded in on us. Most upper-floor windows had decoratively carved wooden balconies painted in vivid pink, white, blue or green. Skilfully contrived murals caught the eye on corners and in tiny courtyard squares. Street vendors pushed wooden carts of ready-to-eat yellow pineapples and scarlet watermelons, local women sported bright sun hats and colourful dresses. Mature jacaranda and mimosa trees cascaded yellow or purple flowers on to the pavements. These cheerful colours were reflected in the people. There were more smiles on faces in Cartagena than we'd seen in weeks.

We were intrigued that many of the ancient house doors boasted large, sturdy, elaborate metal door locks and knockers in the shape of lion's heads, lizards, fish and mermaids. Asking a passerby if these locks were significant he replied they were. 'Lion's heads for military men, lizards for the legal trade, fish for merchants. Each class had its own,' he answered.

'And mermaids and monsters?'

He shrugged. 'Perhaps the monsters were for the slavers.'

The midday heat finally caught up with us as perspiration rolled down our necks, soaking our T-shirts. We found a smart, quiet café; cool as a cave, with white damask tablecloths and bentwood chairs with cushioned seats – luxury for us. A waiter dressed in a white apron passed us a drinks menu with a choice of ten roast coffees including an organic one – we could have been in Paris.

Waiting for our order to arrive, we wandered around looking at the photos on the walls, of the 1920s city with horsedrawn carriages and uniformed soldiers, cutters in the harbour, fish on the quays.

We sat with the coffee in front of us together with a small glass of cold water and a slice of chocolate cake.

Paula sighed appreciatively. 'Maybe it's the coffee of dreams.'

We mused a little, taking occasional looks at each other, sipping our coffee quietly. Had we really travelled all the way from Tierra del Fuego to here on the Caribbean coast?

As far as is known, the original people of Tierra del Fuego were the tall and strong Yangan. When the first European naval expeditions searched the storm-tossed, freezing waters for that elusive passage to the Orient, their sailors crouching wet and exhausted on deck, what they recorded seeing were spirals of smoke from a multitude of warming fires on the shoreline. It was the barefooted natives, the Yangan, tending the fires, apparently only dressed lightly in animal skins – the sailors couldn't see that their skin was thickly coated in solidified whale and seal fat. The tales that seafarers took back to Europe were of superhuman giant savages, whose home they called the 'Land of Fire' – Tierra del Fuego. The Yangan culture and language disappeared only a few years ago. Early work by anthropologists recorded as much as they could of their strange and original language. One of the words they deciphered is unique: no other single word in any language conveys the same meaning, concept or situation. It is *mamihlapinatapai*. It can best be interpreted as a shared look or glance between two people, each one wishing that the other would initiate a subject they both desire to talk about but which neither can bring themselves to start.

Many overlanders do the 10,000-kilometre trip up South America in four months. It had taken Paula and me over four years and 100,000 kilometres. Living so long in less space than an astronaut had brought out every stress and strain. And it was birds that had brought us together each day. Our love for birds had brought us together as teenagers, and kept us together ever since. This love had enabled us to transition into a new life and had forged the strength to make this odyssey to celebrate the wonder of South America's birds.

We had always been able to talk to each other about everything, yet there in the Cartagena café we were unable to mention the one thing that we both wanted to. We sat in a state of *mamihlapinatapai* absorbed in our own thoughts.

A distracted and wandering mind fosters negative self-talk. Had we stayed too long? I wondered. What had we missed? Could we have done more?

'Well,' Paula said, always the optimist. 'Hasn't it been incredible?'

'Beyond anything I thought possible,' I replied.

During our wild travels, we had laughed till we'd nearly died with strangers, late into the night. Some had taken us into their homes, fed us, done our washing and encouraged us. Some had given us their houses to stay in; others had nursed us back from illness. Nature, birds and people had been our common ground; one led us to the other.

'We've been away a long time.'

'Well . . . hurrying nature never got us anywhere.'

We knew that nature thrives on time, as had our slow travels.

We'd been ready to discard our red notebook with its plans, turn around and retrace steps already taken. We had listened to what people had said and, following Guillermo's advice, had trusted them. Birds had shaped our journey; we even carried their totems. We had been led by nature, days spent travelling with a light touch on the land, nights camping under its galaxies of diamonds.

For all these years we had travelled the length of the greatest mountain chain on Earth, from tumultuous icy Antarctic waters and up beyond the equator to the Caribbean. We had endured dust storms, thundering gales, icy mountain tops and skin-searing heat. We'd been pushed into a cage of pumas and shared a shower with a spider the size of a tennis ball. But now we couldn't say the one thing that needed saying to each other. We'd never planned an end point. We had no finishing line to cross.

We couldn't imagine it ending, and the thought had never occurred to us, till now.

'We've done more than we ever imagined.'

'You've repaid your debt.'

'We've done our best for the birds.'

'And for each other.'

'I feel at peace.'

'So?'

'So?'

'I'm tired.'

'Me, too.'

'And missing family and friends.'

'And English beer and cheese.'

We both laughed. Then cried. Then walked back to our beloved truck and the scimitar-like feather waiting for us.

EPILOGUE

In its own distinct way, coming home is just another part of travelling. The wooden gate, creaking from lack of use, swung open as we pushed it. Walking through, we left our bags and hand luggage in a heap among the frosty leaves and simply looked around. Between the oaks and cherries of Valentine's Wood our home stood comfortably as we had left it, waiting for us like a favourite coat. Although longing to get inside, we took things slowly, kicking aside golden leaves between the trees. Snowdrops bright and fresh, with drooping white-capped heads, clustered in groups. A young muntjac deer, unused to being disturbed, barked like a terrier and jumped away only to stop after a moment and look back, surprised at our appearance. Smiling at being greeted by fawn and flower, we walked up the winding path.

Lifting the stone to uncover the key, Paula's mobile pinged, an incoming message from Hernan.

She read it out: 'Annual count of hooded grebes this year shows a small increase in numbers.'

This was great news. So, with memories of grebes pirouetting across a windblown lagoon, we stepped into our kitchen. Home at last.

Our house, called 'The Roost', for that's what it had always been, was as isolated as anywhere can be in the English Midlands, tucked away on the edge of a wood overlooking the Ulverscroft valley in the Charnwood Forest. Paula and I had never lived anywhere else, having built much of it ourselves. The window sills and furniture were from a great yew that had been felled thirty years before in my parents' garden in the next valley. Those first weeks were idyllic, like being on holiday in a place we hardly recognised as ours. Hot showers, spicy foods, Stilton cheese, pork pies and a village pub with draught beer – all things we had missed. Having become used to living a simple life, however, there were times we found ourselves perplexed by the luxury in which we now lived. Everything seemed so spacious – a king-size bed, a huge fridge. We would go into the kitchen, open a cupboard to get a plate and be met with a confusing assortment of choices.

'Why have we got three dinner services?' I asked Paula.

Despite our charity-shop drive on our return some years before, rooms still had cupboards with rarely worn clothes, unused knick-knacks, old DVDs and forgotten games, as well as leftovers from other people's lives.

'Why have we got ten books on British butterflies?' Paula asked me. This was all stuff that we thought had been necessary to our life before we left.

In my mind we had been away for what seemed a lifetime. We had met so many people and had so many experiences. Visions of what we had seen and done filled my head to overflowing and we wanted to tell everyone about them. But people have busy lives of their own to live and we were happy listening about theirs. Time goes so quickly, it seemed to many we'd hardly been gone as long as we had.

A small sign to ourselves that something was very different to how it used to be was the way we spent each day, always having to be outside, in the fresh air, the sky above us, the wind in our hair. Being inside day and night seemed weird, and we threw open the windows. The weather encouraged us – never before have I known a February so perpetually blue and sunny; nature was being kind to us.

What mattered most was remaining immersed in nature, watching woodpeckers and chaffinches, listening to blackbirds and thrushes, renewing acquaintances with these old friends. And, as if by magic, one day a stoat appeared. With a sinuous run the animal would dart about the trees, weaving itself through the crevices and hollows of the stone walls, sniffing after mice and field voles and catching them. *All the years we've lived here*, I thought. *We've hardly ever seen a stoat, and now we're seeing one daily.* Our senses were finely attuned to nature, noticing the minutiae of life; life that had always been there but never seen. Nature was now the drug that infused my body.

We rediscovered the lost skill of watching television – we had to. We didn't want to hide from the world, though there were reasons for doing so. The news about other people's lives was infiltrating our senses in a new and innocuous way. Brexit had been and gone and we'd hardly heard a whisper about it. A thousand world events had passed us by. It dismayed me to be accosted daily with the stream of only bad news: wildfires in California, people dying in Wuhan. As if to counter this, our meal times stretched for an hour or more as we chatted about the things we'd experienced. 'Do you remember the ocelot?' 'And the toucans, for goodness' sake.' These masked the news we tried to put to the back of our minds, painful news we didn't want to hear.

One day, while Paula was in bed enjoying her early morning tea, there came another ping from her phone. It was from Carlos in Colombia saying that the film she had sent him, *Sons of the Savannah*, had been shown to a symposium of Central American farmers and he was delighted with their response to the film. 'Can you use your photographs to put together a bird identification video for us to train national park wardens?' he asked. Doing this meant we had plenty to occupy us, daily reliving our South American dream-life-come-true.

Friends are like dandelion seeds: they need catching and cherishing before they float away. After being away for so long, we caught up with as many as we could, and made plans to visit Richard in Canada as soon as possible. We couldn't wait for that time to come and wanted to experience the spring bird migration in Canada at the same time.

Guillermo would have told us not to plan too far ahead – we should have learnt that lesson by now.

The news we had been dreading came to pass, and weeks after returning home we found ourselves 'locked down' due to the Covid-19 pandemic. Being as free as birds for years, roaming forests and mountains, we now found ourselves as caged birds, unable to mix with the family and friends we'd returned to see, unable to leave the close vicinity of where we lived.

To start with, we didn't think it would affect us that much. We even relished the enforced time at home, feeling immensely fortunate to live in an oasis of nature. Some of our acquaintances were not so lucky. Some of my friends I never saw again. My flute teacher was one, a jovial man who grew up entertaining children with his puppet shows on Scarborough Pier, gone well before his time.

Every night we watched the compulsive but dreaded news. Week by week, Covid accelerating, no one knowing how or when it would end, and still the death toll was rising. Every day the news reported the grim tally of deaths. One evening, when the daily death toll reached 400, I gasped. Surely it couldn't get any worse? It did.

Every week we spoke to friends and family. 'Are you OK?' 'How are you coping?' We managed to catch some dandelion seeds – Zoom calls polishing old friendships to a glow. Every month I fretted at not being able to see Richard.

Friends we spoke to felt trapped by pervasive, news-driven fear and were unwilling or unable to step outside, especially when outside meant facing more brick walls and concrete. They told us they were stressed from months of being isolated from their walks in fields and woods.

I completely understood. I'd learnt the hard way how important nature is to a meaningful, balanced life. People need natural spaces to clear their minds, refresh their spirits, and ground themselves; to find peace in a stressful world.

Paula and I made a series of short films for the local Wildlife Trust on the wildlife in our valley. We hoped this would cheer people up, even alleviate some of the mental anguish of those unable to get out. The weather remained unbelievable: every day sunny, birdsong as never before. I don't ever remember a more glorious spring. Whereas the world of humans had quietened down to that of a medieval soundtrack, the natural world was saying, 'Look out of your window! I'm still here, vibrant and healthy, trust in me and everything will turn out OK!' We need to learn to repay that trust.

Seven years ago it had been nature that I sought to bring back my sanity, as it had done before. During a new life travelling wild through South America, we had immersed ourselves in nature so completely that now we really did feel a part of it. As Claudio, a man who devoted his life to caring for condors, said: 'All nature is to be loved. That means love yourself as well as others, for we are all part of nature, all part of the same world.'

If our journey had taught us anything it was this: love and trust yourself; nature is there for you.

How often are we there for nature?

ACKNOWLEDGEMENTS

Firstly to a 'fairy godmother', Wanda Whiteley, who was instrumental in getting this condor to fly.

The success of our travels in South America was due to all the help we received from the many generous people we met there, as well as the support from family and friends back home.

From Canada, our son Richard and his wife Francina gave us continual encouragement.

Looking after our domestic affairs and freeing us to leave our home was a great team comprising friends, family and neighbours led by Paula's brother, Neil.

For advice on overlanding we were indebted to Peter and Eileen Crichton.

In South America the kindness and warm-hearted generosity from strangers was overwhelming. Many of these acts are mentioned in the book and thanks are due to all the people involved. There are many more people that do not appear in the book to whom thanks must be given.

Cris and Sebastian Torlasco at Andean Roads provided a refuge for us and our truck in Buenos Aires. Santiago D'Alessio welcomed us into the offices of Aves Argentinas, as did all the staff. The committee of the South American BirdFair encouraged us to attend their events where we made so many useful contacts. In Buenos Aires, Silvia Vitale and Carlos Ferrari introduced us to the birds while Irma and Francisco Erize were gracious hosts. We joined Claudio Rodriguez and his delightful family on a boat trip to find seabirds at Mar del Plata. Rosemary Scoffield regularly provided pots of tea and a much-needed washing machine. Alejandro Russo performed miracles on Paula's bad back and the meals with his family were a joy. Graphic designer Agustin Actis helped to give some of our films a more professional look. Jorge Frias was a guy who was worth his weight in gold: his intimate knowledge of Toyota trucks was a lifesaver. Jorge and his wife, Valeria, were generous hosts and even gave us use of their house in Tafi del Valle, enabling us to finally track down the rare Tucumán mountain finch.

In Ibera, Alejandra and Cepi Boloqui were exceptional people who went out of their way to help us and it was a privilege to visit Miranda Collett's Reserve at Don Luis. Julian Baigorria from Iguazu showed us the special birds of the Atlantic rain forest and with Andres Bosso we visited the magical Iguazu Falls. Andy Elias shared his encyclopaedic knowledge of the natural history of Mendoza and was a great host. We enjoyed the company of wildlife photographer Anibal Parera. We learnt about sheep ranching from Sonia and Carlos Amores in Patagonia.

Flavio Moschione allowed us to join him on a bird census of Los Pozuelos Biosphere Reserve. Pedro Chiesa was a good friend on the hooded grebe project and found us a tango show to film in Buenos Aires.

At Mar Chiquita, Lucila Castro was the star of our film and keen birder Miguel Ansenuza provided a warm welcome while our truck was in for repair. Enrique Chumbita showed us how to make *empanadas*. A messy process!

In Chile, Ismael Horta, Fernanda Soffia and Marta Mora, otherwise known as the Frog Squad, showed us – yes! – frogs, and we joined Margarita Ruiz looking for lizards while Cristian Saucedo introduced us to the wonderful Patagonia national park and the work of the Conservation Land Trust. In the far south we visited Ricardo Matus and his project to breed the rare ruddy-headed goose.

During a brief foray into Brazil, Edson Moroni helped us make a film about red and green macaws.

ACKNOWLEDGEMENTS

In the Amazon the warm and friendly Percy Avendano gave us invaluable assistance based on his wide knowledge of the area and its wildlife. In Lima, Alberto Sacio gave us far too many pisco sours.

We met Juan Antonio Ocampo at the South American BirdFair in Colombia. He introduced us to the culture of Colombia as well as its special birds. Lee Calvert provided a luxurious safe haven full of hummingbirds for us in Cali, while Marlyn Zuluaga managed to find a salsa show for us to film.

Essential to the trip was the input from Paula's Spanish teachers, Vanesa Arganaraz and Maria Burgos.

And, of course, thanks are due to the team at September Publishing, whose invaluable expertise has helped to bring my book to you.

¡Muchisimas gracias a todos!

FILMS

I would love you to watch some of the films we made during our travels. They are all on our YouTube channel called The Condor's Feather: https://www.youtube.com/c/Livingwildpics or simply search on Google for 'YouTube channel The Condor's Feather'.

I am usually in front of the camera whereas Paula is director of photography, and also edits the films. The films feature places rarely visited and birds seldom seen.

Part One: A New Life
Life on the Road
Come with us and see what it's like travelling wild in South America.
Travelling Wild in South America
An introduction to some of the wildlife we encountered.

Part Two: Patagonia
Hudson's Patagonian Parrots
Our story of finding the burrowing parrots of Patagonia.
Viva Valdes
Paula speaks to visitors and park wardens to find out why the Valdés peninsula is so special.
Torres del Paine
A brief video of the stunning scenery.
Birds of Patagonia
A sequence of still photos showing the birds of Patagonia.

The Andes
Breathtaking scenery shown in a montage of still photos.

Torres del Paine
A selection of photos from Torres del Paine and the midsummer walk at El Chaltén.

Tango in the Wind
The story of the hooded grebe, the challenges it faces and the team that is trying to save it. Relax with a glass of Argentian Malbec and enjoy this 30-minute film.

Tango Patagonia
Immerse yourself in the tango danced by the hooded grebe.

The Hooded Grebe – Dance Like Nobody's Watching
The meme of the courtship footage that went viral with 50 million views.

Dance-off – Hooded Grebe Style
A visual treat – a selection of photographs of this stunning bird made for a special Valentine's Day event at the Canadian Museum of Nature.

A Conservation Success
A brief look at the Darwin's rhea breeding project.

Baker River
Chile's most famous river.

Carretera Austral
Chile's ultimate road trip.

Bosquepiedra
We travel to the mysterious island of Chiloé for a close look at the nature reserve of Bosquepiedra.

Ratites
The bird family of ratites are found throughout the southern hemisphere. Why are they so special?

Part Three: Condor Country
Mar Chiquita, a Haven for Argentina's Flamingos
An infographic on the three species of flamingos found here.

Mar Chiquita, its Shorebirds
An infographic showing the importance of this site for migration.
Mar Chiquita, What Makes This Place so Special?
The short film that opened the 2018 British Bird Watching Fair highlighting the importance of Argentina's newest national park.
Mar Chiquita, a Place Called Home
An in-depth look at Mar Chiquita.
South American Painted Snipe
One of Mar Chiquita's more elusive birds.
Condor Liberation
A brief glimpse of a condor liberation ceremony.
School
Going to school in El Descanso, Formosa.
The Yellow Anaconda
We take a canoe in search of the yellow anaconda.
Journey into a Flooded Forest
A montage of photographs from the Bañado La Estrella.

Part Four: Land of the Inca
Laguna Pujsa
In the Chilean Andes, Paula finds puna flamingos on a high-altitude lake.
The Rock
Just off the Pacific coast of Chile is a tiny rock full of life. Metres from the driest desert on Earth, birds like pelicans, cormorants and boobies abound.
Cactus
Life in the desert.
The Man who Paints Hummingbirds
Artist Miles McMullan tells of his fascination with hummingbirds.
The Importance of Hummingbirds
Juan Antonio tells us why hummingbirds are so important to him.
Los Amigos
Conservación Amazónica run a biological research centre in the heart of Amazonia. We find out why it is a hotspot for wildlife.

Rhino or Beetle?
A rhinoceros beetle wakes up.
High Hummers
How can wildlife survive at altitudes of over 4,000 metres? Come with us to the highest mountains of South America to find out.

Part Five: Colombia
Salsa
Can hummingbirds dance the salsa?
Working Together
When biologists from Calidris venture into the field they need the help of local people.
Coffee of Dreams
Andres and Paola show us how they make their delicious coffee in a sustainable manner.
Bird Guide Workshop
The NGO Calidris encourages local people to make a living through bird tourism.
Take the Tanager Test
So! How good is your knowledge of tanagers?
Sons of the Savanna
The cowboys of Los Llanos play a pivotal role in the conservation of a rare bird.
A New IBA
Juan Carlos from Los Llanos tells us about the extraordinary responsibility he faces in protecting Colombia's newest Important Bird Area.
Watching and Waiting
What we do best. Patience is a virtue.
Disaster Movie
Disaster strikes!
Shorebirds of the Caribbean Coast
A film we made for Carlos Ruiz to help nature reserve personnel identify shorebirds.

The Blood Red Dance
The vermilion cardinal is intimately connected to the Wayuu people of northern Colombia.

Epilogue
The three films we made for the Leicestershire and Rutland Wildlife Trust on returning home and finding ourselves 'locked down'.
Lea Meadows
Rocky Plantation
Ulverscroft Nature Reserve in May

South America – Our Top Ten Birds
We had a lot of fun narrowing our choice down to ten. We made this film for the 2020 British Bird Watching Fair.

ABOUT THE AUTHOR

Michael Webster is passionate about the natural world. He is a conservationist, birdwatcher and wildlife filmmaker, and throughout his life has encouraged others to share his love of nature.

Michael enjoys the excitement of photographing and filming in wild lands. He is among the few people to have accessed Iran to record bird migration across the Caspian Sea. Travelling independently, he has slept alone with African elephants, tracked lemurs in Madagascar and filmed tigers in India. During their nearly five years in South America, Michael and his wife, Paula, were the first to film the incredible courtship 'dance' of the critically endangered hooded grebe. The footage from their film *Tango in the Wind* had 50 million views on social media and was bought by National Geographic, becoming their second most popular video of 2018. Michael is also the author of *Birds of Charnwood*, described by Sir David Attenborough as a splendid book.

Lecturing all over Great Britain on bird conservation and adventure travel, as well as being a regular speaker at the annual British Birdwatching Fair, Michael can also be found on Facebook at 'Living Wild in South America'.